Killing Off
the Lesbians

Killing Off the Lesbians

A Symbolic Annihilation on Film and Television

Liz Millward, Janice G. Dodd *and*
Irene Fubara-Manuel

McFarland & Company, Inc., Publishers
Jefferson, North Carolina

ISBN (print) 978-1-4766-6816-1
ISBN (ebook) 978-1-4766-2840-0

LIBRARY OF CONGRESS CATALOGUING DATA ARE AVAILABLE

BRITISH LIBRARY CATALOGUING DATA ARE AVAILABLE

Front cover illustration © 2017 Roberto Rizzo/iStock

Printed in the United States of America

*McFarland & Company, Inc., Publishers
Box 611, Jefferson, North Carolina 28640
www.mcfarlandpub.com*

TABLE OF CONTENTS

INTRODUCTION

On March 3, 2016, the CW Television Network in the USA aired an episode of the teen fantasy drama *The 100* entitled "Thirteen." The show had been trumpeted as the first network series to have a bisexual lead in the character of Clarke (the Canadian fantasy show *Lost Girl*, which also had a bisexual lead, was on cable). The show is about "The 100," a group of young people trying to survive on earth in a post-apocalyptic future. Clarke had emerged as the natural leader of this group and was working with Lexa, the commander of the allied Grounder Clans who were the existing inhabitants of earth. By the time the episode "Thirteen" aired the two women had shared a kiss and expressed interest in becoming lovers and partners. In classic star-crossed fashion, they now had to go their separate ways in order to be responsible leaders to their respective people. Meeting up in order to say goodbye, Clarke and Lexa expressed their regret that things could not be different and wistfully imagined they might meet again in a future when their obligations to others had been discharged. The trappings of this traditionally romantic scene were seductive to the audience. There was soft lighting, candles, and a bed covered in fur rugs in which the two women were naked together kissing, smiling, and comfortable in their desire and love for each other.

How far we had come from the grim old days when Xena's love for Gabrielle was all in the subtext or when the girl-on-girl kiss was wheeled in as a cynical sweeps week ratings grab. Or, worse yet, when that episode of *Buffy the Vampire Slayer* had much of the audience "Seeing Red" because Willow and Tara were *finally* shown in bed together only to have Tara immediately killed by a stray bullet meant for the hero of the series. There was so much to celebrate now.

Back on *The 100* it was clear that there could be no rest for the two leaders. Clarke had to leave their bed in order to deal with a new challenge

1

and found herself being shot at by Titus, one of Lexa's advisers who was determined to kill Clarke so that the besotted Lexa would return to her old ways. As Clarke ducked and weaved to evade the gunfire Lexa ran in to see what was happening and was accidently shot dead by one of the bullets meant for the hero. But wait: *what* just happened? What year is it? Haven't we all seen this story before?

Lexa's death was hardly shocking (although it did seem unbelievable) to anyone who had been paying attention to queer women's popular culture websites over the previous couple of years. Most notably, Trish Bendix on the AfterEllen website and Heather Hogan first on AfterEllen.com and subsequently on Autostraddle.com had both been sounding the alarm about the extraordinary increase in the death rates for lesbian and bisexual women on television. In 2014 Bendix identified the fact that in the opening episodes of several dramas writers were choosing to eliminate the lesbian character as a way to move the stories of the heterosexual characters forward (Bendix "Please"). The destruction continued in 2015 with regular or recurring lesbian characters dying violently in shows that originated in Canada, the UK, Europe, and Australia as well as the USA: there was no safe haven. The phenomenon of killing off the women who loved women was identified as the Dead Lesbian Trope, part of the wider "Bury Your Gays" trope. Carrie Lyell expressed her disbelief in *Diva Magazine* in 2015 when Sally Wainwright, writer of the internationally popular television series *Last Tango in Halifax*, suggested that the Dead Lesbian Trope was a myth. If the trope was a myth, why was Wainwright so busy contributing to its maintenance? In addition to killing off Kate McKenzie-Dawson, a pregnant black lesbian on *Last Tango in Halifax*, Wainwright had also written the homicidal/suicidal story arc of the lesbian Helen Bartlett in the ITV police drama *Scott & Bailey*. Her only other lesbian characters were these dead women's partners, left lonely and bereft as the "myth" expects them to be. In 2016 Hogan reminded her readers that "stories exist in imaginary worlds but they are consumed in the real world" where anti–LGBT policies and laws, homophobia and bullying are daily and sometimes deadly experiences for many people (Hogan "Autostraddle's"). There is a sense of urgency in Hogan's posts about the numbers of dead lesbians relative to other characters, as if the window of opportunity to convince the general public that the symbolic annihilation of women who love women is a serious problem might be rapidly closing.

As Vito Russo pointed out in the 1980s, the moving image screen has always been a very dangerous place for lesbians, bisexuals, and gay men. The sheer volume of lesbian and bisexual women's deaths in the 2015–2016 television season, however, was so overwhelming and the response to it so vocal that it drew the attention of more mainstream journalists, with articles appearing in magazines such as *Variety* and *Entertainment Weekly* and on websites such as BuzzFeed. The level of carnage was taken up by public radio broadcasters (NPR in the USA and the CBC in Canada) and analysis of it made its way into *The Washington Post, New York Post, Huffington Post,* and *The Guardian.* This was no longer an issue confined to queer women's media such as AfterEllen.com and Autostraddle.com or the British lesbian lifestyle magazine *Diva.*

To try and get a sense of whether queer women were reasonable to complain or just being over-sensitive, several bloggers crunched the numbers. Line graphs, pie charts and bar charts all revealed the same story in (literally) graphic detail. Women who loved women *were* at greatest risk on the small screen. Caroline Framke, with the assistance of Javier Zarracina and Sarah Frostenson writing on Vox.com, for example, examined all of the deaths on the 2015–2016 television season. They found that nearly 10 percent of character deaths in that season were of LGBTQ women, which far exceeds the proportion of them who appeared as characters in the first place. Of LGBTQ people of color, all of the deaths were of women: given that there were LGBTQ people of color who were men, this is a clear and astonishing difference (Framke, Zarracina and Frostenson). Hogan took a longer view, looking at scripted American television shows for the last forty years. She found that in this period 1,586 shows only had heterosexual characters, compared to 193 that had lesbian or bisexual characters (or 11 percent of all television shows). Of this 193, 35 percent had dead lesbian or bisexual characters and only 16 percent gave them happy endings. That meant a whopping 84 percent ended badly for lesbian or bisexual characters (Hogan "Autostraddle's"). The evidence was indisputable: something was clearly wrong. Writing for *Variety* Maureen Ryan looked behind the scenes for the cause, pointing out that "the vast majority of the most powerful people in TV come from the same subsets of the population, and are typically white, male and heterosexual," with correspondingly limited imaginations.

After a lesbian or bisexual character dies social media, message boards and comments sections on various websites typically fire up with a standard set of responses as viewers try to make sense of what happened. The first of these is distress and a need to express grief over the loss of beloved main characters or shock, irritation, and disbelief over the demise of secondary characters. This general response can be summarized as: how could they? Why are TV and film writers and producers *still* replicating this storyline? We all know it exists, it has been around for decades, representation was supposed to be improving, so why are they doing it? Why are they still choosing to kill the women who love women? In fact, these storylines are so common that after Tara was killed on *Buffy: The Vampire Slayer* in 2002 members of an online forum developed a very clear series of Frequently Asked Questions about the "Dead/Evil Lesbian Cliché" in which they explained that the cliché states that "all lesbians and, specifically lesbian couples, can never find happiness and always meet tragic ends" (www.Stephenbooth.org). Ten years later, in October 2012, Heather Hogan, then a senior editor on AfterEllen.com, drew attention to the predictable storylines for lesbian characters with a witty graphic called "Lesbiland: A TV writer's guide to creating lesbian characters." This guide includes "Token Lesbian Quicksand: Bench her for ten episodes. No one will notice she's missing," the "Psychopath Pit: Surprise! She is an axe-murdering stalker who escaped from an asylum!" and the "Gay Graveyard: Kill her" (Hogan "Lesbiland").

The second set of responses is conciliatory, resisting the outrage of the first set: oh, calm down and stop exaggerating, they say. Straight characters die all the time. Real lesbians die in the real world. We don't want to see utopian storylines in which we are treated differently from everyone else. And then there is the third type of reaction, a response to the first two rather than to the death itself. No, this set of responses say. Straight characters do not die all of the time at the same rates and there are so many straight characters anyway. Thousands of them. Women characters on the whole are slowly diversifying, especially as more women writers, directors and producers gain ground in the industry, so even if one dies the viewer can always change the channel and see another one. The anxious viewer is not hanging all of her sense of possibility onto that one character.

The final response to the responses is perhaps the most interesting, because lesbian and bisexual women are already being treated differently from straight characters and that treatment is far from utopian. So some viewers would, actually, like them to be treated the same. But some viewers would, instead, like them to be treated differently, on their own terms, because women who love women are different from straight women as well as from each other. They would like to see some evidence of that difference on screen and not have it snuffed out, again.

Lapping Up Lesbianism

Many women voraciously devour any film or television series that offers the merest hint of lesbianism. Depending on where they are in the world, they might tweet along to specific shows or rush online to respond to a particular episode. They may write fan fiction to continue the promising story that left them dissatisfied when the credits rolled at the end of a film, or search for fan fiction that depicts the sex that was only implied between their favorite characters. They may "google" the actor who portrayed a lesbian, looking for some evidence of a parallel between fiction and (someone's) real life. Or, again, they might hold tightly to a precious, underdeveloped dramatic moment and bring it out to daydream over in quiet moments at work, in the classroom, or when their children are preoccupied. These women take an indiscriminate approach: they rarely respect the boundaries of genre or format, instead lapping up lesbian possibility wherever they can find it. As one of Jamie Stuart's respondents says in her 2008 study *Performing Queer Female Identity on Screen*, "it's always a treat to see women expressing love/affection for other women.... In a society where such love is kept hidden, I hunger to see evidence that I'm not alone" (209). In contrast to this real-life promiscuity, the by-now quite large number of studies of lesbian representation in film and television and of online communities built around particular television shows tend to remain relatively narrow in their focus. Such disciplined examination provides many rich and complex analyses that tease out the context and meaning of particular representations, but frequently it cannot examine the broader significance of the—limited—range of lesbian representations available for viewers to consume, nor their responses to them.

In this book, we mimic the variegated approach of women seeking lesbian characters and storylines, looking across genres, at work coming out of different nations, at the industry which produces the stories, and at the fandoms who engage so vociferously with them. For many women, their encounter with fictional characters and storylines (whether in literature, on TV, film or online) is their first encounter with lesbian possibility. Sara Ahmed argues that "we might become lesbians because of the contact we have with others as well as objects, as a contact that shapes our orientations toward the world and gives them their shape" (94), and so these characters and their stories matter not just for women who are lesbians, but for all women.

There has been a great deal of scholarship which examines the representation of lesbians on both small and big screens. From Andrea Weiss's 1992 book on *Vampires and Violets* to the 2012 special issue of the *Journal of Lesbian Studies* on Global Lesbian Cinema edited by Daniel Farr, scholars have been dissecting the mainstream typology of on-screen lesbians using a variety of theoretical frameworks. Watchdogs, such as GLAAD (formerly the Gay and Lesbian Alliance Against Defamation) in the USA, and publicly accountable broadcasters, such as the BBC in the UK, have studied the incidence of lesbian, gay and bisexual representation on screen. For example, GLAAD issues annual reports on the state of the industry: *Where we are on TV* and the *Studio Responsibility Index*. The BBC produced a report on the *Portrayal of Lesbian, Gay and Bisexual People on the BBC* in September 2010 with a follow-up in 2012 to review what improvements had been made. Studies such as these acknowledge that there are, overall, more lesbians on screens now than there were in the past, although numbers do go down as well as up between one year and the next, and many lesbians appear in reality shows rather than scripted ones. However, as the studies caution to various degrees and as Brigitte Rollet argues in her analysis of lesbians on French television, there is a danger that "quantity is therefore seen as synonymous with progress, a simplistic and questionable approach for a much more complex issue" (86). Rebecca Beirne, too, suggests that "progress" in representations of lesbians is non-linear. Thus, she argues, the 1931 German film *Mädchen in Uniform* is more complex in its portrayal of lesbian desire in a homosocial setting (a girls' school) than is *2 Girls*, the 2005 film from Turkey (Beirne, "Teen," 261).

Several of these analyses mention two lesbian characters that have tended to endure through the decades. One is evil and the other one dies. In the past they were not infrequently the same character: what Stephen and Kath dub the "Evil/Dead Lesbian" (www.stephenbooth.org). These characters have been appearing in films and television series since early on in the lives of each medium. The evil one experienced a brief heyday in the 1990s but had largely disappeared by the end of that decade. However, the dead one shows no signs of vanishing. Vito Russo briefly reviewed the appearance of these characters, alongside their gay brothers, in his *Celluloid Closet*. Subsequent authors acknowledged their existence (although they, like him, tended to conflate dead dykes with dead queens) but with a few exceptions, until Lexa died, they tended to dismiss the "Dead Lesbian" as a tired stereotype before turning their attention to other questions including the rise in domestication (or baby) storylines and the whitewashing, de-butching, and tendency to turn straight which was the fate of many supposedly lesbian characters. Nevertheless, every time it appears, the Dead Lesbian Trope is critiqued online by fans and cultural commentators on websites such as AfterEllen.com, Autostraddle.com, Vox.com, and TV Tropes.org, although there is no existing full analysis of just how widespread (transnationally and across genres of TV and film) this cliché is, why it remains, nor a detailed discussion of fans' responses to it. We suggest that the ongoing on-screen practice of killing off the lesbians is deeply political, and cannot be divorced from a "real world" or "IRL" in which lesbian subjectivity is hard to achieve and lesbians are murdered or take their own lives.

Dana Heller argues that there have been two stages in the development of queer television studies: the first examines visibility politics and the second tackles postvisibility politics, with the coming-out episode (or "The Puppy Episode") of the *Ellen* sitcom on ABC in 1997 as the watershed (Heller 665). The name of the largely defunct lesbian and bisexual women's popular culture site AfterEllen.com nods to this seismic shift. In terms of *responses* to on-screen depictions of lesbians and bisexual women, however, there have been four broad stages. The first was the pre–1970s when women tended to respond privately and extract what they needed to sustain their sense of self, even from the most disheartening storylines. Following the rise of the New Social Movements, the 1970s and 1980s saw the formation of lesbian and gay activist groups, such as the National Gay Task Force (later National Lesbian and Gay Task Force) in 1973 and the Gay and Lesbian Alliance Against Defamation (now simply GLAAD) in 1985. These groups created a mechanism for lesbians and gays to collectively demand less deeply offensive portrayals on film and television and to have input to improve representation. In the third stage, during the 1990s, "lesbian chic" was momentarily all the rage, with a growing number of lesbian or bisexual characters on mainstream screens as well as the development of independent lesbian film and New Queer Cinema. In this context community responses began to shift towards an analysis of the impact of heterosexism and heteronormativity on the limited existing representations.

From the 2000s onwards, particularly since *The L Word* (2004–2009), increasing numbers of industry workers seemed only too pleased to be applauded for their lesbian or bisexual characters and to receive public recognition from established organizations such as GLAAD. As Elaine Atwell remarks, industry professionals "collect the GLAAD awards like Greek gods courting temple sacrifices. They eagerly repeat the stories of how their characters gave real life people the courage to come out [...] But when we dare to object, when we express fatigue or frustration with being force-fed the same tired clichés again and again, then the same queer women who formed a vital part of their fan base become a nuisance" (Atwell, "Last"). Atwell's frustration with the refusal of industry professionals to accept critique goes straight to the heart of the problem. At least since the emergence of the "Xenaverse" in the mid 1990s women have expected to engage in a dialogue with writers, producers and even actors.

These expectations rose proportionately with the exponential growth of social media. Although take-up rates for this new level of access to people in the industry are uneven, it has brought with it a heightened sense that showrunners need to justify their actions and viewers can share their otherwise quite isolated responses to characters and shows.

Starting with Terry Castle's groundbreaking study, *The Apparitional Lesbian*, we first review the literature that discusses the phenomenon of the dead and/or evil lesbian and its transfer from literature to the screen. This cliché is extraordinarily widespread, and the idea of intertextuality, by which one text (book, film or television show) references others helps explain the cumulative impact of watching all the dead lesbians pile up. To give a sense of its scope and scale Chapter 1 looks at examples from different genres as well as films and television series from many nations, including those in North and Central America, Europe, Africa, Asia, and Australasia.

The Bechdel Test, created by the cartoonist Alison Bechdel, asks whether a film has two women who talk to each other about something other than a man. In Chapter 2 we argue that a film or television series which passes the Bechdel Test with flying colors (rather than scraping through the test while audience members argue over the microseconds of dialogue shared by the women characters) is likely to promote subtextual readings. In this chapter we examine the role of so-called subtext, in which characters who are not, apparently, romantically or sexually involved on screen can be "read" against the grain as being coupled. Historically, this strategy of reading for "variance" formed a crucial component of the lesbian survival kit. By the 1990s it was effortlessly transferred to the internet by viewers who responded enthusiastically to the phenomenon of *Xena: Warrior Princess*. This practice has expanded dramatically since then. Naomi Rockler argues that audience members can produce oppositional readings of a text (rather than the "dominant ideology of a culture"). Some texts lend themselves to this process, because they have "strategic ambiguity" where the author deliberately makes multiple readings possible. In these types of films or television series "the dominant reading of a strategically ambiguous text often promotes dominant ideology, while other readers may decode the text within an oppositional framework" (Rockler 93). Such skill can develop over time for viewers who participate (even passively) in fan fiction communities, but engaging in a subtextual lesbian relationship does not protect characters from death, and we consider how the communal pleasures of a subtextual reading can be snuffed out by writers and producers.

The question of the roles played by industry professionals then leads us to consider the film and television industries in Chapter 3. We review the rise of lesbian chic and the shift towards postfeminism, and argue that the limited numbers of women in key roles, as studio bosses, producers, directors, writers or advertising executives has the effect of reproducing a narrow perspective, which assumes that diverse and more challenging depictions of lesbians (or women in general) with complex storylines cannot succeed. This is in spite of evidence that there is a large audience for a different set of stories, as the success of *The L Word, Pretty Little Liars, Orange Is the New Black* and *How to Get Away with Murder* demonstrates (although most of these shows also sacrifice characters).

In the short Chapter 4 we take a brief detour through "real life." One of the most common ways to dismiss critiques of the Dead Lesbian Trope is to point out that these are only fictional people and so viewers who become invested in them must be emotionally stunted and are making a fuss over nothing. We question that naïve (or cynical) response by reviewing the evidence that lesbians and bisexual girls are worse off than all of their peers, suggest that the damaging impact of saturation messages on them as well as on older women must be taken seriously, and consider forms of resilience.

Chapter 5 considers the various ways in which "it gets better," the importance of out lesbian actors, and the advances and limitations in stories told about women who love women. Here we take a close look at *Orange Is the New Black* as an example of an attempt to tell a different set of stories about same-sex love and women's community. Unfortunately, the promise of this approach is derailed by the showrunners' decision to kill off the character of Poussey Washington in order to draw attention to the Black Lives Matter movement.

Chapter 6 extends our analysis to consider how lesbian-focused fandoms organize. We argue that over the last twenty years lesbian fandoms have developed into complex spaces which provide an alternative to more formal advocacy groups such as GLAAD. The Lexa Pledge, an initiative started in 2016 to try and get writers and directors to promise not to kill off their lesbian or bisexual characters is only the most recent example of this type of organizing.

Finally, we turn to examples of fan fiction which reanimate dead characters, disregard their deaths, or place the characters in alternative universes, as a form of resistance to all of the dead lesbian storylines. Resistance here is defined not just as the insistence on a life-affirming story for lesbian characters, but as the re-telling of that same life-affirming story across fandoms by writers whose work appears in multiple fandoms over time.

The dead lesbian character is not, then, just an example of lazy storytelling. She is a tired but persistent figure who haunts lesbians and other women with the message that their lives and stories are expendable. While women who work in the entertainment industry struggle to challenge the narrow and frustrating versions of women who appear onscreen, fandoms pick up on the nuanced and pleasurable interactions of women whose stories pass the Bechdel Test. Femslash community has been developed and is sustained through the hard work of fandom elders, and these communities refuse the dead lesbian storyline, insisting, instead, on a world of alternative possibilities.

1

THE EVIL/DEAD LESBIAN— WHAT A CLICHÉ!

"As soon as the lesbian is named," wrote Terry Castle in 1993, "she is dehumanized" (6). Castle is referring to works of Western literature, but the process she identifies applies to on-screen women as much as to those appearing on the page. Dehumanization is a key strategy of oppression. It turns complex human beings into simplistic stereotypes in a black-and-white universe where good naturally triumphs over evil (perhaps after some nail-biting sequences in which the outcome seems doubtful). It reassures us that there is a natural order which is (of course) the existing power structure. For women, this "natural order" tends to be based on two inter-connected ideas. The first is that women are naturally heterosexual and derive their sexuality from men, or what can be called heteronormative thinking. As Martha Lauzen, David Dozier and Nora Horan point out, "traditional gender stereotypes posit that men represent the ideal or norm against which women are judged. As such, women become the perpetual other, valued primarily in their relations to others, men in particular." As they go on to argue, "when multiple programs across the broadcast and cable spectrum repeat these gendered roles, they assume the air of truth and credibility" (Lauzen, Dozier and Horan 201). The second idea is that lesbian possibility is a dangerous abnormality that threatens the very foundations of the existing social order. Kevin Moss and Mima Simić assert that "the real lesbian is a menace, too much of a menace to be allowed to write the plot herself, to take a lesbian subject position" (279).

There is evidence that many women's sexuality is mutable, it can change depending on the social context, and that "variable patterns of same-sex and other-sex desire and behavior may emerge in any woman over time" (Diamond 6). Lisa Diamond suggests that "contextual changes over the life course (such as intimate relationships) can redirect women's sexual-developmental pathways at any point" (13), and more women seem to be taking advantage of these pathways. For example, the third British National Survey of Sexual Attitudes and Lifestyles (Natsal-3), undertaken from 2010–2012, indicates that while only 3.7 percent of women had had any sexual experience with another woman in 1990–1991 (when Natsal-1 was conducted) by the time of Natsal-3 that proportion had jumped to 16 percent. A report on the health of lesbian, gay and bisexual youth in British Columbia by the McCreary Centre Society found that over time the number of female youth defining themselves as bisexual nearly doubled (Saewyc et al. 12). One possible explanation is that "the portrayal of women's increasing independence and choice of diverse sexual lifestyles in the media could have increased both inclination to engage in, and willingness to report, experiences. The demographic and social changes provide new opportunities for women and their sexual lifestyles, as shown by the increased numbers of partners and greater likelihood of same-sex experience reported by Natsal-3 participants" (Mercer, et al., 1792). Given this, it becomes clear that exposing women to lesbian possibility really can open up women's sexual horizons.

One technique to reassure men (and women) of the very naturalness of the heteronormative order and to limit the potential disruption posed to this order by lesbians is to insist on a sharp distinction between lesbians and all other women (with bisexual women disappearing altogether). For example, Sophia Davidson Gluyas argues that Australian films of the 1970s contain lesbian relationships but that they are easy to overlook. "A reason the lesbian dynamic to the friendships in these films is able to be so successfully rendered invisible is, quite simply, because we never see them have sex" (Gluyas 98–99). Naomi Rockler makes the same point about the film *Fried Green Tomatoes* (Jon Avnet, USA, 1991). In this adaptation of Fannie Flagg's novel *Fried Green Tomatoes at the Whistle Stop Café* the central same-sex couple of Ruth and Idgie are rewritten as friends rather than lovers. Rockler argues that "viewers who read the film through the dominant ideological framework that defines lesbianism as sexual behavior, as opposed to identity, are unlikely to define the women's relationship as a lesbian relationship" (91). In her study of audience responses to the film, Rockler found that seven out of ten viewers "did not believe that Idgie and Ruth were lesbians. Reflecting the dominant definition of lesbianism as sexual behavior, the simplest reason viewers gave was because the film contains no overt evidence of a sexual relationship" (Rockler 96). As Gluyas puts it, "until a woman explicitly defines her sexuality on screen, she can always be read as not-not heterosexual" (Gluyas 103). The reductive assumption that what makes a lesbian is only her (visible) sexual activity means that other forms of women-centered intimacy are automatically read as heterosexual.

Another technique to limit lesbian possibility is to dehumanize the lesbian character. There are two common ways to achieve this. One is to make her expendable, to kill her. On the surface, the explanation for her death does not have to be because she represents danger—it can be a tragic or heroic death, the expiration of a cipher whose killing provides an opportunity for other characters to develop dramatically. The other way to dehumanize her is to make her evil, a negative and unsympathetic force with which the audience (readers or viewers) cannot identify. Sanja Laćan argues of post-communist cinema, "in this cultural context the cinematic lesbian is a 'doubly metaphorical and doubly "voiceless" subject' since she is a repository of the content provided by straight (usually male) directors and screenwriters who have no interest in depicting her as a real lesbian and for whom she is ultimately a disposable metaphor" (Laćan 231).

Arguably, the Dead Lesbian made her very first appearance in Western literature in a 1706 story by Daniel Defoe, *The Apparition of Mrs. Veal*. Castle claims that this is an "archetypally lesbian story" (30). In the story, the ghost of one woman, Mrs. Veal, visits her living friend, Mrs. Bargrave: the implication in the story is that they loved each other but were estranged by Mrs. Veal's decision to move away to look after her brother. After her death, Mrs. Veal's ghost reconciles with Mrs. Bargrave (who is unaware either that her love is dead or that she is interacting with an apparition) but, because she is incorporeal, the ghost evades the kiss that Mrs. Bargrave attempts to plant on her lips. As Castle explains, because of "the kiss that doesn't happen, the kiss that *can't* happen, because one of the women involved has become a ghost (or else is direly haunted by ghosts)" the story seems to be "a crucial metaphor for the history of lesbian literary representation since the early eighteenth century" (30). Following from this early example, at least in the Western tradition, lesbian characters frequently exist only as phantom figures, sometimes literally as ghosts, sometimes as women whose sexuality is suggested but not quite clarified, their purpose and their lives obscure. They are "elusive, vaporous, difficult to spot—even when she is there, in plain view, mortal and magnificent, at the center of the screen" (Castle 2).

For centuries in Western fiction the lesbian—or the woman who seems to exert a fascination over other women characters, even if her sexual identity is never specifically named—has tended to come to a sticky end or to find herself alone and abandoned. In her comprehensive assessment of *Sex*

Variant Women in Literature Jeannette Foster tracks down virtually every example of women-loving-women in Western literature from Sappho to the publication of her own book in 1956. Foster's emphasis on "variance" rather than specific lesbian or bisexual identity is useful because it covers all women who desire women. Having discussed the quality of the various works she studied, Foster concludes that "the age-long prejudice against variance, deriving as it does from religious taboo, retains something of the hysteria which motivated witch-burning and inquisition. For this reason the whole subject is surrounded by a surcharged atmosphere to which no sensitive mind is impervious" (Foster 349). Furthermore, she argues, while some stories do try to champion the lesbian, others paint them as monsters:

> negative writing of better quality presents less-sinister characters, but manipulates circumstances to the end that variant experience shall always prove disastrous. In *Mme Adonis* and *Die Schwester* the relatively sympathetic title figures meet violent death; in *Méphistophéla, The Island, The Captive,* and *Pity for Women,* they end in madness or severe neurosis. In minor French tales of the last century, variant couples destroy one another by excessive physical indulgence, and in virtually all censorious novels they bring much harm or suffering to those with whom they are associated [Foster 349–350].

In the USA during the 1950s and 1960s, with the rise of the cheap paperback novels or pulp fiction which were widely available in drugstores and at bus and train stations, fictional lesbians' grim outcomes continued: punished for the attractive possibilities that they represented, they were contained by murder, rape, accidental or sacrificial death, or marriage. Sporting titles such as *Women in the Shadows, Odd Girl Out,* and *Twilight Lovers,* the pulps were "generally cautionary tales: 'moral' literature that warned females that lesbianism was sick or evil and that if a woman dared to love another woman she would end up lonely and suicidal" (Faderman, *Odd* 146–147). In spite of this many women did read them, trying to extract a sense of identity and possibility from between the covers. With those covers depicting half-undressed women gazing hungrily at each other, pulps were "readily available to women of this generation, in 'dizzying' quantities and at locations close to home" (Keller 386).

In some ways the pulps mirror the television depictions of same-sex desire today. Like television shows, they are genre fiction and products in the media landscape (Keller 395). Because they sat in racks in the local drugstore they were easy to access, titillating, and created in order to make money. For example, *Women's Barracks* by Tereska Torres, published in 1950, had sold 2.5 million copies by the 1970s (Keller 389). While about 90 of the 500-odd lesbian pulps were written by women and were "pro-lesbian," even these tended to have negative consequences imposed by the editors which damned the "real" lesbian and saved the supposedly heterosexual woman she had seduced (Keller 390). Nevertheless, mimicking those studies which suggest that women's sexuality is mutable, "often the books suggested that lesbianism was so powerful that a heterosexual woman only had to be exposed to a dyke and she would fall (though she was usually rescued, rather perfunctorily, by a male before the last pages—in which the real lesbian was shown to be doomed to suitable torment)" (Faderman 147).

In parallel with these pulp fiction stories, films and television shows are ultimately controlled by men (and sometimes women) who justify killing off their lesbian characters with stale excuses. They too tend to punish the more overtly or unapologetically lesbian characters, such as Lillian on the Canadian historical police procedural *Murdoch Mysteries*, who is shot by the jealous husband of her former lover, or Connie in the British Second World War home front show *Homes Fires*, whose ship is torpedoed while she is sailing across crossing the Atlantic. In the U.S. drama *The Wire* two lesbian characters exist in two different death worlds based on whether their self-presentation can be assimilated into heteronormativity or is unapologetically lesbian. The first, the police officer Kima Greggs, is relatively economically mobile. She is married to a woman, Cheryl, with whom she raises a child, she is feminized for a significant portion of the show, and her sexuality is normalized via the similarities she shares with her male counterparts. Snoop, on the other hand, is a gang member who rises to a reasonable position of power in her squad due to her marksmanship and her cool demeanor towards death and killing. She is only seen wearing baggy clothes and cornrows. She is never emotional, she is never feminized during the show, and she is never linked romantically to any partner. Although Kima is shot in the first season, she survives. Snoop, on the other hand, is shot dead by her protégé. This pattern is commonplace. As Kevin Moss and Mina Simić note about post-communist films which depict same-sex love, "the restoration of the heterosexual order is either fully established through marriage and children (in *Fine Dead Girls*), or suggested by the stated impossibility of being homosexual *here* (in *Take a Deep Breath* and *Another Way*)" (Moss and Simić 278). In these examples one of the women in the depicted same-sex relationship is bisexual and it is she who survives, "while the exclusive homosexual, unredeemable, is uprooted— symbolically admitting that in this kind of a celluloid universe queerness is completely (perhaps justifiably, as a mere metaphor) disposable" (Moss and Simić 279).

Hollywood films communicated much the same message. Patricia White points out that "Hollywood studio product was the nation's most significant mass cultural discourse for the first half of [the twentieth] century; at the height of Hollywood's cultural hegemony in 1946, ninety million Americans attended the movies weekly" and in 1927 women formed 83 percent of movie audiences (White 3). Between 1930 and 1968 what these women could see on the big screen was limited by the Motion Picture Production Code, also known as the Hays Code, under which "sex perversion or any inference to it is forbidden" (qtd. in White 1). The Hays Code was bizarrely worded to try and control what could be understood through on-screen images: "even the play of connotation was forbidden by the Code; the awkward formulation ('inference to,' rather than 'reference to' or 'implication of') implies an attempt to legislate the *viewer's* potential impression of homoerotic content" (White 1, emphasis in original). The Hays Code thus pushed women to work hard at subtextual interpretation in order to see the specter of lesbianism haunting the twentieth-century cinema screen.

Castle elaborates on the characteristics of this specter, where lesbianism only appears under specific conditions: "one woman or the other must be a ghost, or on the way to becoming one. Passion is excited, only to be obscured, disembodied, decarnalized" (35). Kaite Welsh, writing in the major British national newspaper *The Guardian* remarked that "in television, it seems lesbians are acceptable as ghosts or flashbacks, but never living people, never the survivors." Some on-screen couples explicitly enunciate this "ghosting." In season four of the BBC drama *Call the Midwife* the nurse Delia and midwife Patsy are sitting in a café talking about the barriers to their relationship when Delia remarks that "I sometimes feel as if we're ghosts. Half with each other but mostly without." Later Patsy reassures her: "We're not dead and we won't live as we were. We'll find a way to be together." But Patsy's hope for a solution is largely misplaced. When Foster's catalogue of doomed women, publishers' constraints on pulp fiction, and the restrictions of the Hays Code are taken together, this long history is a form of "symbolic annihilation," a term used to describe the fact that specific groups are either not or are barely represented in the mainstream media. As Gerbner and Gross explain in an essay which laid the foundation for later feminist and lesbian and gay analyses of television and film:

> representation in the fictional world signifies social existence; absence means symbolic annihilation. Being buffeted by events and victimized by people denotes social impotence; ability to wrest events about, to act freely, boldly, and effectively is a mark of dramatic importance and social power. Values and forces come into play through

characterizations; good is a certain type of attractiveness, evil is a personality defect, and right is the might that wins [Gerbner and Gross 182].

Symbolic annihilation therefore ensures that women who desire women are completely absent from stories, destroyed through the narrative, or rendered insubstantial and ineffectual through "ghosting." For example, reviewing films from the 1960s that contained barely acknowledged and clearly repressed lesbian characters, Vito Russo comments that "since most lesbians were invisible even to themselves their sexuality, ill-defined in general, emerged onscreen as a wasted product of a closeted lifestyle" (158). And even when it has been filmed, same-sex desire can still be symbolically annihilated by cutting the scenes that depict it. The lesbian relationship in *Love Actually* (Richard Curtis, UK, 2003) is relegated to the deleted scenes found on the DVD version. As Eva Krainitzki notes, this relationship ends in death anyway—with one older woman left alone (Krainitzki 17). In *Buffy the Vampire Slayer* (1997–2003) what Stephen Booth calls "the one and only truly sexual moment—Willow ducking her head under the sheet and Tara moaning—was cut from 'Seeing Red' by UPN" (www.stephenbooth.org). The scenes showing the relationship between Patsy and Delia in *Call the Midwife* are mostly cut from the version aired in North America on the PBS network, presumably because they are deemed less important than the other storylines and something had to be dropped to adjust the running length in order to accommodate commercials.

This Plot Reminds Me Of...

As Patricia White, Elaine Marks, and Eva Krainitzki all argue, intertextuality is crucial in understanding how and why certain storylines are relentlessly repeated and how women interpret them. Intertexuality is a term first coined by Julia Kristeva in 1969. It means that every text (written in her case, but also film and television texts) refers to other existing texts. It is in dialogue with them in multiple ways, including structure, plots, tropes, and characters—rewriting, mimicking, rejecting and creating narratives in opposition to them. Part of how readers and viewers make sense of a text is through their recognition (conscious or not) of the familiarity of those other texts. In commenting on the screen adaptation of her novel *The Color Purple*, for example, Alice Walker wonders if:

viewers realize that Olivia is not named after Oliver Twist (as implied in the film) but from a line in Virginia Woolf, "Chloe liked Olivia," which appears in *A Room of One's Own*, a book that made me happy to be a writer, and bolstered and brightened my consciousness about the role other women, often silenced or even long dead, can have in changing the world [Walker 41].

White provides an example of how this intertextuality influences lesbian representations in film. In 1929 Radclyffe Hall's British novel *The Well of Loneliness* was published, a novel featuring a masculine lesbian protagonist which catapulted to international notoriety because it was banned in Britain. Two years later the film *Maedchen in Uniform* (Leontine Sagan, Germany) came out, based on a play by Christa Winsloe set in a girls' school, about a student who was in love with her teacher. Around this time, MGM studios wanted to make a biopic about the 17th century Swedish Queen Christina, who refused to marry, dressed in men's clothes and was in a long-term relationship with her lady-in-waiting, the Countess Ebba Sparre: the result was *Queen Christina* (Rouben Mamoulian, USA, 1933). As White explains:

> Although *Queen Christina's* plot resonates intertextually with [Radclyffe] Hall's novel, when the film's producer Irving B. Thalberg suggested to [Greta] Garbo's friend screenwriter Salka Viertel that putting a hint of lesbianism into the film might be "interesting," the intertext he invoked, according to Viertel's memoirs, was neither the actual queen's life history of relationships with women nor Hall's quintessential lesbian novel, but the quintessential lesbian film *Maedchen in Uniform* (Germany, 1931). "Does not Christina's affection for her lady-in-waiting indicate something like that?" [17].

This common process of one film or TV show referencing a previous one is a strand in the intertextuality that structures lesbian representation. Castle briefly refers to another: the "rampant intertextuality" of contemporary lesbian writing, in which current novels enact the re-reading, re-writing, and referencing of earlier (homophobic) texts that depicted lesbians. She suggests that the overall effect of this intertextuality is to make readers "feel suspended, as it were, within a single lesbian Ur-text, replete with plots and counterplots, conjurings and reconjurings" (Castle 64). This concept of an Ur-text helps explain the power of the Dead Lesbian cliché. White discusses the intertextuality created by Hollywood producers, while Castle is referring to the way it is used by lesbian writers. It is also functions for television viewers and for fan fiction writers. Thus viewers, who may start watching a show precisely because it has a lesbian character or subtext, add that experience to all of the previous ones they have watched (generating, in effect, an Ur-text littered with dead or evil lesbians). In addition, fan fiction writers and readers re-write and reinterpret shows so that when they are watching the on-screen version the alternative interpretations (or the kisses and sex scenes that are missing from the television screen) are also present in their minds, creating the impression that the lesbian storyline is much more clearly delineated than it really is and rendering the cliché even more powerful. Intertextuality reinforces the impact and power of each of the stories which, individually, they do not possess.

Given this disheartening history of symbolic annihilation, why do women continue to devour any portrayal of women who love women? Castle makes the point that "it is a curious fact that for most readers of lesbian literature, at least until very recently, it has seldom mattered very much whether a given work of literature depicted love between women in a positive or negative light: so few in number have such representations been over the years, and so intense the cultural taboo against them, that virtually any novel or story dealing with the subject has automatically been granted a place in lesbian literary tradition" (64). Keller makes the same point about lesbian pulp fiction: "pulps seem to prove that an oppressed group finds the fact of representation more important than the homophobia of that representation" (Keller 405). This argument can be extended to film and television representations—rather than rejecting the tired and dehumanizing tropes, women seek them out and include them in our canon of lesbian representation, watching a TV show even if it only has the hint of a lesbian or bisexual character. As Andrea Weiss argues:

> because the dominant culture offers lesbians so few images to identify themselves with, the rare surfacing of these images has had exaggerated importance and invariably has come to hold a special place within the lesbian subculture. Although such images are constructed within the contours of the dominant heterosexual culture and its reliance on models of pathology, the meanings attached to the images have been frequently transformed, either through women's involvement in production (as in the case of *Mädchen in Uniform, Borderline, The Wild Party*) or, more frequently, within the lesbian spectator's imagination [Weiss, *Vampires* 28].

Perhaps because of the paucity and poverty of on-screen same-sex desire, viewers are often obliged to imagine more than is actually there, to create backstories and Alternate Universe (or AU) versions of particular characters. In Castle's phrase, they have "tended simply to 'pick out the subject-matter' of lesbianism, regardless of surrounding context, in order to retrieve it for their own subversive ends" (Castle 64). The problem is that while reading or watching for the subject matter that she can transform, the reader or viewer is very likely to find herself exposed to a wealth of Dead Lesbians.

Spoilers?

To paraphrase the Nigerian writer Chimamanda Adichie, the danger of telling only one story is deadly. The "spoiler" is a term used to describe a piece of information, such as a plot point, about a television show that is shared prior to the airing of the relevant episode. The information "spoils" the viewer's pleasure in the show because instead of simply enjoying the dramatic tale, they already know what is going to happen. With shows airing in multiple time zones and on different continents as well as the use of social media to share information, spoilers are ubiquitous. But the essence of a spoiler is that it affects the viewer who cannot see or imagine what is coming next in the show. For those watching the women characters who become erotically and emotionally entangled with other women, no such thing as a spoiler can truly be said to exist: if a character dies, the viewer already knew that would happen. If she is safe one week, it is doubtful she will be the next. This certainty—or lack of spoilers—exists because these characters seem to die at alarming rates which becomes more apparent when tracing the appearance of the Dead Lesbian cliché across film and television, not just one or the other. The cliché is considered part of the "Bury Your Gays" trope, which refers to "the problem [that] gay characters are killed off *far more often* than straight characters, or when they're killed off because they are gay" (tvtropes.org). In a fuller exploration of the components of what he described as the Evil/Dead Lesbian cliché, Stephen Booth explains that it is the idea "that all lesbians and specifically lesbian couples can never find happiness and always meet tragic ends. One of the most repeated scenarios is that one lesbian dies horribly and her lover goes crazy, killing others or herself" (www.stephenbooth.org).

The scholarly literature has tended to present a progress narrative, in which the cliché is mostly in the past (along with her doomed cousin from pulp fiction). Rebecca Beirne analyzes twenty-seven films made between 1931 and 2007 which depict teenage lesbian desire. She finds that regardless of the time period and the country of origin there are basically three types of lesbian teen film: subtextual (in which lesbian desire is hinted at but partially renounced); tragic; and coming of age. She notes that the more tragic stories are, at least in her survey, now less common in all countries (although she does warn that progress is not linear). All of the studies point to the same trend: there are now more lesbians on screen. However, the extent of the increase, and whether it signals a shift away from killing the lesbians and towards complexity, depends on the national context, on the genre, the rating or classification a film receives, and whether the television shows are free to air, accessed through premium pay services via cable or satellite, or on streaming services such as Netflix.

Lucille Cairns studied lesbian desire in francophone films and found that French Belgian and French Canadian films (directed by women) have a "generally more upbeat, lesbo-affirmative take" than do metropolitan French films, or the single film from Senegal (*Karmen Geï*, dir. Joseph Gaï

Ramake, 2001) in which Angelique, the lesbian, kills herself. In her study of lesbian characters in Hispanic Caribbean films (from the Dominican Republic, Cuba, and Puerto Rico) Consuelo Martinez-Reyes finds that lesbian characters are starting to appear in Cuban and Puerto Rican but not Dominican films. None of them die, but she also notes that only the films (two shorts) directed by women "construct female *individuals* who are willing to open a space in which to express female homosexuality on their own terms" (303). She notes that the other feature-length films refuse to actually show lesbian desire (it takes place off screen) and they incorporate it (via threesomes) into an extension of men's heterosexuality. By being invisible and re-centered around heterosexual men, Martinez-Reyes argues that same-sex desire is rendered not threatening to them nor to the national discourse, represented as a patriarchy. Sanja Laćan makes a similar point about post-communist films. In these, lesbianism "disappears behind the masculine vision of the world" because, as women, they are defined through the stories told from patriarchal and heteronormative perspectives (Laćan 231).

Of course, there are different genres in both film and television and some of these do lend themselves to more death and destruction than others. Horror, crime dramas, science fiction and fantasy (including vampires and zombies), and soap operas are likely to contain character death. On the other hand, school stories (or films set in schools) seem to be an almost lesbian-specific genre and while these frequently combine both the dead and the evil lesbian they can also introduce alternative storylines. Nevertheless, while lesbians and bisexual women are appearing more frequently on our screens the outcomes for some groups are worse than for others regardless of genre. By any measure, lesbian and bisexual characters who are not white seem to be in the greatest peril. In American film and television, women of color are rare enough on screen anyway except in Black ensemble pieces such as those that deal with the period of slavery or the Civil Rights movement. As Nina Cartier explains, "we have yet to arrive at a place in representation where a critical mass of different roles has been reached and a wider swath of the spectrum-that-is-blackness is *ubiquitous*, because we have yet to be fully accepted as people in a society that loves our 'cool' but denies us our humanity in the form of equal access to the ways and means of success in this society" (Cartier 152).

To understand why fictional black lesbian deaths exist at a different order of annihilation from those of their white cousins means digging into the deep layers of meaning attached to black women in the context of North America with its history of enslavement. Black feminist theorist

Patricia Hill Collins explores the controlling images that abound in media representations of black women—the mammy, the matriarch, the welfare queen and the jezebel. "While the mammy typifies the Black mother figure in White homes," Hill Collins highlights, "the matriarch symbolizes the mother figure in Black homes. Just as the mammy represents the 'good' Black mother, the matriarch symbolizes the 'bad' Black mother" (75). The mammy is the desexualized devoted servant of her white masters as portrayed by Juanita Moore's Annie Johnson in *Imitation of Life* (Douglas Sirk, USA, 1959). By contrast the matriarch is a "failed mammy" (Hill Collins 75), because she is assertive and domineering, even to the point of emasculating her male partners. This failed mammy, brought to the screen in the character of Carolyn, the mother in Spike Lee's *Crooklyn* (USA, 1994), takes the brunt of the failure of the black family. Her death is different from that of the mammy and is not deeply mourned. In fact, as bell hooks notes, "life not only goes on without her, it is more harmonious" (56).

Also a failed mammy, the welfare mother signifies the intersection between gender, class and race. Typically portrayed as a problematically fertile unwed woman, the welfare mother is an unemployed state-dependent who passes on her laziness to her many offspring. Portrayed by Diahann Carroll in *Claudine* (John Berry, USA, 1974), this controlling image racialized the cycle of poverty by which under- or unemployed black women needing state assistance had to forego marriage or romantic relationships in order to maintain a semblance of financial stability. Mo'Nique's portrayal of Mary Johnston in *Precious* (Lee Daniels, USA, 2009) as having a pathological sexuality draws similarities to the final controlling image that Hill Collins introduces: the jezebel. This hypersexualized controlling image is one of the most pervasive in contemporary representations of black women. Iconized as the hoochie-mama, the gold digger and the freak, this image signifies the sexual deviancy of black womanhood. This controlling image is most popular in hip-hop music videos, "hood" films, and reality television shows such as *Bad Girls Club* and the *Love and Hip Hop* franchise. This controlling image depicts black women at the margins of sexuality with sexual appetites that masculinize them and remove them far from the heterosexual norm.

The black lesbian fits into these images of black women at the points where masculinity meets sexual deviancy. As Manthia Diawara points out, Queen Latifah's character Cleo in *Set It Off* (Gary Gray, USA, 1996) takes on the figure of the racialized thug or gangsta popularized in the 1990s via a boom in "hood" films. For Hill Collins the thug or gangsta are controlling images of black working-class men. Thug masculinity, which reduces black men's "athletic bodies" to the personification of crime, is commodified and marketed by gangsta rap and characterized by "cool." This "black aesthetic of cool" is "an aesthetic of death [that] mimics death itself" (Diawara 272) in its stoic lack of fear. This proves true for masculine black lesbians as well, as Queen Latifah summons this lack of fear—the flirtation with death—in her glamorous death scene in *Set It Off.* In this scene, three women, Cleo, Stoney and Frankie are engaged in a high-speed chase after they have robbed a bank. Cornered in a tunnel by a cluster of flashing police cars, helicopters and press vehicles, Cleo, as the get-away driver, stops to think. She decides to sacrifice herself to save her friends, orders them out of the car and drives out of the tunnel. Personifying "cool" she stops again, this time in the middle of the fleet of police cars, lights a cigarette, pumps the hydraulics on her vehicle to make it spring up, and accelerates a final time. The police officers fire repeatedly at her vehicle. The now-wounded Cleo bursts out of her car, automatic in hand, and the police spray her with bullets. Unlike the other two women Cleo, who comes with the accouterments of a real thug (gang affiliation, arms-dealing associates, and hot young girlfriend) dies in a blaze of glory.

The death of Snoop from the HBO television series *The Wire* also employed the cool "aesthetic of death" (Diawara 272). Snoop (played by Felicia Pearson) is a gang member who rises to a reasonable position of power in her gang due to her marksmanship. She has killed numerous people and maintains a cool demeanor towards death. Her lack of fear of death appears in her last scene when she drives into an alley with her protégé, Mike, who tells her he needs to urinate. Parking in an alley, she looks over to Mike who seems hesitant. She asks him "what now, motherfucker, you shy?" knowing full well she is about to be killed. Mike pulls out a gun and aims it her. After a calm discussion between the two characters about Mike's impending death (due to gang dynamics), Snoop glances in the side mirror of her SUV. "How my hair look, Mike?" she asks as she runs her hand over her cornrows. "You look good, girl," he responds as the next frame shows a long shot of the SUV parked in the alley. A spark, followed by the sound of a gunshot, implies Snoop's death. While Snoop's death is a tender moment shared between a teacher and her student, Cleo's death is a spectacle. As Kara Keeling explains, the glorified death of this bank robber is a "stark and bloody, aestheticized manifestation of bourgeois state power" (40). Thus, although Cleo and Snoop both transcend the role of the mammy, matriarch, welfare mother, and jezebel, they fall easily into the trap of the cultural role of thug masculinity and the death promised by that role.

Black femininity brings on a different set of meanings for lesbians. Unlike the masculine black lesbian, who is afforded some capacity to transcend the controlling images of black women, the black feminine lesbian is trapped within these cultural roles. These feminine women-loving women are versions of the jezebel role in its contemporary form of the "gold-digging hoochie" who attaches herself to an affluent man. A stock character in hip-hop culture, the gold-digger, is mysteriously sexy, maniacally manipulative, and has an insatiable taste for the finer things in life. The show *Empire* includes the character of Camilla Marks who is a gold-digger and opportunist. Her own (authentic) sexuality is erased by her desire for capitalist success. In fact, Becky, the executive assistant at the recording label Empire, refers to Camilla as a "gay for pay tramp." Played by the former supermodel Naomi Campbell, Camilla is the older girlfriend of Hakeem Lyon, one of the sons of Lucious Lyon, the show's gangsta rapper turned media mogul. Camilla and Hakeem's relationship is as romantic as it is pathological, making Camilla a hybrid figure of the matriarch and jezebel. Through a series of the type of plot twists popular in melodrama, Camilla leaves Hakeem only to return after a few months as the wife of Mimi Whiteman, Lucious's business partner. The plot thickens as Mimi announces that she is dying and leaves her share of Empire to her loving wife Camilla, who uses her position to make Hakeem the new CEO. Camilla resumes her relationship with Hakeem and divulges to him that she is only using Mimi. The young Lyon records this—along with a sex tape—which he then sends off to Mimi. With her plan now backfiring catastrophically in her face, Camilla kills Mimi. Lucious breaks in and records Camilla while she is cleaning up her condo in an attempt to stage her wife's murder as a suicide. Threatening to send the video out, Lucious succeeds in psychologically manipulating Camilla to drink poison, which kills her instantly.

Asked to comment on why she had killed off the two women lovers on her show, the *Empire* showrunner Ilene Chaiken argued that:

> I would say that Camilla is not a lesbian character. Camilla was, if anything, an opportunist, which is quite different from being a lesbian. If anything, the lesbians should wish for a character like Camilla to be killed off since she just preyed on a powerful lesbian in order to fulfill her heterosexual ambitions [qtd. in Wagmeister].

Chaiken's statement symbolizes the erasure and vilification of black bisexual women and reifies the racialization and sexualization of villainy. The concept of "villainy" was deployed in the construction of the figure of the "black rapist," a character used to justify killing or lynching black men after the emancipation of slaves in the USA. Based on racist white claims about the supposed bestial sexual appetites of black men, the "black rapist" was a cartoon villain that united white men across class lines in their shared violence, which they rationalized as necessary to protect "their" white women and the "purity" of "their" race. Just as lynching the black rapist was framed as an act of justice, Chaiken frames the death of this bisexual black character as an act of justice to be celebrated by lesbians.

The concept of villainy is not the only way in which representations of black women's sexuality in general are fraught. "Like all women on-screen, she represents a lack, and doubly so. Like her white female screen counterparts, she is not a man, and thus not a person. At the same time, nor is she fully a woman, since the fact of her epidermis prevents her from fully entering the realm of desire. Nobody wants to be her (except perhaps the black women in the audience), and nobody wants her" (Cartier 152–153). Evelyn Hammonds concurs that "Black women's sexuality is often described in metaphors of speechlessness, space, or vision, as a 'void' or empty space that is simultaneously ever visible (exposed) and invisible and where black women's bodies are always already colonized" (Hammonds 142). In other words, the black woman almost never gets to tell her own story and her sexuality always means something else. Since lesbians are dehumanized through an emphasis on their sexual activities, and given that "the one power of black women was indeed sex, in every trope that has represented them in the media" (Cartier 154), then the black lesbian becomes a symbol of extreme sexual excess, threatening to spill out beyond the limits of what can be seen to exist. Her death is particularly reassuring, then: once dead, she cannot threaten the politics of respectability or silence that structure heterosexual Black women's lives, nor white people's collective fantasy that Black women are merely background figures (the supporting cast) in the symbolic landscape. Black lesbians or other lesbians and bisexual women of color thus remain a tiny proportion of women characters: Marlon Rachquel Moore surveys their recent incarnations and found a total of ten on U.S. television shows since 1976, although there have been a few more. That these characters are so expendable and their deaths are justified by drawing on long-held racist claims is a troubling demonstration of the intersection of race and sexuality in limiting what can be allowed to exist on screen and therefore be considered a real-life possibility.

Adding to Moore's list and the women discussed above, some examples of lesbians or bisexual women of color who die are Shana in *Pretty Little Liars* who is shot by one of the Liars and Maya, also in *Pretty Little Liars*, who is murdered by a stalker (a black man killed by another Liar). Tosha is shot during a heist in *The Wire* (2004) and Tara is killed by a vampire on *True Blood* (2014). Clementine is killed by a monster in *Hemlock Grove* (2013); Kate is hit by a car on *Last Tango in Halifax* (2015); Carolyn is crushed to death in *Under the Dome* (2016); and Kira gets Julia to assist in her suicide in *The Magicians* (2016). In the much-lauded *Grandma* (Paul Weitz, USA, 2015), Elle's black partner, Violet, does not even make it onto the screen: she is already dead before the action of the film starts. Other women of color are also symbolically annihilated: Sandy in *ER* dies from injuries sustained working as a firefighter (2004); Nadia in *Lost Girl* is killed by the main character, Bo, who is the lover of Nadia's girlfriend, Lauren (2012). Toshiko is shot on *Torchwood* (2008). One of the only Māori lesbians on television, Jay, is murdered on the New Zealand soap opera *Shortland Street*. On the one hand, these characters suffer similar fates to those of the white women: it is simply hazardous to express sexual or erotic desire for another woman character. On the other hand, the paucity of black or other lesbians of color on television or in film at all makes their deaths even more shocking—and predictable.

Old women (typically white) belong to another group which is particularly unlikely to make it through a film or TV show alive. In her study of films with older lesbian characters (aged 60 and over), Eva Krainitzki finds "a specific pattern of storylines involving terminal illness, mourning, and widowhood, with a seemingly inevitable unhappy ending" (Krainitzki 14). Like younger women, these characters are isolated rather than belonging to any wider lesbian friendship or political community. In *Hold Back the Night* (Philip Davis, UK, 1999) Vera dies of her terminal illness after her partner Jo has already died. Abby dies after a fall in *If These Walls Could Talk 2* (Anderson, Cooledge and Heche, USA, 2000), leaving her partner Edith homeless and in financial ruin. Lovers Hannah and Rachel are separated in a nursing home in *Hannah Free* (Wendy Jo Carlton, USA, 2009). While this lesbian-made film does complicate lesbian lifestories, it nevertheless ends with the death of Rachel. Dotty dies of natural causes just after marrying Stella in *Cloudburst* (Thom Fitzgerald, USA/Canada, 2011), and in *Tru Love* (Wade Gasque, USA, 2014) Alice drops dead on the train home after her night in bed with her daughter's lesbian friend Tru. Krainitzki asserts that "through the guise of old age, the systematic erasure of lesbian characters gains a new level of cultural acceptability, making the 'ghosted' old lesbian the most visible cultural representation" (14).

The deaths of these women of color and older lesbians form part of a longer intertextual history where the lesbians rarely make it to the final credits, although they are revealed as evil or die for a variety of reasons. In one of the early films depicting lesbian desire, the 1936 film *Club de Femmes*

(Jacques Deval, France) the lesbian Alice is a murderer who is banished to a leper colony. Martha in *The Children's Hour* kills herself when she realizes that the vicious rumor that she is a lesbian is, in fact, true (William Wyler, USA, 1961); a falling tree kills Jill in *The Fox* (Mark Rydall, Canada/USA, 1968); and Chun is killed during a battle with the protagonist Ainu—although she also manages to kill her with a poisoned kiss—in *Intimate Confessions of a Chinese Courtesan* (Chor Yuen, Hong Kong, 1972). In *Picnic at Hanging Rock* (Peter Weir, Australia, 1975) Miranda goes missing at Hanging Rock and Sara, left behind, kills herself. Éva is shot trying to escape from Hungary while her lover Lívia is left paralyzed in her bathtub after being shot by her jealous husband in *Another Way* (Károly Makk, Hungary, 1982). In seventeenth-century Mexico, Sister Juana Ines de la Cruz dies from the plague after being brutally punished by the Catholic Church for her writing in *I, Worst of All* (María Luisa Bemberg, Argentina/France, 1990).

The film *Basic Instinct* proffers not just one but two Evil/Dead lesbians (the murderer Roxy who is killed in a car crash and the stalker Beth who is murdered) in addition to Catherine, the psychopathic bisexual serial killer (Paul Verhoeven, USA, 1992). In *Crush* (Alison MacLean, New Zealand, 1992), the disabled Christina manipulates a teenage girl, Angela, to help her to murder her lover Lane, who had left her in the wreckage of a car crash. A car crash kills the main character's wife and her lover in *Golden Balls* (Bigas Luna, Spain, 1993) and Eunice is both a murderer and kills herself in *Butterfly Kiss* (Michael Winterbottom, UK, 1995). Lucy overdoses in the aptly named *High Art* (Lisa Cholodenko, Canada/USA, 1998), Paulie jumps to her death from a roof in *Lost & Delirious* (Léa Pool, Canada, 2000), and Diane (or Betty) shoots herself in *Mulholland Drive* (David Lynch, France/USA, 2001).

In *Fine Dead Girls* (Dalibar Matanic, Croatia, 2002) Iva is raped by her neighbor Daniel, who is enraged that she is not interested in him. When her lover Marija confronts Daniel they fight and she accidentally kills him. The couple's other neighbors then form a mob and kill her in revenge (Iva subsequently vanishes into heteronormativity—she marries a man and has a child). In *Emotional Crack* (Lancelot Imasuen, Nigeria, 2003) Crystal falls in love and has an affair with her abusive husband Chudi's mistress, Camilla. When their relationship is threatened, Chudi "saves" Crystal from Camilla who then kills herself in jealousy and despair. Miss Murgatroyd is murdered in *A Murder Is Announced* (John Strickland, UK, 2005), although because her murder is so predictable it is not the one that is announced. Two couples are executed by the state for being lesbians:

Valerie and her partner in *V for Vendetta* (James McTeigue, USA/Germany, 2006) and An and Min in *The Chinese Botanist's Daughters* (Dai Sijie, France/Canada, 2006). In *Cracks* (Jordan Scott, UK/Ireland, 2009), the manipulative teacher Miss Green sexually assaults her student Fiamma, when the latter is drunk, and subsequently prevents her from receiving medical aid—basically killing her—because she is afraid that Fiamma will expose her.

Sara dies during childbirth in *Viola di Mare* (Donatella Maiorca, Italy, 2009) and Sydney dies of cancer in *Running on Empty Dreams* (Nitara Lee Osbourne, USA, 2009). In *Love Crime* (Alain Corneau, France, 2010), Isabelle murders her boss, Christine, with whom she is erotically obsessed. Chloe falls from a window to her death in *Chloe* (Atom Agoyan, USA/Canada/France, 2010). In *Soongava: Dance of the Orchids* (Subarna Thapa, France/Nepal, 2012) Kiran is murdered by her brother to maintain their apparently progressive family's honor. Cancer brings about *A Perfect Ending* for Rebecca (Nicole Conn, USA, 2012), while assisted suicide is Val's choice of a *Happy End* (Petra Clever, Germany, 2014).

Biopics too may include death scenes that emphasize the impossibility of enriching lesbian lives. *Reaching for the Moon* (Bruno Barreto, Brazil, 2013) dramatizes the real-life relationship between the Brazilian architect Lota de Macedo Soares and American writer Elizabeth Bishop. Macedo Soares did die of an overdose while visiting Bishop in New York in 1967, but in the filmed version of this death she takes her life immediately after being rejected by Bishop and discovering that Bishop has taken another (younger) lover: her lesbianism thus directly causes her death.

Certain genres appear to deliberately center the Evil/Dead Lesbian. Vampire and horror movies are obvious examples, but so too are blaxploitation films. Angelique Harris sampled twenty of these which were made between 1969 and 1974 in order to examine how they depict lesbians and gay men. As she explains, these films employed Black people in a full range of occupations, and targeted and "entertained black audiences who were excited to see representations of themselves onscreen in leading roles" (Harris 218). Because "everything perceived as not being 'black' in these films is scorned, including homosexuality," Harris argues that the lesbian characters:

> are not only used to glorify the [hetero]sexuality of the lead character; they are also used to dehumanize the villains, making their often brutal deaths more palatable for the audience. All of the lesbian and gay villains in these films are violently killed, and in many instances, they are killed in a much more brutal fashion than their heterosexual villainous comrades (unless the villain is a white man). These queer villains or

"monsters" are unsympathetic characters who, in one way or another, block the protagonist from obtaining their set goal [228].

The lesbian characters in films such as *Black Mama/White Mama* (Eddie Romero, USA, 1973), *Women in Cages* (Gerardo de León, USA/Philippines, 1971), and *Cleopatra Jones* (Jack Starrett, USA, 1973) are "shot, beaten, killed by a sword, raped and murdered" (Harris 228).

The on-screen Death of the Lesbian has become, in effect, one of the "basic cultural assumptions that make a show 'entertaining'—i.e., smoothly and pleasingly fitting dominant notions (and prejudices) about social relations and thus demonstrating conventional notions of morality and power" (Gerbner and Gross 189). As Moss and Simić put it more bluntly, lesbian characters "still have to affirm the stereotype of tragic lesbian destiny straight audiences find comforting" (281). Occasionally, a film will use this "basic cultural assumption," or the comfortable sense which the audience has that the lesbian must die (even heroically) in order for the film to be satisfying, to effect a sort of feint. *A Marine Story* (Ned Farr, USA, 2010), for example, leads the audience to believe that Alexandra, the lesbian ex–Marine who was discharged under the Don't Ask, Don't Tell policy of the United States military, has been killed in a meth-lab explosion. The implication is that she sacrificed herself to destroy the lab (and the criminals running it), who have attacked and possibly left for dead the troubled young woman, Saffron, whom she has been mentoring. In fact, both women survive the explosion: at the end of the film they are shown to be thriving in their new lives and Alexandra is in a settled relationship with another woman. In another example, Corky, the butch lesbian from *Bound* (Wachowskis, USA, 1996) helps her girlfriend Violet steal from the latter's gangster boyfriend Caesar. The audience is encouraged to believe that Violet may have been using Corky and will let Caesar kill her, but actually Violet kills Caesar and chooses Corky over a new male admirer, Mickey.

Occasionally films use the murderous lesbian in a new way, challenging the idea that she is evil and even encouraging the audience to root for her. In Lucia Puenzo's *The Fish Child/El niño pez* (Argentina-Paraguay, 2009), Lara, the lesbian daughter of a wealthy Buenos Aires family intends to kill herself after she sees her domineering father (a powerful judge) having sex with her lover Ailin, who is the family maid. However, when her father helps himself to the poisoned drink she had prepared for herself, Lala does not warn him that it is deadly, in effect killing him. After Ailin has been arrested for his murder, Lala rescues her by shooting the corrupt police chief who is torturing Ailin, and the two escape to Paraguay in what Lala optimistically suggests will be their happy ending. If one reason why the lesbian is so often cast as a killer (who has to be killed) is to emphasize her potential to terrorize men in their unjustified assumption of power, a sheer threat to patriarchy, then Puenzo's film makes this fear explicit and champions the lesbian (whose side the audience is encouraged to take) in her initially inadvertent but certainly literal destruction of the patriarchy.

Such clever deployment of the trope is rare, and on television shows the dead lesbian is alive and well. On television her effect is arguably more powerful than in films, because viewers invest in the characters who appear week after week in their living rooms or on their laptops or other devices. When Tara is shot on *Buffy the Vampire Slayer* or Maya on *Pretty Little Liars* is murdered by a stalker, their deaths feel like a betrayal of the future because they are. And when incidental lesbian characters die or murder other people during the evening crime dramas, they remind us that erasure is the constant companion of women who love women. The litany of regular or recurring characters in recent television shows who are sexually involved with other women and who die is astonishing. In March 2016 the U.S.–based website Autostraddle began to document them. Not counting women who only appeared in one or two episodes, they initially listed 142 examples and immediately had to start adding more.

To give some examples, in addition to Tara and Maya, Hanna dies from kidney failure after she was injured in an argument with her ex-husband in the German soap opera *Verbotene Liebe* (2004); after a particularly horrific betrayal, Gina shoots her ex-lover Helena in *Battlestar Galactica* (2006); Marissa has a relationship with Alex Kelly and then dies in a car crash on *The O.C.* (2006); and Jay is murdered by a serial killer in the New Zealand soap opera *Shortland Street* (2007). The grieving mother of a child shoots the doctor Marina dead in front of her lover Esther in the Italian series *Terapia d'urgenza* (2009). June Stahl murders her lover Amy Tyler in order to frame her in *Sons of Anarchy* and is herself murdered in retaliation for an earlier crime she committed (2010). Cat is hit by a car in the British show *Lip Service* (2012) and Crisabel in the Spanish series *Tierra De Lobos* is accidentally killed during an argument with her lover's husband (2013). Alisha is shot dead in *The Walking Dead* (2013) and Alice dies from lack of insulin in *Under the Dome* (2013). Kenya Rosewater is murdered by her lover Stahma in order to appease her husband in *Defiance* (2014); in the mini-series *Ascension*, Samantha Krueger is betrayed and shot in the head (2014); and the paramedic Leslie Shay is killed in an explosion on *Chicago Fire* (2014).

The list goes on: Naomi dies from an aggressive form of cancer in *Skins: Fire* (2013) and Bullet is murdered in *The Killing* (2013). Silvia is shot dead on her wedding day, dying in the arms of her new bride on the Spanish series *Los Hombres de Paco* (2010). Reyna Flores is riddled with bullets on *Matador* (2014). Sophie's lover Maddie is killed after being caught in an explosion on the British soap opera *Coronation Street* (2015). Charlie is stabbed to death in *Supernatural* (2015) and Ruby is killed when a helicopter crashes in another British soap opera, *Emmerdale* (2015).

Even when a character does not die or turn evil, lesbian futures can be jeopardized. Sara Lance is pierced by a quiverful of arrows on *Arrow* (2014); in the Canadian television series *Orphan Black* Delphine, the ex-lover of Cosima (one of the clones) is shot in a parking lot (2015); and Rose is a murderer who is herself strangled on *Jane the Virgin* (2016). All three of these women are subsequently resurrected, but the damage to their relationships and the viewer's feelings had already been done. In *Call the Midwife* Delia does not die when she is hit by a car but she does lose her memory, including the recollection that she was in a relationship with Patsy (2015). Although the two recovered their relationship in season five, fan distress over their separation was intense: suspended in the Ur-text of ghosted relationships, no viewer had any reason to place their faith in the show's producers. As TheGayUK wrote in an opinion piece on 15 April 2015, "for a long time now gay viewers have complained by *[sic]* the lack of happy gay couples on TV, lesbians in particular have felt hard done by with several TV shows killing or 'turning straight' lesbian characters. So with hardly any TV representation and coming hot on the heals *[sic]* of *Last Tango in Halifax* 'lesbian hit by car' plot-line, repeating this on *Midwife* hit hard" ("Tragic"). And even though they are no longer the "ghosts" that Delia sensed they were in season four, they are still decarnalized: while every significant heterosexual couple is permitted an on-screen kiss, Patsy and Delia have not had one.

The lesbian of the week, who frequently makes her appearance in crime dramas, police procedurals, medical dramas, or as a ratings grab during "sweeps week," also struggles to reach the credits without falling prey to some catastrophe. For example, in *Dark Angel* the Black lesbian Original Cindy finally gets a girlfriend who is almost immediately killed. In *Blue Murder* a veterinarian, Ruth, was having an affair with another woman and was contemplating leaving her husband before she was murdered (2009). One half of a lesbian couple on the last episode of *Emily Owens: MD* (2013) dies, Emily and her lover on *Teen Wolf* (2013) are murdered just before they have sex, and one half of a lesbian couple on the British show *Endeavour* (2013) is murdered when she is mistaken for her girlfriend. And, when they are not being extinguished, lesbian and bisexual characters do more than their fair share of betraying and murdering other characters. Maia on *Shortland Street* murders one man and is eventually committed to a psychiatric institution. Beth Jordache in the British soap opera *Brookside* helps her mother murder her abusive father, and then dies in prison. Mandy is a con artist who dupes Princess Eleanor on *The Royals*. In a study of lesbian characters on French TV between 1995 and 2005 Brigitte Rollet found just 20 of them in total, of which four are victims (either murdered or raped), two are killers, and two are suspected of being criminals. Women who find themselves in prison on the small screen also need to be wary. The Australian show *Prisoner: Cell Block H* kills Franky and Sharon (1980) and then Bea in the remake *Wentworth* (2016). *Bad Girls* kills Shaz (2000), Al (2004), and Natalie (2006), *Orange Is the New Black* kills Tricia (2013) and Poussey (2016), and Elise dies in the French-Canadian show *Unité 9* (2015).

Some shows kill off more than one woman who loves other women. *Pretty Little Liars* is the most obvious, killing Maya (2012), Shana (2013), and Sara (2016), but there are more. Patty kills her deceitful ex-girlfriend Veronica and then takes her own life in *La Reina del Sur* (2010). Both Gaia and her lover Lucretia die in the swords-and-sandals series *Spartacus*, the first murdered (in 2011) and the second killing herself (in 2012). Susan dies and Bizzy kills herself on *Private Practice* (2011). Angela and Louise are shot dead together on *Boardwalk Empire* (2011), to punish Angela's husband. On the ground-breaking *The L Word* Dana dies of cancer (2006) and Jenny ends up dead in a swimming pool: the speculation over the cause of her death fuels the entire story arc of the show's final season (2009). *True Blood* kills off no less than three of its bisexual characters: Tara (2014), Sophie-Anne (2011) and Nan (2011). The *American Horror Story* series ramps up the body count over time: Wendy is murdered in *Asylum* (2012), Lucy and Alice die in *Freakshow* (2014), and Sally, the Countess, and Natacha all die in *Hotel* (2015). In the British supernatural series *Hex*, Thelma, who is in love with her straight best friend Cassie, is murdered (2004) and remains on the show as a ghost, quite literally "ghosted" with her lust decarnalized. In order to try and control her another character, Malachi (the supernatural offspring of Cassie and a fallen angel), kills another lesbian, Maya, because Thelma had expressed interest in her (2005). Now ghosts together, Maya and Thelma pursue a spectral relationship until Maya's body is decapitated, which annihilates her ghost. Not satisfied with killing two lesbians and turning both into ghosts, *Hex* insists on killing one of them twice over, ensuring that the disembodied Thelma is left truly alone.

Sometimes shows create complex storylines to justify the death of the lesbian or bisexual character and to invoke her evil twin. In 2009 in *Hollyoaks*, a British soap opera, Lydia cuts the cords of her lover Sarah's parachute. She had intended to cut those of Sarah's close friend (and one-night stand) Zoe, and then tries to get Zoe blamed for the murder. In the 2015 Brazilian mini series *Felizes Para Sempre?* Denise is clearly characterized as evil because she had earlier precipitated the suicide of a married woman whom she had seduced and dumped, and she also unceremoniously left her own wife when she found out Denise had a secret life as a sex worker. After a tangled plot, in which Denise has separate relationships with a married couple, the husband (now her ex-lover) shoots her dead but is prevented from also killing his ex-wife (her current lover). In the U.S. show *Legend of the Seeker* Cara is in a complicated (platonic) relationship with her former enemy Kahlan. In the show's final season Cara's former lover Dahlia rekindles her sexual relationship with Cara in order to come between the two women and to try and bring Cara back to her side, against Kahlan. Kahlan subsequently kills Dahlia, but not before Dahlia has killed Cara in an alternate timeline (2010). In the first season of the Australian show *Miss Fisher's Murder Mysteries* (2012) Hettie accidentally kills her former lover Daisy while the two are arguing because Daisy broke off their relationship in order to take up with Dr. Mackenzie, another lesbian who is one of Phryne Fisher's closest friends. Hettie then murders her boss, Gaskin, in order to frame Dr. Mackenzie for murder as a way to punish her for "stealing" Daisy.

The Canadian television series *Murdoch Mysteries* recycles its lesbian storyline and the idea that the lesbian may be a murderer. In season seven (2013) the jealous husband of her lover, Pauline, drives the lesbian Sarah to jump to her death out of a window. Detective Murdoch suspects Pauline in the death but his future wife, Dr. Julia Ogden, defends her: "she's a sapphist, not a psychotic" she snaps. In season nine (2015), Lillian, the lover of Dr. Emily Grace, is murdered by her former lover's jealous husband. Once again, the lesbians are suspected: Emily (briefly) in Lillian's murder (because the partner is the most likely suspect), and Lillian in the "death" of the man who eventually murders her (the local detectives have concealed the fact that he did not drown after she and her former lover had struggled with him on a boating expedition).

At least since the infamous "Seeing Red" episode of *Buffy the Vampire Slayer*, women seem particularly endangered immediately after having sex with—or even just kissing—each other. In 2002 Andy Mangels raised the question of whether "Lesbian Sex = Death?" in an article in *The Advocate*, and Stephen Booth points out that "one of the most overused features of the lesbian cliché is that the death is generally directly associated with the act of lesbian sex. Usually it occurs soon after a real or implied sex scene in order to cement the connection" (www.stephenbooth.org). This connection is not typically made when heterosexual characters die. There are several examples of this lesbian sex (or kissing) = death storyline. Angela and Louise appear to have just had sex on *Broadwalk Empire* when they are murdered: Angela is lying on the bed in her underwear, half asleep and smiling, while Louise comes out of the shower. In *Murdoch Mysteries*, Lillian and Emily are depicted in their bedroom, with Emily lolling around in her underwear on the bed watching Lillian getting dressed. They kiss and Emily says "I love you." Cut to the very next scene: Lillian is shot dead. In *The 100* Clarke and Lexa are shown having sex just before Lexa is killed. Bea makes Ferguson stab her after she has finally had sex with Allie. *Person of Interest* even "kills" Shaw twice. In season four she finally kisses Root and is immediately gunned down, and in season five she leaves their bed after having sex and kills herself shortly afterwards. Although in neither case was she *actually* dead (she survived the first shooting and the second took place in virtual reality), the impact on viewers is heightened by the storyline's snug fit into the existing Ur-text.

Occasionally, a television series—perhaps inadvertently—helps its lesbian character to articulate the wider problem that she and her sisters face. *Les Revenants* is an award-winning French television series, remade in the USA as the short-lived *The Returned* (2015). The show depicts a small, isolated French town, where a number of people return from the dead. One of the main characters, Julie, is a lesbian. Seven years prior to the events depicted in the show, she was attacked by a serial killer and she has not recovered from this trauma. Although she continues to work as a nurse she lives in isolation, having split up from her partner Laure who is a lieutenant in the local police force. One of the dead people, a small boy she calls Victor, selects Julie as the "fairy" who will look after him. His presence in her life helps Julie to establish that she wishes to live and she restarts her relationship with Laure. However, once the townsfolk have accepted that the returned people are indeed dead rather than joyful miracles, Julie asks Mrs. Costa, one of the revenants. "How can you tell if you're dead?" Mrs. Costa gazes at her for a moment then responds: "It doesn't take long to realize." Julie leans forward and almost whispers "because sometimes I wonder if I'm..." but does not complete the sentence. Much later, after Julie and Victor have moved in with Laure and the two women are kissing and starting to have sex, Julie is more explicit about what troubles her. She suggests to Laure that she believes she too may be a revenant:

LAURE: You're not like them. I know you're not.

JULIE: You don't understand. You have no idea. I'm not scared to be like them. It's the opposite. For years, I've felt incapable of living. What if it's because I'm dead? [*Les Revenants*, "Adele"].

The point here is that this living character already feels that she must be dead because it is the only logical explanation for her situation. In other words, she may have been dead all along, which in American slang means to be marked for death, or destined to die, unable to escape her fate. Certainly, by the end of the season she has chosen to accompany Victor when he joins the ranks of the dead people, and Laure, along with most of the gendarmerie, has vanished (presumed dead) after a night spent protecting the living from the hordes of the returned. The U.S. version of the show avoids this trope, keeping the two women alive and together at the end of season one and banishing Victor from their lives instead. However, since the U.S. version was not renewed the dead lesbian remains while the living ones are cancelled.

Deliberately Doomed or Careless Mistake?

The convoluted history of the screen adaptation of Lillian Hellman's 1934 play *The Children's Hour* provides good evidence that the lesbian is deliberately doomed. The play is based on a real-life account of two women who ran a private school in Scotland during the nineteenth century which was also the subject of Lillian Faderman's book *Scotch verdict*: Miss Pirie and Miss Woods v. Dame Cumming Gordon*. Accused of lesbianism by one of the pupils, the play examines the scourge of lies and whispers and their capacity to destroy livelihoods and lives (those of the schoolteachers and of the pupil). Once the possibility of lesbianism has been articulated one of the women, Martha, realizes that she is in fact attracted to her friend and co-worker Karen, and kills herself as a result of this devastating realization. Adapted for the screen during the era of the Hays Code, the film version had to recreate the drama of the original without inferring lesbianism. The result, *These Three* (William Wyler, USA, 1936), turns the story into a heterosexual love triangle. The play was adapted for the screen again, this time reinstating the lesbian accusation, as *The Children's Hour* in 1961. What is crucial here is the different outcome in each version: in the heterosexualized version Martha does not kill herself, whereas in both lesbian versions she does. As White points out "the very fact that *These Three*'s Martha doesn't have to die shows how gratuitous and calculated queer movie deaths are (the Code requires that crime and vice must be paid for)

[…] Having the lesbian pass for straight in this film saves her life" (White 5).

The lesbians or bisexual women in other genres are also deliberately targeted. Harris notes that in blaxploitation films gay men are typically depicted as humorous and played for laughs, in the role of "jesters," whereas lesbians are violent and evil, thus "scoundrels," and are therefore killed. "The lesbian characters portrayed in these films are more likely to be cruel and villainous than the gay male characters," and "the frightening and sadistic lesbian is one character that repeatedly emerges" in them (Harris 224–226). Harris argues that in the film *Coffy* (Jack Hill, USA, 1973), the titular character (played by Pam Grier) "has easily been able to defend herself in a variety of situations," but when confronted with a butch lesbian, "Coffy did not even attempt to fight with her. This scene suggests Coffy was so afraid of the big, black, butch Harriet that she actually runs from her" (Harris 224). However, Cleopatra Jones (also Pam Grier), who is "tall, thin, suave, black, heterosexual" is not afraid of white lesbians: she despatches both Mommy, who is "a racist, overweight, older, white lesbian, who kills any employee who disobeys her," and the Dragon Lady, "another brutal white lesbian dope smuggler" (Harris 224–225).

Harris argues that in a several blaxploitation films set in prisons lesbianism is deliberately portrayed as predatory and threatening. In *Women in Cages*, for example, Alabama (Pam Grier yet again) is a prison guard in the Philippines, "has taken on many women as lovers in the film, who, in addition to the other women in prison, she seems to enjoy torturing. For example, while having sex with her Filipino lover, an inmate in the prison, Alabama begins to violently whip her" (Harris 226). The decisions to make the lesbians seem threatening and brutal, in order to justify their subsequent annihilation, was intentional. According to Harris, Jack Hill, the director of *Coffy*, "shot the lesbian character from the floor up to make her appear much larger and more intimidating than she actually was" (Harris 227). In addition, Harris suggests that lesbian sex is clearly marked as deviant and despised in these films, and the inmates who resist it at any cost are deemed more moral (Harris 227).

Post-communist and Nigerian films perform similar deliberate strategies to erase the threat of lesbian possibility and restore patriarchal heteronormativity to the nation. In order to do this the lesbian characters "experience unrestrained violence that frequently eliminates their representation not only from the framework of a particular film, but also from the civil societies and liberal democracies of the Western Balkans" (Laćan 231). Lindsey Green Simms and Unoma Azuah comment that *Emotional*

Crack was written by a woman and directed by a man: Emem Isong and Lancelot Imasuen respectively. Isong was inspired by being romantically pursued by another woman. Green Simms and Azuah note that "Isong knew that creatively there were many ways for the film to end, but she also insisted that in order for *Emotional Crack* to be acceptable in Nigeria, there had to be a way to salvage the marriage of Crystal and Chudi" (41–42). Thus the film's creators acknowledge that Crystal's death is uncalled for. Although one can cite the illegality of homosexuality in Nigeria, due to its conceptualization as "un–Nigerian" (Green-Simms and Azuah 32), this excuse is too similar to those made by directors who reside in other nations. The Croatian film *Fine Dead Girls*, for example, "presents lesbianism as a choice inspired by the influx of Western products and ideas, rather than as a phenomenon rooted in local communities" (Laćan 231).

An additional way in which killing the lesbians seems deliberate rather than a careless accident is that it seems to be the storyline of choice when an actor is leaving a show anyway. Characters can be written out in multiple ways. Georgina Reilly, who played Emily Grace on *Murdoch Mysteries*, for example, was leaving the show in order to relocate from Canada to the USA. The show's writers created a storyline where she and Lillian had decided to move to London, England in order to join in the suffragette movement there. There was no reason why they should not have followed through on this story, since after Lillian was murdered Emily left anyway. Equally, Leslie Shay could have been transferred to another Fire House on *Chicago Fire* instead of killing her, and since Sarah Shahi had to take a potentially lengthy maternity leave from *Person of Interest*, the writers could have selected from a range of alternative exits for her character instead of the one they did choose.

Conclusion

As the number of lesbians on screen increases, the pace at which they are annihilated accelerates. Since 2013, English-language television seasons have been particularly tough for lesbians and bisexuals. As Trish Bendix pointed out on Afterellen.com, "there were at least nine queer female characters killed off their prospective shows in 2013 alone," (Bendix, "Please"), and things only got worse from there. Various television shows had established regular or recurring characters with whom audiences were familiar. These included Leslie Shay on *Chicago Fire*, Lillian on *Murdoch Mysteries*, Charlie on *Supernatural*, and Sara Lance on *Arrow*. In the 2014 season opening episodes of *Chicago Fire* and *Arrow*, two of these characters were killed off. Although Sara was later resurrected, she set off on her own adventures in *Legends of Tomorrow*. Shortly afterwards both Lillian and Charlie died. Disbelieving audience members and critics aired their pain and astonishment online in blogs with titles such as "Please stop killing us! The state of lesbians and bi women on TV" by Trish Bendix and "Fandom Fixes: Just stop killing all the black lesbians, OK, 'Pretty Little Liars'?" by Heather Hogan.

Following on from this wholesale symbolic annihilation Sally Wainwright—who dismissed the Dead Lesbian Trope as a "myth"—killed off Kate, a black lesbian no less, on *Last Tango in Halifax*. She had already annihilated the lesbian from another of the television shows she penned, *Scott & Bailey*. In the final episode of that show's third season, the deeply troubled lesbian Helen Bartlett kidnaps DCI Gill Murray, clearly intending to murder Murray and kill herself. In the end she only takes her own life. On *Last Tango in Halifax*, meanwhile, Kate was killed in a car crash. Wainwright's decision to kill yet another lesbian character even prompted a response from the mainstream media, in addition to all of the lesbian and queer women's sites that were already hoarse from protesting over the preceding months. Kaite Welsh writing in *The Guardian* remarked that Kate was "the latest victim of the dead lesbian cliché" and provided "yet more evidence that lesbians in TV exist to be sacrificed for the plot." This was one more example of a show "privileging heterosexual narratives and contributing to misogyny in popular culture by using a woman's death as a means of manipulating audience emotions" (Welsh). Apparently surprised by the very predictable outrage of viewers, Wainwright tried to justify her choice in an interview with Carrie Lyell in the British lesbian magazine *Diva*:

> It was a narrative decision, it was a storyline decision. I was really sad. It was a big decision, a huge decision, and one I didn't really want to make because I didn't want to lose Nina [Sosanya]. I didn't want to lose the character. I actually wrote two versions of episode four—one where she didn't die [Lyell, "Last"].

This justification did not satisfy frustrated viewers, especially given that two months later Lyell had to ask "Did Call the Midwife just do a Last Tango in Halifax?" The debacle over Lexa's death in *The 100* crystalizes the pain and frustration that weary viewers increasingly feel over the repetitive, predictable nature of the dead lesbian storyline. "Fans revolt after gay TV character killed off" the international BBC News site recorded in March 2016, and Jason Rothenberg, the creator of *The 100*, felt pressured to apologize to the fans and claimed he was not aware of the Dead Lesbian Cliché (Prudom), a claim which echoes that of the *Buffy* creators more than a decade earlier (Mangels 70). Given that viewers are only too well aware of these dehumanizing and commonplace tropes (just watch any show with an intimate relationship between women to see it), these public denials of complicity by those in the film and television industries seem disingenuous at best.

In thinking about pop cultural representations about black women in North America, Nina Cartier remarks that "I feel a great sense of fatigue. My fatigue emanates from watching every black female image carrying the burden of all the ideological work for all black women. My fatigue rises as I wonder not only when a critical mass of black female representations will occur so that a wider spectrum manifests but also why black women's roles have to become ubiquitous for that wider spectrum to even occur in the first place" (Cartier 156–157). The same fatigue applies to lesbian and bisexual representations (who of course can be women of color too). The fact that this pattern, whether in the allocation of death via suicide, murder or accidental death, repeats itself in television series and films all over the world should strike a penetratingly deep chord. Writing out of existence women who love women in general and black and ethnic minority lesbians and bisexual women in particular might be a justifiable "narrative decision," but this does not make it any less of a social and political decision.

2

THE SUBTEXT WILL NOT PROTECT YOU

On September 4, 1995, viewers tuning in to try out a new television series were told that a land in turmoil was crying out for a hero. She was called Xena, and while the opening credits claimed that it was her courage that would change the world, it was actually her relationship with her soul mate, Gabrielle, that changed the lives of many viewers, generated a massive (fan) fiction industry, and reconfigured how on-screen relationships between women were interpreted. Through the latter process the show *Xena: Warrior Princess* (hereafter *XWP*) mainstreamed the idea of lesbian subtext. Chapters 6 and 7 discuss the on-going ripple effects of community organizing and fan fiction as responses to the symbolic annihilation of lesbians, but here we concentrate on what started it all: the subtext. Overwhelmingly, scholarly analyses of lesbian representation since the rise of second-wave feminism tend to focus on how *lesbians* represent themselves, examining how filmmakers negotiate the treacherous shoals of cinematic conventions in order to reach authentic, alternative ways of being on-screen. We will discuss some of the challenges to that process later in the book. The vast majority of people, however, will never see a lesbian-made alternative film or TV series. They are stuck with mainstream messages and have to engage in practices of decoding what the film and television industries have encoded for them.

Reading for the Subtext

In 1981 *Jump Cut* published an essay by Edith Becker, Michelle Citron, Julia Lesage and B. Ruby Rich which explicitly named the concept of lesbian subtext. It was reprinted in the 1995 *Out in Culture* anthology edited by Corey Creekmuir and Alexander Doty and remains a key framework through which to consider lesbians' relationship to film. Becker, Citron, Lesage and Rich argue that in the absence of meaningful or authentic portrayals of lesbians on screen, "the most important viewing strategy has been to concentrate on the subtext, the 'hidden' meaning, of commercial films. The notion of the lesbian subtext depends on the knowledge, suspicion, or hope that some participants in the film (director, actress, screenwriter) were themselves lesbians, and that their perspective can be discerned in the film even though disguised" (Becker et al. 30). This definition came out of the specific historical context of Hollywood film in the pre-internet age, when information about stars and directors had to be gleaned from gossip. Women who were part of a lesbian subculture or who had developed sufficient "gaydar" to be able to recognize a fellow Sapphist often depended on gossip to provide clues about a person's status. They also operated on the assumption that women who did not fit recognizably into a heteronormative straitjacket might have a secret or "hidden" life in the closet.

A good example of the role of gossip is the character of Sylvia Scarlett, played by Katharine Hepburn in the film of the same name (George Cukor, USA, 1935). When dressed (very convincingly) as a young man, Scarlett evoked in the viewer what the character of Michael Lane in the film described as "a queer feeling when I look at you." That enunciation of a "queer feeling" was important because it acknowledged the underlying frisson of strangeness created by the combination of the whole audience being "in on the joke" (that the boy is a woman) and at least some audience members being acutely aware of the fact that the "boy" was Hepburn, who was already divorced and had been in a relationship with Laura Harding since 1930. Although her relationship with Harding was basically over by the time she filmed *Sylvia Scarlett*, for years gossip magazines had drawn attention to the fact that they were often seen together and lived together. In December 1933 the *Los Angeles Times* even included Harding in a feature about the "husbands, wives, and lovers" who were actively involved in promoting their partners' careers (Mann 200–201). This gossipy background information was significant because, as Andrea Weiss explains, certain stars such as Hepburn "often asserted gestures and movements in their films that were inconsistent with and even posed an ideological threat within the narrative." This meant that for some audience members at least, selected films could provide "the opportunity to see in certain gestures and movements an affirmation of lesbian experience—something that, however fleeting, was elsewhere rarely to be found, and certainly not in such a popular medium" (Weiss, "Queer," 292).

Although Becker, Citron, Lesage and Rich's definition of subtext is based on extra-textual knowledge (via gossip) about a film's actors and directors, in the 35-odd years since they created that definition the meaning of the term has mutated considerably, in part because of the effect of *XWP* and in part by linking up with ideas borrowed from lesbians' consumption of literature. Sherrie Inness claims that when they are reading material that is targeted at heterosexuals, lesbians are likely to "look for meanings that lurk behind the text's apparently heterosexual surface, knowing that lesbian experiences, whether in fiction or reality, are rarely overt" (Inness, *Lesbian* 83). As a result, the sense that there is something unseen but secretly encoded is no longer based on the idea of a lesbian perspective being covertly introduced by the actors or director. Instead, the idea of "lesbian subtext" involves reading for a relationship between two characters which is unacknowledged on-screen but which seems to be implied, sometimes through codes, sometimes through intertextual references. Although the characters may be involved in maintext relationships with men, the series which evokes a lesbian subtext will contain ambiguous storylines which are open to multiple readings, and some of these allow an engaged audience to read against the grain to see a relationship between characters which is never explicitly named on the screen.

Stuart Hall explains the processes of "encoding/decoding" through which meaning-making in television shows occurs. In his foundational essay on this process Hall explains that "the institutional structures of broadcasting" attempt to "encode" the particular message(s) of a show, transforming that message into a discourse which makes sense within the ideologically "dominant cultural order" (123). However, this ideological message is not communicated seamlessly, even when its content has been so naturalized as to seem to reflect reality rather than ideology. Instead, audience members have to decode the messages. Hall argues that it is possible for a decoder-receiver (a viewer) to interpret the message in a way other than that intended by the encoder (a writer, producer, director, actor). Hall considers three potential decoding positions: the "dominant-hegemonic," the "negotiated code," and the "oppositional code" (125–127). Television studies have elaborated extensively on these codes but for the purposes of reflecting on lesbian subtextual readings, their basic forms help to explain three potential responses to the representation of relationships between women characters who have not been explicitly named on-screen as lesbian or bisexual.

The first of these, the "dominant-hegemonic," is based on the concept of hegemony which can be defined as "the capacity of a dominant group to control not through visible rule or the deployment of coercion or force but through the manufacture of consent which ensures the willingness of people to accept their subordinate status" (McDowell and Sharp 121). The process of manufacturing consent takes place through civil institutions such as the media. The "dominant-hegemonic" discourse is received by this type of viewer virtually undistorted, just as it left the dream factory. In terms of lesbian subtext, the hegemonic or powerful commonsense message (what Hall calls the "preferred code") is that heteronormativity is natural and inevitable and that lesbians are masculine, highly visible (and therefore easily targeted), only sexual, and better off dead. This viewer does not perceive any subtextual connection, because lesbian desire would be announced via a sexual relationship or recognizably butch character.

The second, "negotiated" position "acknowledges the legitimacy of the hegemonic definitions to make the grand significations (abstract), while, at a more restricted, situational (situated) level, it makes its own ground rules—it operates with exceptions to the rule" (Hall 127). Or, put more simply, the negotiating decoder accepts the dominant (hegemonic) message about heteronormativity but she or he can also see in individual (localized or situated) examples the possibility that two women could be in love without them necessarily posing a danger to the heteronormative order. Such a reading is likely to see the two women as born-that-way lesbians, even if it would take a dramatic incident for the characters to realize their true natures—they may have been closeted even to themselves and they may remain resolutely closeted on screen. A show such as *Once Upon a Time* lends itself to a negotiated reading for a relationship between the characters of Emma Swan and Regina Mills, who co-mother Henry. In early seasons their initial hostility, bonding together over making magic and saving Henry, and reliance on each other to make necessary tough decisions, primed willing viewers to see in their relationship the potential for romance, even if the characters themselves do not yet realize it. Because of this mixture of the hegemonic and oppositional, or locally specific challenges to the hegemonic discourse, the negotiated code can be full of contradictions.

The third or "oppositional" position recognizes that the hegemonic message exists but outright refuses it. This viewer "detotalizes the message in the preferred code in order to retotalize the message within some alternative framework of reference" (Hall 127). Inness claims that "lesbian readers search for the lesbian subtext that speaks to them and their experiences. Lesbians read and interpret aspects of a text that heterosexual readers might not notice in the same way [...] they are constantly involved in altering the entire text" (Inness 83). Thus, "when lesbians read, they actively disassemble the dominant heterosexual plot" (Inness 83). Femslash fan fiction writers are particularly adept at this, but for a general subtextual reading of films and television shows the oppositional code means that some viewers consistently "see" a lesbian relationship between characters which is not visible to other viewers. Subtext tends to become visible over time and therefore is more likely to be read into television series rather than into films, although there have been some notable exceptions such as *Rebecca* (Alfred Hitchcock, USA, 1940), *The Uninvited* (Lewis Allen, USA, 1944) and, more recently, *The Devil Wears Prada* (David Frankel, USA, 2006). Key examples of shows which can easily be read through an oppositional code are *XWP*, *Rizzoli & Isles* (in the bond between the titular characters), and *Warehouse 13* (in the connection between Myka Bering and H.G. Wells).

A film or television series which passes the Bechdel Test with flying colors is likely to promote both negotiated and oppositional subtextual readings, because women characters share a lot of screen time talking to each other, frequently without any men present, and often without referring to men at all. They may even discuss their relationship with each other. Similarly, a show which is "strategically ambiguous" may also lend itself to subtextual interpretation. "Strategically ambiguous" texts are those in which the creators have deliberately incorporated multiple meanings (or polysemy) into the text. As Rockler explains, "the dominant reading of a strategically ambiguous text often promotes dominant ideology, while other readers may decode the text within an oppositional framework (in an active manner that overlaps, somewhat, with resistive reading)" (Rockler 93). For example, as Weiss says of the film *Queen Christina* (Rouben Mamoulin, USA, 1933), "although Hollywood attempted to purge the story of Queen Christina from the taint of lesbianism, the sub-text left itself wide open to possible lesbian readings" (Weiss, "Queer," 293).

Pre-Xena Warrior Princess *Subtextual Readings*

The *practice* of reading for a lesbian subtext was already well-established before Xena met Gabrielle: viewers learned to decode under the Hays Code. The impact of the Hays Code meant that viewers had to develop skills in subtextual reading in order to "see" lesbian possibility. As Vicki Eaklor points out, the Code "did not mean that people who might be recognized as lesbian or gay disappeared from the screen, but rather that their queerness would be coded in ways recognizable to viewers attuned to stereotypes or 'inside knowledge'" (Eaklor, "Kids," 156). Although superficially the Hays Code appears to be a straightforward example of moral repression, Rhona Berenstein among other scholars argues that it was a productive mechanism. That is, rather than banning something that already existed, its codifications and the correspondence and negotiations around what it permitted actively *produced* the idea of what it was supposedly censoring. It also produced knowledge about what to look for in order to see what was not depicted. In her close study of documents about *The Uninvited*, Berenstein argues that "self-regulation added to the signifying scope of films—versus limiting that scope—by actively contributing to the rewrite process" (Berenstein 19). Correspondence between self-appointed moral guardians, filmmakers, and members of the Production Code Administration attests to the complex negotiations through which men decided what could be shown and what it was supposed to mean.

Two key sets of encoding emerged under the Hays Code. The first set was based on gender inversion, or the idea that lesbians were unnaturally masculine. On screen this idea manifested itself in the masculine-coded woman, who might wear tweed, pants or sensible shoes, have short hair, and be direct, hearty, or no-nonsense. She would almost certainly be brunette rather than blonde, and possibly taller or otherwise larger than her feminine-coded screen mates. The assumption that the "real" lesbian is the masculine woman (in life and on screen) makes these women visible as lesbians, and this set of ideas "reinforce the popular conceptions that homosexuals are easily recognizable (in obvious cross-gender appearance and/or behavior) and thus, since relatively few people seem to fit this description, relatively rare" (Eaklor, "Seeing," 327). The second set of encoding was more dynamic and based on the interactions between characters, including emotional bonds, physical closeness, and exchange of looks, as well as blocking of shots, reactions of other characters, plotlines, and so on. Weiss suggests that in *Queen Christina* the "interaction between Queen Christina and Countess Ebba relies on sexual innuendo within their dialogue and gestures, revealing the desire of the two women for each other and the frustration of having duty and responsibility interfere with that desire" (Weiss, "Queer," 293), while according to Patricia White it is the combination of both sets of codes that make Mrs. Danvers in the thriller *Rebecca* so eminently readable as a lesbian in love with her deceased mistress.

These combined codes could evoke a potent sense of desire in women viewers in complex ways. It takes work to assert the existence of a lesbian subtext and then to maintain that it is there when other viewers dismiss or deny its possibility. Rockler points out that several scholars caution that in this process "the work necessary to perform oppositional readings must be outweighed by pleasure, and audience members must be rhetorically skilled enough to recognize the textual cues or 'codes' that signal polysemy" (92). Equally, in their *Studio Responsibility Index* looking at LGBT representation in film, GLAAD notes that they count some films as LGBT inclusive which might not appear to be so. This discrepancy is because "certain characters must be subjectively interpreted to be seen as LGBT, require external confirmation of the filmmakers' intentions, or rely on pre-existing knowledge of source material or a public figure on whom a character is based" (GLAAD, *Studio* 5).

Nevertheless, there is evidence that lesbian and gay audiences do take pleasure in their collective decoding skills as well as in the need for these readings. In her analysis of the film *Muriel's Wedding* (P.J. Hogan, Australia, 1995) Jill Mackey suggests that part of the pleasure that lesbian viewers get from reading a film for a lesbian subtext (which here she restricts to the definition based on extra-textual gossip) or a countertext (which Mackey defines as "a reading strategy that appropriates the film for lesbian's pleasure") "lies in the act of appropriation itself." She claims that this appropriation "makes us part of the in-joke. It demonstrates the power of the viewer against the tyranny of the text" (Mackey 100–101). Private feelings of desire provide another motivation to do the work of believing in the subtext. These feelings can be a secret passion which fuels daydreams of a different kind of life which is not a stretch because film and television condition viewers to long for one anyway, preferably by buying the carefully placed products. Once extended beyond the personal this passion can generate (fan) community formation and dialogue, which fan fiction and femslash organizing then reinforce, providing even more satisfaction in the shared conviction that a subtext exists.

Adapting the Maintext into Subtext

The need to read for subtext should only have lasted as long as the inference of lesbianism was banned from the screen. In the post–Hays Code era, Hollywood filmmakers were finally safe to depict lesbian relationships on-screen: indeed, there had been some loosening of the restrictions in 1961. The decision in the 1980s to adapt two novels with significant same-sex relationships should, therefore, have marked the beginning of the end for subtext as the dominant representation of lesbian desire. However, in both film adaptations these relationships were eviscerated and turned from maintext into subtext—almost as if the Hays Code was still in place. The films were *The Color Purple* (Steven Spielberg, USA, 1985), adapted from Alice Walker's Pulitzer Prize-winning 1982 novel of the same name, and *Fried Green Tomatoes* (Jon Avnet, USA, 1991), adapted from the 1987 novel *Fried Green Tomatoes at the Whistle Stop Café* by Fannie Flagg. The former was a major Hollywood film by an enormously successful director (Spielberg had already helmed the blockbusters *Jaws*, *Close Encounters of the Third Kind*, and *E.T.*) and was entirely about African Americans.

There was an enormous outpouring of anger towards the film, particularly from African American protestors who picketed the Academy Awards where the film had received nominations in eleven categories, including Best Picture (it did not win any Oscars). Walker herself recorded that "from the moment word went out that there would be a movie, it was attacked by people who loathed the idea" (Walker 22). Most critics were angry at the film's depiction of Black men, accusing Walker of being anti-man and bitterly attacking the film for making African American men look like one-dimensional, violent clowns. Allen Woll suggests that the level of controversy had a major impact on the acceptance of African American actors and directors in Hollywood and that the industry's interest in adapting other novels by African American writers slowed as well (Woll 207). Analysis of the film therefore tends to be more on its depiction of Black people's lives rather than lesbianism (as if the two can be separated).

What is special about the film *The Color Purple*, however, is that in her book *The Same River Twice* Alice Walker, who was closely involved in the adaptation, documented her reaction to the film, the responses to it, and her reflections on the ways in which the novel and film differed from each other. She therefore provides insight into the role of the industry in managing representations of same-sex desire and her own ideas about how to present an authentic relationship between the characters of Shug (Margaret Avery) and Celie (Whoopi Goldberg). As she explains, she had "wanted to give my family and friends an opportunity to see women-loving women—lesbian, heterosexual, bi-sexual, 'two-spirited'—womanist women in a recognizable context" (Walker 170). In the novel, Celie and her husband's mistress Shug fall in love and have a sexual relationship that is precipitated by an erotic kiss. The film is much more circumspect. Referring to her mother, Walker wrote that "I did not want her to miss the love between women in *The Color Purple*. And so I lobbied for a kiss. I refused to believe intolerance for anyone was my mother's true nature. (In the movie almost all the women kiss each other, making the kiss between Celie and Shug less significant.)" (Walker 168). Thus a profoundly erotic scene in the novel, around which Celie's burgeoning sense of self develops, is reduced in the Hollywood version to an emotional exchange on a par with others in the film. This makes the same-sex sexuality much less visible and powerful. Walker remarks that "there are telling moments in the film when the censor's knife scars the scene." Dissecting a scene in which Celie and Shug sit in separate seats in a vehicle—Celie in the rumble seat and Shug in front—Walker asserts that this is a misrepresentation of the deep connection between the women-loving women that she had originally wanted to depict. Celie "had met the woman with whom she would spend the rest of her life: they both knew it. They would have shared a seat, at least" (Walker 220).

Walker did write her own script for the film but Spielberg went with the script by Menno Meyjes. As Walker explained, in her version "it was clear that the women loved each other. It was clear that Shug is, like me, bisexual. That Celie is a lesbian" (Walker 35). Furthermore, Walker's script included one thing "which the film avoided entirely, [which] is Shug's completely unapologetic self-acceptance as outlaw, renegade, rebel, and pagan; her zest in loving both women and men, younger and older" (Walker 25). That clarity and complexity is missing from the film version and, instead, viewers have to dig for it underneath what Spielberg promised Walker would be a "tasteful" kissing scene.

More has been written about the fate of the lesbian relationship in *Fried Green Tomatoes* than in *The Color Purple*. For *Fried Green Tomatoes*, several authors have carefully demonstrated how the maintext lesbian relationship between Ruth (Mary Louise Parker) and Idgie (Mary Stuart Masterton) in Fannie Flagg's original novel was rendered subtextual in the film version. Rockler nicely summarizes the problem: "through the use of strategic ambiguity, *Fried Green Tomatoes* transforms Idgie and Ruth's relatively unambiguous lesbian relationship from the book to an ambiguous relationship" (104). However, by embracing intertextuality even lesbians who had not read the book were quick to spot the lovers at the center of the film, even if other viewers noticed nothing. Eaklor points out that "both anecdotal and some printed evidence suggest that if anyone sees Ruth and Idgie as lesbians, it is lesbians" ("Seeing," 325). In the novel, Idgie's brother Buddy is already long dead before Ruth and Idgie meet and fall in love when Idgie is a teenager and Ruth arrives to teach at the church summer school. The young women share an intense experience (the bee charming episode in both book and film) and after this Ruth can no longer suppress her feeling for Idgie. Ruth leaves, concerned that Idgie's love is merely an adolescent crush whereas her own is only too real and could endanger both women.

In the film, however, Ruth first loves Buddy (when Idgie is much younger) and some years after his death returns and transfers her affection to Idgie. Lu Vickers analyses the differences between the book and film and claims that this particular revision suggests that "the movie wants us to believe that the women's relationship revolves around their mutual love of Buddy, and that given his loss, they may as well settle for each other" (Vickers 7). In the book, Ruth and Idgie bring up their son Buddy Jr., and live together for nearly twenty years, except for a period when Ruth moves out because of Idgie's lying and need to feel unencumbered (Flagg 255). In the film Ruth does not last that long: she dies of cancer while Buddy Jr., is still young. These adaptations alter the story sufficiently that it can be incorporated into a tale that matches the "dominant-hegemonic" coding for a sizeable number of viewers. Eaklor comments on the (in)visibility of the couple and points out the possibility that "if there is a 'real' lesbian here, it is Idgie, the 'tomboy' who never grows out of either loving Ruth or ignoring males (except as pals)" ("Seeing," 327), while Jan Whitt amusingly remarks that "even though Idgie is a lesbian and chooses to wear pants, suspenders, ties, and vests, it is still possible for members of the audience to refer to Idgie as a 'tomboy' and avoid dealing with her lesbianism entirely" (50). For those who do manage a negotiated decoding, the adaptation communicates the message that lesbian relationships may be deep, meaningful, and supported by the whole town, but they are inevitably short-lived and tragic.

Both of these films reduced a clearly acknowledged lesbian relationship (in the novels) to subtextual relationships (on screen) that could only be seen by viewers practicing negotiated or oppositional decoding. In another example, from television, a lesbian relationship was technically encoded as the "dominant-hegemonic" meaning but was rendered so ambiguous that viewers had to actively engage in either negotiated or oppositional readings to believe in it. In her study of New Zealand lesbian representation, Alison Hopkins examines the relationship between the characters Maia and Jay on the New Zealand soap opera *Shortland Street*. Neither of these two characters was supposed to be interested sexually or romantically in men: they are lesbians, not bisexual or heterosexual. However, the show's creators introduced "strategic ambiguity" into their storylines: the characters rarely experienced support for their relationship from other characters; numerous homophobic incidents and commentary from other characters went unchallenged; the two women displayed little intimacy; and both were sexually paired with men. Maia's co-worker Mark sexually harassed her, behavior which she treated as flirtatious evidence of his love for her, and Jay had sex with Norman so that she could get pregnant, as well as with her business partner Dylan.

By studying the responses of viewers via the "Streettalk" online forum, Hopkins was able to ascertain that the majority of "viewers prefer to read heteronormatively, aided by the ambiguity the scriptwriters intentionally created around Maia and Jay's sexuality" (Hopkins 166). Some of these viewers rooted for Maia and Mark to become a couple and for Jay to get out of the way, or they wanted Jay to stay with Norman and leave Maia. Hopkins also conducted focus groups with a variety of viewers, and notes that many of her "lesbian focus group participants complained about the lesbian stereotypes, representation, and plot arcs that reinforced heterosexuality, particularly within *Shortland Street*. Despite this, participants and fans acknowledged they continued watching the characters" and that "despite the overwhelming weaknesses in Maia and Jay, lesbian viewers identified with the characters because they explicitly identified as lesbians" (Hopkins 202–203). However, although these two were explicitly named as lesbian, these viewers still had to engage in some reading for subtext. Hopkins explains that "the ideological inflections of heterosexuality were so overwhelming in the construction of Maia and Jay it is necessary to actively read the lesbian sexuality into the lesbian characters" (176). This meant that to read these lesbians *as* lesbians required reading against the grain—a tactic normally reserved for subtextual readings. However, while being—essentially—heterosexual characters they were not treated in the *same* way as the actually heterosexual ones. Even when the lesbian couple had a major storyline about a Civil Union they only had, on average, half the number of on-screen kisses that heterosexual characters enjoyed.

These three examples indicate that while, in theory, from the late 1960s onwards films and television shows could depict lesbians on screen without too much fear of censorship, the "institutional structures of broadcasting" (Hall 123) remained unwilling to show women's same-sex relationships as complex, qualitatively different from heteronormative relationships, embedded in women's and/or lesbian communities, and sexual in ways that were not designed to titillate heterosexual men. To *see* this kind of complexity required viewers to continue to watch for the subtext, and they found it in *Xena: Warrior Princess*.

Mainstreaming the Subtext

The mainstreaming (or perhaps "maintexting") of lesbian subtext began—and, arguably, was completed—with *Xena: Warrior Princess*. The series ran for six seasons until June 18, 2001. It had a total of 134 episodes and was syndicated in 115 nations (Silverman 33). It was the number one new syndicated show on U.S. television and by 1998 it had become one of the top ten television series in syndication worldwide (Morreale 79). It was set, as the opening credits explained, "in a time of ancient gods, warlords and kings" but was loose with chronology and geography. The action of the series ranged across different time periods, including ancient Greece and the Roman Empire, the 1940s, the present day, and reincarnations at some point in the characters' future. It also dealt in alternative timelines. The characters traveled across fictionalized versions of Greece, the Roman Empire, China, India, Scandinavia (for episodes loosely based on Wagner's Ring Cycle opera), and Japan. In addition to fighting warlords, Roman emperors, and villagers' bigotry, Xena and Gabrielle battled and sometimes allied with mythical beings, supernatural forces, and various gods. From its inception the series used what was considered at the time to be a daringly postmodern approach, mixing mythology and spiritual texts with events from history and bastardized versions of characters and storylines from film, television, opera and theatre to generate a highly intertextual series. Sara Gwenllian Jones documented its:

> own self-conscious postmodernism, its constant and deliberated blurring of the boundaries between history and fiction. At the same time, by building on its own mythologic, by opening and irreverently challenging and reworking historical orthodoxy, the series reinforces its own status as a highly politicized interpretative space by inviting its audience to ask itself, "what if…?" [Gwenllian Jones 404].

The show was a massive (and unexpected) international success, even though its co-creator and producer, Rob Tapert, said that "*Xena* was a very tough sell to the syndicators" because "everyone believed there was no market for a woman superhero" (Weisbrot 19). It was particularly popular with lesbians. On the twentieth anniversary of the first episode one of the writers for AfterEllen.com, Dana Piccoli, reflected on the show's significance, stating that "*Xena* lived just beyond the borders of subtext and more than once leapt completely over it." She claimed that "these were two women who loved each other fiercely, and for a generation of lesbian and bisexual women, that meant everything" (Piccoli). Introducing her book about the impact of *XWP* had on fans, Nikki Stafford averred that "their friendship was like nothing I had ever seen on television" (Stafford viii). Indeed, the entire show was unlike anything else on television at the time. Nadine Crenshaw tried to capture what was so different about Xena herself. Typically:

> female action stories simply inserted a woman into the basic male archetypical narrative. At the same time, television producers made them almost too feminine. Wonder Woman's hair was always perfect—and worse, she looked as if she cared about such

things. In contrast, if Xena were to have her clothes yanked off while fighting, she wouldn't shriek and try to cover herself. She'd just keep on fighting, probably with more fierceness and fury than before [Crenshaw 55].

Xena herself (Lucy Lawless) is a former warlord who possesses nearly supernatural fighting skills and a fierce reputation earned during her years as a brutal "Destroyer of Nations." In the first episode, having forsworn her fighting life, she is obliged once again to pick up her sword and chakram (a sharp-edged circular throwing weapon from India) in order to protect the villagers of Poteidaia from being terrorized by a warlord. It is during this rescue that she meets Gabrielle (Renee O'Connor), an aspiring bard who is keen to escape her arranged marriage and village life in order to see the world and have a chance to be herself. As she explains to her sister Lila, "I'm different from everybody else in this town [...] I don't fit in" ("Sins of the Past"). With a combination of youthful bravado and hero-worship, Gabrielle follows Xena and persuades the warrior princess to let her tag along on her travels. This first episode establishes Gabrielle's idolization of Xena and the next few mine their relationship in a fairly conventional (and often amusing) dynamic of larger-than-life hero and her sidekick who gets into scrapes, needs rescuing, and helps the hero learn something about herself. While a familiar trope, this dynamic was nevertheless rare (perhaps even unique) for two women, and some segments of the audience—already attracted by the novelty of an action show with two women leads—quickly identified a subtext running underneath the surface narrative.

In an interview with Rob Tapert in the national feminist magazine *Ms.* in 1996, Donna Minkowitz explained that he "spontaneously brings up the possibility that Xena also has love relationships with women" and he "proudly tells me that the show 'has become a favorite with gay women' and that some lesbian bars have special *Xena*-viewing nights. (So do a number of women's prisons.) 'Early on, the studio came down on me, because they wanted to make sure no one perceived Xena and Gabrielle as lesbians,' the producer says. He doesn't seem to be trying very hard to accede to their demands" (Minkowitz 75). As Jeanne Hamming remarks, "the circuitous relationship that has formed between the series and its fans has created a character who hovers always on the threshold of the closet, or to put it more boldly, who is both in and out of the closet at the same time" (Hamming para. 29).

Xena: Warrior Princess had a profound effect on the visibility of lesbian subtext in multiple ways. Characters, story arcs, individual plotlines, dialogue, and blocking of shots all provided material that could be interpreted using existing codes in order to see what was never technically there. These elements both consolidated the previous work of Hollywood films and fixed them as proof of an intentional subtext (rather than wishful thinking) in many viewers' and commentators' minds. But the show dramatically exceeded these predictable processes of encoding/decoding for several reasons: its women-centeredness; its witty use of intertextuality (the show was often categorized as "camp"); and the explosion in the use of the internet to form fan communities.

Within the encoding/decoding framework already set up in the western context via Hollywood film, the characters of Xena and Gabrielle could effortlessly be read as a romantic couple. Xena is tall, dark-haired, and a taciturn warrior. Gabrielle is shorter, blonde, and a garrulous bard. Terry Castle argues that "by refusing to undergo the symbolic emasculation that Western society demands of its female members—indeed depends upon— the woman who desires another woman has always set herself apart (if only by default) as outlaw and troublemaker" (Castle 5). The converse appears to hold as well, with the outlaw who troubles dominant stories set apart as most likely to be a woman who desires another woman. The characters of Gabrielle and Xena, respectively, seem to map onto this formula. Even in season one, before any media had picked up on the fan buzz around their relationship, the two women put their connection with each other first. Season two consolidated and amplified the components of the show that influenced the mainstreaming of the subtext. Most significantly, Xena and Gabrielle shared what Andrew Leonard called "the kiss that shook cyberspace" (Leonard 1), cementing the decoding that understood them to be lovers.

By season three their relationship was in trouble, with a "Rift" that started when Xena began to take Gabrielle for granted, got much worse when Gabrielle lied to Xena about killing her demonic child Hope, was exacerbated when she got jealous over Xena leaving her to do the bidding of her former mentor (and possibly former lover) Lao Ma, and was torn asunder when Hope murdered Xena's son Solan and in retaliation Xena lassoed Gabrielle and dragged her behind her horse in an attempt to kill her (a scene dubbed the "Gabdrag" by shocked fans). A musical episode allowed them to express their love, heal the rift and reestablish the terms of their relationship just in time for Gabrielle to sacrifice herself in order to save Xena's life at the end of season three. In many ways this season confirmed that the power of their love for each other was at the heart of the show, although viewers could interpret that any way they saw fit.

Following a shamanistic search for her in the underworld at the begin-
ning of season four, a broken-hearted Xena was ecstatic to learn that
Gabrielle was still alive and they were reunited. However, with shades of
Stephen Gordon's treatment of Mary Llewellyn in Radclyffe Hall's novel
The Well of Loneliness, Xena spent much of the season trying to push
Gabrielle away, even into the arms of another woman, the crusader Najara,
to prevent the death she had seen in a vision of their future. In spite of
their best efforts to overcome this destiny, both women were crucified at
the end of season four.

Together in the afterlife at the beginning of the next season, they were
brought back to life by the spirit of Xena's arch enemy Callisto. Now pregnant through Callisto's intervention (one is tempted to say with Callisto's
baby) and back in their mortal lives, Xena had to adjust to the new dynamic
in her relationship, as Gabrielle (initially startled and feeling somewhat
betrayed by this inexplicable pregnancy) began to take on more of a pro-
tective role. Their stint in the afterlife, as well as their earlier experiences
of reincarnation in season four, confirmed that they would be together for
eternity as soul mates. Nevertheless, season five had its ups and downs, as
Gabrielle transformed into a warrior poet and Ares, the god of war—who
had been courting Xena since season one—now made a play for Gabrielle's
loyalty in order to win over Xena. With the birth of their daughter Eve,
Xena and Gabrielle were faced with existential questions over how to raise
her while protecting her from both general violence and the targeted pursuit
of the Olympian gods who believed (correctly) that she would bring about
their downfall. Unfortunately, a ploy to fool those gods went awry and
Xena and Gabrielle slept in suspended animation for twenty-five years
while Eve grew into a brutal warrior (renamed Livia) and then, through
divine intervention, a prophet of monotheism. In a plot worthy of Greek
tragedy, while possessed by the Furies Gabrielle stabbed Eve to within an
inch of her life, Xena nearly brained Gabrielle with her chakram, and Ares
sacrificed his immortality in order to save both of them while Olympus
literally fell around them.

The sixth and final season was even more dark, dealing with loss,
ghosts, the effects of vengeance, Xena at risk of replacing Mephistopheles
in Hell, the Wagner-inspired Ring cycle complete with relentless Valkyries,
restoring the godhood (and thereby cosmic balance) of Ares and his sister
Aphrodite, the goddess of love, and the grim reality of battlefield sacrifices
as Gabrielle tried to protect her Amazon sisters. To the devastation of
innumerable fans, the series ended with Xena's gory death, leaving her soul
mate to continue with only her ghost as company.

A World of Women

If Becker, Citron, Lesage and Rich were at least partially right that "the world of women is banned from film" (28), this dictate was blown clean off the small screen by *XWP*. The remarkable woman-centeredness of the series reinforces its lesbian subtext. There certainly are plenty of recurring male characters on the show. In addition to Ares, there is comic relief in the form of Joxer; Borias, who is Xena's former lover and father of her first child, Solan; Eli the messenger of peace; the Roman Emperors Caesar, Brutus, and Mark Anthony; Autolycus the king of thieves; and Beowulf (who is in love with Gabrielle), as well as numerous weekly villains and victims, but there are also an extraordinary number and diversity of female characters with whom both Xena and Gabrielle have complex relationships. During her journey to becoming a terrifying warlord Xena encountered several powerful women, from each of whom she learned important skills that contribute to her almost unstoppable ability.

Two of these women make relatively brief appearances: M'lila, who saved her life in "Destiny" and taught her the "pinch" technique she uses to temporarily paralyze her opponents, and the Amazon Cyane who taught her how to fight in tree tops and offered her the chance to join the Amazons. Xena's life is more intertwined with those of Alti and Lao Ma. The disgraced Amazon shaman Alti uses her supernatural power to try to both claim and destroy Xena in a series of reincarnations, and she also teaches Xena shamanism ("Adventures in the Sin Trade, Parts I and II"). Lao Ma—who keeps her husband Lao Tzu in a coma, rules the land of "Chin" in his place, and has written the *Tao Te Ching* under his name—rescues Xena, names her as her "warrior princess," and teaches her to control her emotions and move objects with her mind ("The Debt, Parts I and II"). Lao Ma is such an important figure in Xena's life that she leaves Gabrielle to fulfill her mentor's posthumous request to assassinate Lao Ma's son, the Green Dragon, in season three.

Had *XWP* had stopped there—with two women leads and four significant women mentors—it would have been remarkable enough, but it did not. Instead, the complex network of women around Xena and Gabrielle continued to grow. Sara Crosby called this network "an enabling feminist community" and argues that, until the troubling finale, this community supports the journey of Xena and Gabrielle in "finding love and freedom and bringing this empowerment to other women" (172). Gabrielle becomes an Amazon queen and finds a ready-made, complicated sisterhood of women, including Ephiny who is an important friend who rules in

Gabrielle's absence, Amarice who passes as an Amazon in order to find community, the shaman Yakut, and Velasca and Varia, both of whom challenge Gabrielle's right to be queen. With the Amazons Gabrielle has to learn how to manage the Hobson's choice of leading a threatened nation of warrior women when she has embraced non-violence as her personal philosophy. The Amazons also provide a home for Xena and Gabrielle while they bring up their baby daughter.

Two women try to displace Xena in Gabrielle's affections: the maniacal religious crusader Najara, and a spy for the Norse god Odin, Brunhilda, who falls in love with Gabrielle during the Ring cycle. Other significant female figures in the couple's lives include Xena's mother Cyrene, Gabrielle's sister Lila, and the goddess Aphrodite. Finally, Callisto is the complicated enemy of both women: she hates Xena because the warrior princess killed her family, and Gabrielle hates her because she murdered Gabrielle's (for-one-night-only) husband. After several seasons of pursuing and forming uneasy alliances with each other (even exchanging bodies), Callisto's soul is redeemed by Xena and in turn Callisto's spirit makes Xena pregnant with her daughter Eve.

These communities of women bolstered the lesbian subtext because they harkened back to long-forgotten women-centered scenarios. White suggests that "early 1930s urban melodramas, musicals, and comedies offered probably the last context in which any viable urban social milieu could be signified: best friends, roommates, chorines, and golddiggers thrived in reference to new codes of sexual morality and female 'continguity'" (White 147). These communities of women were suggestive because Xena and Gabrielle spent the series learning to define themselves (in relation to each other) and were part of widespread women-centered networks. Their focus and attention was not on men and they did not define themselves in relation to men.

Another technique by which the idea of subtext was mainstreamed was through intertextuality. The intertextuality of the series seems to have been a source of pleasure for almost all viewers, but it held particular resonance for lesbians who were already comfortable and skilled at intertextual interpretation. In the show, as Gwenllian Jones demonstrates, intertextuality works in two ways. First, it draws the viewers' external knowledge of other texts in towards the show, so that they bring rich layers of additional meaning to their decoding. Second, it pushes viewers outwards from the show, as they track down the original sources of the stories utilized by the series.

Some intertextual references were deliberately aimed at perceptive lesbian audience members. For example, at the end of the season four comic episode "The Play's the Thing" set in the ancient Greek theatre business, Minya (Alison Wall) and Paulina (Polly Baigent, who was also Lawless's body double) says to Gabrielle and Xena that "I never would have met Paulina if it wasn't for you. In fact, the two of you made me realize something deep down about myself. I guess I always knew, but just didn't dare admit. Yes, I'm a [pause] thespian!" She then grabs Paulina's hand and they run off together. Gabrielle stands in for the audience by confirming with Xena that Minya did, in fact, say "thespian." "Yeah, thespian," Xena retorts. "Why, what'd you think?" implying that Gabrielle, and the audience, had assumed that Minya would say "lesbian." Not only does this exchange playfully taunt the audience with what is not said, it also makes an intertextual reference to lesbian crooner k.d. lang's practice in the early 1990s of announcing to her concert goers that she was "lebanese," in order to simultaneously tease and avoid publicly coming out, a tactic also used by Ellen DeGeneres and later referenced by *Glee*. Rumors circulated on and off that lang wanted to make a guest appearance on *XWP*, and in March 1999 *TV Guide* reported the non-news that the producers did want lang to be on the show but that the hints she might do so were unfounded.

Over several years there was also recurring discussion about a "Sappho" episode. Sappho was the famous poet from the Greek island of Lesbos whose name and birthplace gave western culture the language of Sapphism and lesbianism. In 1998 Greg Cox, reflecting on the subtext, suggested that "once Sappho herself appears, as is reportedly in the works for next season, all bets are off. Says Lucy Lawless (Xena), who intends to play the part herself, 'she gets a hankering for Gabrielle, and Gabrielle doesn't know how to handle it'" (Cox 6). At the end of 2000 the website *Whoosh!* was still providing updates on a possible "Sappho" episode which would be co-written by Rob Tapert and fan fiction author Melissa Good. These were all examples of intertextuality that were designed to keep certain audience members in on the joke.

The History Left Out of the History Books

More important in terms of the show's power to fix subtext as a visible component of the television spectrum was its cavalier approach to historical veracity, by which "familiar historical and mythological events and figures are rearranged into unfamiliar configurations; perspectives are skewed; agency, relations, and outcomes are reconfigured; 'Other' voices speak" (Gwenllian Jones 405). Such skewing of perspectives and rearranging of narratives sounds a lot like an "oppositional" decoding, and the show reinforces that approach to "dominant-hegemonic" stories. In the show itself "orthodox versions of the past are constituted as inherently unstable and incomplete, and the audience's imagination is directed toward the possibility of multiple untold histories that at any moment might resurface" and which thereby "throw 'official' accounts of the past into crisis" (Gwenllian Jones 405). The hegemonic version of heteronormativity, of course, relies on a particular commonsense version of history (something that was done by heroic men) as well as limited ideas about how heterosexual relationships should function, that women lack community because they are in competition for men, and by "separating off the *lesbian* as a being not only defined by, but limited to, her sexuality" (Becker et al., 29). By creating the conditions through which, in order to enjoy the show and "get" the intertextual jokes, viewers needed to watch the show with a sense of that "possibility of multiple untold histories," *XWP* effectively pushed the majority of viewers to question those commonsense views, or to detotalize "the message in the preferred code in order to retotalize the message within some alternative framework of reference" (Hall 127). Both the show and its fans engaged in "tactics of seizure and salvage, appropriation and revision" (Gwenllian Jones 406).

Many lesbians at least were, arguably, already skilled in some of these tactics. In analyzing the films by lesbian Hollywood director Dorothy Arzner in the 1930s, Judith Mayne suggests that there is "a process of lesbian detection—an effort to rethink and reconstruct the various images and gaps and silences of the past" which women undertake in order to feel connected to a larger, historical lesbian community (*Directed*, 177). The remarkable effect of *XWP* was to develop those detection skills in other viewers too. Thus the message or master narrative that viewers were rejecting was not the message of the show itself—it was the hegemonic message (about women's weakness and male-centered worlds as naturally dominant throughout history) that the show itself was detotalizing. As Gwenllian Jones argues, through postmodern intertextuality and creation of alternative possibilities *XWP* tells a different version of what may have happened in the past, makes this alternative appealing and entertaining, and thereby suggests that "history" is just the commonsense story we have been told, not a comprehensive and neutral account.

One could argue that viewers performing this reading were actually engaged in a "dominant-hegemonic" decoding of the show (receiving the message of the show as its producers had encoded it), but that argument does not quite hold for two reasons. First, the show itself deliberately avoided encoding a dominant message, with producers, actors, and fans all acknowledging that multiple readings of *XWP* were possible and encouraged. Joanne Morreale argues that the contradictions in the show and its "postmodern format, enable viewers from different subject positions to read their own meanings into Xena" (Morreale 80). Second, the show itself performs an oppositional reading. If the Hays Code was "productive," producing the idea of what it was supposed to merely ban, *XWP* actively *produced* the idea of learning to actively look for and construct alternative meanings.

Xena-Mania

An additional factor which had a major impact on the ability of *XWP* to mainstream lesbian subtext was the way the show was taken up by popular media as a fascinating phenomenon that needed to be discussed and analyzed in detail. Instead of being an obscure subcultural experience, Xena-Mania hit global newsstands. "Xena-Mania: Why Is TV's Warrior Princess a Hit with Women?" asked the cover of *Ms.* in July/August 1996. In the accompanying article Donna Minkowitz attempted to capture what was making this highly unusual show so popular with both men and women, and also examined the extent to which Xena could be a feminist icon. Even at this stage (the first season had just ended) the show had so many meanings that Minkowitz could not reach any specific conclusion about it, a pattern of indeterminacy followed by the academic scholarship that discusses the show as well.

Ms. magazine was particularly quick off the mark with their cover story, and mainstream interest did not show any signs of abating during the next few years. For example, Morreale quotes the CEO of the USA Network Kay Koplowitz, who was trying to manage the implications of this complex character, suggesting that "forceful women characters must strike a balance between strength and femininity" (Morreale 81). A cover story in *Sci-Fi Magazine* in 1997 confirmed how extraordinarily popular the show was with a vast array of viewers before posing the question: "why are we all so damned intrigued?" (Stanton and Werksman 18). They argued one reason was that when Xena, who had first appeared on *Hercules: The Legendary Journeys*, was given her own show "delightfully, they didn't dilute her complex character one iota" (Stanton and Werksman 20). An article in *Psychology Today* in 1998 situated *XWP* in the context of other shows with complex women heroes, including *The X-Files, Buffy the Vampire Slayer*, and *La Femme Nikita*. It argued that male action heroes "just aren't flexible enough to handle the conditions that Buffy, Nikita and Xena deal with. To handle, that is, the Nineties." Instead of waiting for men to adapt, "Young America, the big audience for these shows, seems willing to let warrior women lead in the realm of the betwixt-and-between, morally, sexually, every which way" (Ventura 61).

Overall, then, *XWP* mapped perfectly—if unexpectedly—onto the zeitgeist. Lawless herself suggested that the show met a need for strong women heroes: although she didn't explicitly refer to second-wave feminism, she acknowledged that young people in the 1990s had been exposed to a much fuller range of roles for women than the previous generation. Lawless also acknowledged the advocacy role of the fans. She claimed that it was largely due to their efforts in "bombarding" talk show producers with requests to feature Lawless on their shows that *XWP* had so much coverage (Stanton and Werksman 22). She appeared on major U.S. talk shows such as *Rosie O'Donnell* and *The Tonight Show* and on October 17, 1998, hosted *Saturday Night Live*. Such extensive publicity for *XWP* was consistently maintained. Even by 2000, *The Hollywood Reporter* put the show on its cover and "labeled its 100th episode as must-see television" ("Xena Draws," 5), while the February 2000 conference of the U.S. National Association of Television Program Executives was reported to have "credited *Xena: Warrior Princess* for the proliferation of female-led action series on our television screens" ("Girls," 9). Scholars also took up this point in collections of essays such as *Athena's Daughters* edited by Frances Early and Kathleen Kennedy, *Fantasy Girls* edited by Elyce Rae Helford, *Action Chicks* edited by Sherrie Inness and her book *Tough Girls: Women Warriors and Wonder Women in Popular Culture*.

After Lawless broke her pelvis while taping a sketch for *The Tonight Show with Jay Leno*, Renaissance Pictures was "flooded" with get-well wishes. "Seldom did even major American television stars get this kind of attention, this kind of outpouring of concern" (Crenshaw 85). Commenting on the fan reaction to Lawless's accident, *Sci-Fi Magazine* called it "so overwhelming that the actress posted an open letter on the Internet, thanking them for their wonderful generosity" (Finch 24). While direct communication between stars and fans via the internet and social media is now commonplace, it was extremely unusual in 1996. In a book about *XWP* published at the end of season three Greg Cox devoted a chapter to "Xena: The Phenomenon," highlighting key examples of Xena fandom and merchandising which "are expanding by leaps worthy of the warrior herself: conventions, fan clubs, comic books, novels, fan fiction, Web sites, and even a special attraction at Universal Studios Theme Park in Orlando, Florida" (Cox 223).

In 1997 Nadine Crenshaw suggested that "it was undeniable, the show had caught a wave. The recent premiere of *Xena* in France had a fifty-share viewer rating, meaning half of the sets in use were tuned in to the warrior princess" (Crenshaw 90). Debates and discussions about its formative power continued and "in the absence of any clear sign, so far, of disapproval from Xena's rights-holders, Universal Studios and Renaissance Pictures, Xenites have freely created a festival of Xena glory online" (Leonard 2). Lesbian media too participated in emphasizing the phenomenal impact of the show. *Girlfriends* magazine acknowledged the "puppy episode" of *Ellen* (aired on April 30, 1997) had 30 million viewers, but that *XWP* was more of a "lesbian cult phenomenon" (Findlay 28–29). Heather Findlay suggested it offered a major counterpoint to *Ellen*'s appeal to an "assimilationist gay movement," attracting instead a "true-blue and blue-collar" fan base (Findlay 29). In these varied ways the series generated an enormous and ongoing amount of interest and engagement at every level.

Are They or Aren't They?

Practically each story or publication seemed to want to take up the vexed question of whether there was a subtext hidden in the show, thereby continuously re-circulating it for re-consumption. Cox, for example, points out that "no discussion of the show would be complete without mentioning its celebrated lesbian subtext" (5). Capturing the "strategic ambiguity" of the show, Cox explains that "many viewers prefer to view this deep and abiding friendship as strictly platonic, a perfectly valid interpretation that is quite consistent with the events depicted on the screen [...] another segment of the audience, however, eagerly reads between the lines, looking for signs of an even closer, more physical union. And sometimes they don't have to look very hard" (6). This is because *"Xena: Warrior Princess* takes things one step further by occasionally teasing its devout (and well-publicized) lesbian following with a provocative line or scene, while simultaneously remaining open to more innocuous interpretations" (Cox 6). Cox includes a text box filled with quotes from actors and producers on "this prickly issue": all of them fuelling the idea that since the maintext is based on the fact that Xena and Gabrielle love each other, the audience can interpret that love through their own preferred reading.

There are multiple examples of this interpretive tactic being encouraged. Jeanne Hamming, for example, refers to an interview that Lawless gave to the men's magazine *Maxim* in 1999. In this interview Lawless responded to the inevitable subtext question by saying "we like to have the audience make up their own minds about that. That interpretation seems to work for some people, and if it ain't broke, don't fix it" (qtd. in Hamming para. 10). In *Xena Magazine* of September 2000 O'Connor "offer[ed] her take on the all-important subject: the show's subtext." She emphasized that the key aspect of the show was the love between Xena and Gabrielle, and that "it ruins the show if we say yea or nay. Also, that's what's exciting about it as well: everyone can watch the show and see an aspect of themselves in the characters" whereas some audience members would be alienated by a definitive position (Barker 22). Rob Tapert reflected that it would be difficult to maintain the show's impetus if the couple had sex. He referred to the "Ellen effect," the idea that a large audience—indeed, up to 30 million—would watch a show to see the lesbians as a spectacle, but that afterwards they would quickly lose interest. Furthermore, he claimed that after the episodes in season two which really toyed with the lesbian subtext ("The Quest" and "A Day in the Life") the executives had pressured the creative team to stop doing it (Nazzaro 16). In reality, however, they simply switched to an arguably even more powerful and complex representation of the women as eternal soul mates. Stoddard Hayes also wrote an extensive analysis of what she called the "intense and ambiguous relationship" between Xena and Gabrielle and included a helpful "Do They or Don't They?" text box. Hayes pointed out that "within the series itself, the evidence is deliberately inconclusive," but that it was "impossible to imagine either of them forsaking the other to fall in love with anyone else" (Hayes, "Who," 46). She quoted Tapert who emphasized that "both *Xena* and *Hercules* have gone out of their way not to pass judgement on people for their race, creed, colour or sexual preference" (Hayes, "Who," 46). An *Xposé Special* on *XWP* in 2000 pointed out that "the speculation over their alleged lesbianism only heightens the show's interest and popularity" (Kate Anderson 12).

Discussion of the subtext focused primarily on Xena and Gabrielle, but could extend to other characters as well. Jacqueline Kim, who played Lao Ma, referred to conversations she had with R.J. Stewart, one of the writers, about her character and her sense that the show wanted the women to be close romantically (Hayes, "Jacquelin," 44). Paris Jefferson, who played Athena in season five, reflected on the relationship between Athena and her "chosen warrior" Ilainus (played by Musetta Vander). She argued that the two loved each other, and even though the show did not explicitly show the nature of that relationship, "the director of that episode, Mark Beesley, wanted to cultivate that relationship to a point" (qtd. in Bassom 43). Certain scenes and storylines also played up the idea that lesbianism was part of the show, with season two laying much of the groundwork. Gwenllian Jones aptly describes a scene in "Girls Just Wanna Have Fun," for example, as one in which "vampirical Bacchae dressed in lesbian S&M chic dance to hip-hop in a barbarian-retro nightclub" (Gwenllian Jones 404). This season also disposed of Gabrielle's overnight husband, thereby putting to rest any homophobic inference that she stayed with Xena out of immaturity or because she had had no better (male) offer.

Season two also included the kiss in "The Quest" as well as "A Day in the Life," the episode which follows the pair through a typical day. As Greg Cox claims, "this episode provides a feast for subtext fans," including O'Connor's ad-lib when Gabrielle is asked whether Xena would marry: "no, she likes what I do," as well as their scene bathing together in a hot tub. "Let us not forget that in the Xenaverse a hot bath is almost always a prelude to romance" (Cox 125). Although season three concentrated on setting up the "Rift" (which itself arguably only makes sense if the characters are estranged lovers), it also found the time to include some nods to the subtext, such as Gabrielle sleeping in Xena's arms and apparently giving her a hickey in the Groundhog Day–inspired "Been There, Done That," and the deepening of the fundamental love triangle between Xena, Gabrielle, and Ares.

By the final season, perhaps knowing that there was little left to lose, *XWP* had almost completely abandoned any attempt to suppress the subtext and included multiple episodes that seemed to insist on a reading of Xena and Gabrielle as lovers as well as soul mates. In what Hayes called "a last treat for the subtext fans" the season six episode "Many Happy Returns" has a scene in which Xena gives Gabrielle a poem by Sappho (quoting a real fragment of Sappho's verse) (Hayes, *Xena*, 133). Other episodes played on the idea that some fans embraced the subtext or that viewers wanted to know, once and for all, whether Xena and Gabrielle were lovers. A large portion of the episode "You Are There," for example, consists of an anachronistic TV reporter called Nigel trying (and failing) to get a scoop on the exact status of their relationship.

The episode "Send in the Clones" provides another example which openly plays with the subtext. It is an inventive clip show set in the present day, in which a reincarnated Alti is working with seemingly reincarnated Minya and Paulina to reanimate cloned versions of Xena and Gabrielle. The team (which includes a male Joxer fan) prepare clips from the television show in order to stimulate the clones' memories and they argue over the correct balance of storylines to show. "I feel very strongly that Gabrielle is the most important relationship in Xena's life," the Minya character gushes, while the Joxer fan groans that "if you start talking about subtext I'm gonna barf." Later, Minya suggests that Xena "needs a dose of Gabby—that'll jump start her heart." Once the clones have woken and are watching more clips, the on-screen Xena kisses the on-screen Gabrielle. The cloned Gabrielle looks uncomfortable while the cloned Xena settles more comfortably into her chair to watch and appreciatively smirks "all right!" Later, cloned Gabrielle protests that "they've taken liberties with my scrolls," and cloned Xena agrees. "Yeah, and what are they trying to say about our relationship anyway?" "Who knows?" retorts cloned Gabrielle. This exchange provides a perfect (and self-referential) commentary on how "strategic ambiguity" works.

In terms of intertextuality, "Send in the Clones" also has Minya think to herself that she will "play them a full season of old Ellen episodes" which acknowledges the only openly lesbian television series that had existed up to that point. In spite of this explicit acknowledgment of the subtext, throughout its run the balance struck by the show "perpetuates the series' marketability by maintaining the tension between secrecy and openness" (Hamming para. 21). Hamming suggests that "the anxiety of indeterminacy—the crisis of 'not knowing for sure'—has the effect of continually regenerating the (very profitable) desire-producing circuit created between Xena and its fans" (Hamming para. 21). Some observers saw the indeterminacy as more than just a ratings grab. Lori Medigovich writing for a lesbian readership in *Lesbian News* argued that "perhaps the lesbian subtext was exactly what was needed [...] Perhaps those characters showed that there is much more to lesbian love than just sex" (Medigovich).

Subtext for Everyone

XWP was groundbreaking in that it formed the bridge between narrow definitions of subtext as based on extra-textual material recognizable to subcultural lesbians in the know, and the approach popularized via the internet which was the idea that any viewer could detect lesbian subtext through a story carrying the relevant markers that *XWP* taught them to look for. In *XWP*, the extra-textual material was introduced into the show by staff working on it. The most prominent of these was Liz Friedman, a lesbian who was one of the producers and writers of the show. Hamming states that the "lesbian subtext was not intentionally written into the show's story-line by its producers, but was rather deciphered by lesbian consumers and then routed back to the show where it was taken up by the cast and eventually the writers" (Hamming para. 14). Friedman corroborates the existence of this circuit. She acknowledged that they had not deliberately written Xena as a lesbian, but they quickly responded to fans' interpretation. In an interview she gave to the national gay magazine *The Advocate* in August 1996, she confirmed that the show had starting writing "sapphic double entendres into scripts" (Stockwell). Calling Xena and Gabrielle "a perfect little butch-femme couple," Friedman was quoted as promising that "Xena's lesbian fans can look forward to lots of gal-pal action in stories to come" (Stockwell). Friedman was one of the writers (with Vanessa Place) responsible for the final season's episode "Many Happy Returns" which saw Xena give Gabrielle the poem by Sappho. Deliberate ad-libbing, in-jokes, and intertextual references all facilitated what Hamming called "an unusual participatory relationship between fans and cast members, made possible, in part, by the emergence of online chat forums" (Hamming para. 17). This relationship perhaps reached its zenith when the prolific and popular Xena fan fiction author Melissa Good was invited by Steven Sears, one of the show's main writers, to write the episodes "Coming Home" and "Legacy" for series six.

The cumulative effect of the mainstream media's fascination with the subtext, the showrunners' desire to maintain indeterminacy, and the immense online Xenaverse shifted the terms of reading for subtext, which has remained a key framework through which to decode the series and its legacy. When *The Complete Illustrated Companion* was published two years after the show ended it included a text box entitled "Do they or don't they?" which consisted of cautiously indeterminate quotes from people involved in the show (Hayes, *Xena*, 154). Those quotes dated from when the show was still on the air, but once it had concluded the constraints vanished too. Speaking to *Lesbian News* in 2003, Lawless "outed her former alter ego" by stating that the couple's relationship was "Gay, Gay," and that by the end of the show she was convinced that the pair were married (qtd. in Medigovich). In an interview for *Girlfriends* magazine with Lawless and O'Connor in 2004, Carson Hunter asked whether, looking back, the actors thought of their characters as gay. Both agreed that they did: O'Connor argued that "they were a couple, and they will always be a couple," while Lawless said that "by the end, there was no doubt anymore in my mind that they were [lesbians]" (qtd. in Hunter 46). In a final example, an *Entertainment Weekly* article in 2016, which performed double duty by celebrating fifteen years since the final episode and promoting the possibility of a rebooted show, reviewed the impact of the series. Lawless remarked on the power of the show for marginalized communities who had never before seen themselves on screen, while both O'Connor and Tapert acknowledged that they went as far as they could within the constraints set by the studio (Abrams). These post-show pronouncements effectively "revealed" that there had been a lesbian relationship at the heart of the show and that, therefore, those who could "see" it at the time were right. In sum, the combination of the unique qualities of the show and the widespread media attention it garnered consistently reinforced the idea of lesbian subtext.

Gwenllian Jones summarizes the relevant components of the show: "a powerful, charismatic, and complex female hero; a central lesbian-inflected relationship; an explicitly postmodern take on history and mythology; an excess of intertextuality; and the complementary hypertext technologies of the internet" (Gwenllian Jones 410). This list more or less codifies what made the show extraordinary and because it was unique and garnered so much attention, why it made lesbian subtext so visible. Never had a show (or film) that was *not*, technically, about lesbians generated so much discussion and debate about lesbianism from lesbians, bisexual women, women who were coming out, and all of their straight allies as well as from homophobic commentators who fretted over whether the whole heteronormative and patriarchal order was now under threat. The invisible lesbian had finally and dramatically appeared "in plain view, mortal and magnificent, at the center of the screen" (Castle 2). No longer based on secret knowledge possessed by those "in the know," the very idea that (as long as it remained unnamed) a lesbian relationship could underpin a popular television show had fully arrived in mainstream consciousness. Unfortunately, the key word in Castle's formulation was "mortal."

FIN

The end of *XWP* was horrifying to an enormous number of viewers. This most exuberant of shows had killed and resuscitated both Xena and Gabrielle several times, including the crucifixion of Gabrielle by Xena in a parallel, evil universe on a crossover episode with its sister show *Hercules*. But now it decapitated Xena and prevented Gabrielle from restoring her to life in the two-part series finale "Friend in Need" which fans quickly shortened to "FIN." Terry Castle explains that, in literature, because one of the women has become a ghost the two women who are in love with each other cannot kiss. This technique "derealizes the threat of lesbianism by associating it with the apparitional" (Castle 62). As she says, "how better to exorcise the threat of lesbianism than by turning it into a phantom?" a question many fans asked themselves as they watched the closing scenes of *XWP* where the mortal Gabrielle is accompanied by the ghost of Xena.

In her analysis of the role death scenes played in the show (written before that fateful finale) Kate Goodman argues that because these scenes "are filled with intense moments of physical intimacy and words of love," they allow "the use of the language and physical expressions of love in the form of comfort and grief. It is the vehicle which enables the writers to bring subtext into maintext but in seemingly socially acceptable circumstances" (Goodman para. 7 and para. 2). In her close reading of the death scenes as moments where love can be expressed (without invoking the "Ellen effect") Goodman examines the kiss in "The Quest." She notes that since this kiss occurs in an "unreal atmosphere" (Xena's spirit is inhabiting the body of Autolycus) "the writers are playing with the homosexual taboo in a daring way. Because Xena and Gabrielle's bodies do not really touch, their 'kiss' is within acceptable bounds. In other words, the women can exchange a romantic kiss as long as one of them is dead" (Goodman para. 17). Or, put another way, once the finale confirmed (at least in Lawless's mind) that the pair were (maintext) lovers, it removed their carnal connection permanently.

Other scholars have examined the wider implications of the annihilation of Xena. Vivian Sheffield provided an extensive analysis of "A Friend in Need" for *Whoosh* in 2004. With the prominent subheading "Three Years Later and It Is Still with Us," the piece carefully reviewed the finale and the justifications given for it by both Tapert and R.J. Stewart. Sheffield concluded that their explanations were illogical, that the finale essentially depicted an unfamiliar Xena, and that it obliterated the previous six seasons which had focused on the love between Xena and Gabrielle. Sheffield argued that this was extremely troubling for long-term fans and effectively undermined the pleasure taken in the show up to that point: it was a betrayal. Sara Crosby and Kathleen Kennedy both examine roots of that sense of betrayal, situating it in the stifling limits of just war theory (Crosby) or the "purity of liberal categories of justice and evil" (Kennedy 327). Both argue that the show emphasized feminist community as a powerful redemptive and transformative force in contrast to the "bargain for turning women into objects that solidify patriarchal power relations" (Kennedy 322). In effect, they suggest that until the finale *XWP* had consistently gone where no other show had dared. It challenged the legitimacy of patriarchy by presenting a viable (and compelling) alternative community of, as Kennedy characterized them, "Amazons, peasant girls, slaves, prostitutes, goddesses, disobedient daughters, and men who seek justice" (317), all living complex lives with multiple meanings. FIN therefore represented a failure of imagination, not just in telling their stories, but in recognizing that their telling had, in fact, ignited a similar (more contemporary) community in the real world.

Becker, Citron, Lesage and Rich caution that some subtextual readings can become "fantasy projections" which completely lose sight of the original text and imagine alternative readings that are simply too far from that original to be supported by it (Becker et al. 31). This refers back to Hall's argument that while a text may be polysemous, "if there were no limits, audiences could simply read whatever they liked into any message [...] the vast range must contain *some* degree of reciprocity between encoding and decoding moments, otherwise we could not speak of an effective communicative exchange at all" (Hall 125). In other words, neither "strategic ambiguity" nor polysemy in a text can lead to an unlimited plurality of meanings. What is interesting about responses to the *XWP* finale is that many viewers, and even Lawless herself, decided on an alternative reading that the end of the show did not support. Lawless was quoted as saying that Xena's death "is a huge regret on my part, because we didn't realize really what it meant to people. We thought, 'Oh, that's a really strong ending.' No. I just say to fans, 'Let's pretend that never happened'" (qtd. in Abrams).

Crosby and Kennedy both note that many fans simply rejected the ending altogether. In other responses, fans engaged in "fix-it" activities, taking up where the show left off and "fixing" the unacceptable ending. The Australian Xena Information Page (Ausxip.com) hosted "Subtext Virtual Seasons" written by fan fiction writers including Melissa Good, and by the end of the virtual "Season Seven" two-part opener (named "A Friend Indeed") Xena was restored to life and the pair had resumed their travels. These creative refusals of the suddenly (and for many, inexplicably) "dominant-hegemonic" encoding of *XWP* perhaps point to just how successful the show had been. Arguably, the ones who had engaged in a "fantasy projection" which exceeded the narrative logic of the show were not the subtext fans who grieved and then wrote Xena back to life. Instead, they were the show's producers who took Xena's story too far away from its core for it to make any sense. The "encoders" had switched roles and become failed "decoders."

Be Careful What You Wish For

Xena: Warrior Princess was exceptional for the way it flooded the small screen with multiple communities of women and strong support for the central relationship. It was also credited with kick-starting the now commonplace trend of shows with women action heroes. Subsequent (non-action) television series have not sustained its women-centeredness, but many shows are about independent women who have strong bonds with other women, even when they may also have male love interests. Extensive on-screen time, ambiguous—even flirtatious—dialogue, and emotional intimacy between women characters is necessary to suggest that they may be more than platonic friends. In particular, as White asserts in a different context, "these characters are defined in relation to work (implying economic and social self-reliance) and with female communities [...] the semiotic overlap of these types with lesbianism is strongest in the lack of attribution of romantic attachment to men. This is often compounded by a sarcastic, flippant, or superior resistance to male values" (White 146).

Many post–*XWP* representations of women show them as active, self-reliant (if often flawed), working, and not attached to any specific man, particularly on television where the woman cannot settle down with a man because otherwise the TV series may quickly reach narrative closure. Noticeable examples of independent women characters where subtext logically appears include shows such as *Rizzoli & Isles* (between Jane and Maura), *Stargate SG-1* (between Sam and Janet), *Legend of the Seeker* (between Kahlan and Cara), *The X-Files* (between Dana Scully and Monica Reyes), *Star Trek: Voyager* (between Captain Janeway and Seven of Nine), *Warehouse 13* (between Myka Bering and H.G. Wells), and *Once Upon a Time* (between Regina and Emma). As the phenomenon of reading for subtext has become a standard practice when watching television, viewers express their commitment to particular "ships," the terms for relationships which can be either canon or subtextual. Fuel is added to the fire of any given "ship" not just through "shipping wars" on the internet (many of which become extremely vitriolic) but through pronouncements by actors and showrunners.

While *Variety* criticized the producers of *The 100* for what they called a masterclass in what NOT to do in response to the Bury Your Gays trope, the CBS cerebral science fiction drama *Person of Interest* is exemplary of how to maximize symbolic annihilation while appearing to engage in a progressive and positive dialogue with hopeful fans. This is a complicated example. The show included many strong women characters with complex storylines, but in season two it brought two of them together. Sameen Shaw (played by Sarah Shahi) and Root (played by Amy Acker) are both strong but very emotionally damaged women. It is inconceivable that either woman could be in a meaningful relationship with a man, if that relationship needed to make sense as part of a traditional narrative reinforcing the gender order.

When they first met in the season two episode "Relevance" their dialogue and interactions are dangerous and flirtatious. This dynamic continued throughout their subsequent encounters. The actors later explained that they quickly realized the writers and directors were keen to encourage a subtextual interpretation of their relationship. The pair became known as "Shoot" and was very popular with the show's audience. Their flirtatious relationship was much discussed by cast members and fans at various fan conventions and the couple won the Zimbio March Madness Challenge, an online vote to choose a favorite TV couple (www.zimbio.com). However, the reason why this is a complex example is that in season four the pair basically acknowledge their love for each other and kiss immediately before Shaw sacrifices herself in order to save her team. The show deliberately left this apparent death ambiguous, with Root speaking for some of the audience by being convinced (correctly) that Shaw remained alive but captured by the team's enemy, while two other team members, Harold and Reese, stood in for the portion of the audience who believed Shaw could not have survived. The ambiguity made a certain sense: rather than being written out merely in order to explore the emotional impact on the other characters, Shahi needed to take a potentially lengthy maternity leave. But for viewers, knowing that the actor and producers hoped that Shahi could return before the show got cancelled only partially mitigated the impact of juxtaposing the kiss with the shooting. It mirrored too closely the Ur-text of women dying immediately after kissing or having sex with another woman. And learning not to trust that such a character will return is also part of an on-going pattern. Viewers familiar with that particular Ur-text had already dealt with the false hope that there would be a "fix-it" *Xena* movie, and that Kenya Rosewater could not possibly *really* be dead on *Defiance*.

The final season of *Person of Interest* did manage to bring Shaw back, but perhaps not quite in the way that Shoot fans had hoped for. For much of the final season Shaw was being held captive by the team's enemies and subjected to mind control experiments. In the episode entitled "6,741" the audience watches Shaw escape from her captors and reunite first with Root and then with the rest of the team. They retire to an apartment where the team leaves Shaw in Root's care. The two women have athletic sex, each remaining true to character by trying to top the other.

This was a dream come true for many fans. Having started with mild sexually charged flirtation, fans leapt onto Shoot and showrunners had rewarded them. The depiction of their relationship progressed from scenes of increasingly obvious flirtation, to the reactions of the other team members which legitimized the idea that they shared a particular bond, to scenes when they indicated that they felt more than (just?) sexual interest in each other. And now, finally, there was an actual sex scene. The showrunners had clearly been listening and had turned subtext into maintext. But then something went horribly wrong. Shaw began to suspect that her mind was being manipulated (a feeling only too familiar to some audience members) and she ran away. When Root finally caught up with her in a playground Shaw shot herself, afraid that if she did not she would kill Root. At this point, viewers discovered that it had all been, in effect, a dream. Shaw had just gone through version 6,741 of a virtual reality simulation. They did learn through the episode that Root was Shaw's "safe place," which confirmed what she felt for Root (Root's love for her was already well established). But they (and Root) had just watched her apparently die for a second time.

For many fans this was a complicated mess that was hard to understand, although some of them valiantly gave the showrunners the benefit of the doubt. At least the subtext was now maintext, they on the whole concluded, and settled in to watch the next episode. However, after Shaw had *really* managed to reconnect with the team, it was *Root's* turn to die while protecting another team member, Harold. The consolation prize here was supposed to be that the artificial intelligence (The Machine) which over the previous three seasons Root had loved, learned from, protected, and for which she had functioned as its analogue interface with humans, now decided to use her voice as its own. Thus in theory Root lived on. Some fans tried to reassure themselves with this form of immortality but others were unable to get away from the fact that she was, in fact, dead. So here was a show which had turned subtext into maintext and given the fans what they wanted, only to kill off each of the women who loved each other—one of them not just once, but twice.

Conclusion

Explicitly named lesbian relationships do now appear on screen. However, as we demonstrated in Chapter 1, they are also limited in their depictions of same-sex love and carry a disproportionate risk of death. With the exception of the new women's prison dramas such as *Orange Is the New Black* (the pilot was also co-written by Liz Friedman) or *Wentworth*, viewers still have to look for shows with recognizable subtext to find (somewhat) women-centered community and complex same-sex relationships. In looking for subtext, "one finds a textual universe filled with lesbian interpretations and lesbian meanings. Studying this universe starts a person along the long and laborious path of decentering heterosexuality as the 'norm'" (Inness, *Menace* 100). The subtext has been one of the only places where complex relationships between women seem to thrive. The pleasure of reading a television series through a subtextual filter is a crucial element of women's engagement with lesbian possibility and shared community. Whereas looking for it used to be the province of those in the know, *XWP* mainstreamed it sufficiently to encourage non-lesbians to also see its possibilities. Taught by *XWP* and the media attention generated around it to decode lesbian subtext, viewers can find lesbian possibility in the increasing number of shows that depict independent, strong, and complex women. Unfortunately, the subtext does not protect characters from troubling fates, where their futures are closed off by some very final deaths.

3

WHO POISONED
THE BOX OFFICE?

The summer of 2016 saw a handful of blockbuster films which included the barest whisper of a suggestion that some of their characters were queer. Benjamin Lee, writing in *The Guardian*, named these as Sulu and his husband in *Star Trek: Beyond* (Justin Lin, USA, 2016), Doctors Okun and Isaacs in *Independence Day: Resurgence* (Roland Emmerich, USA, 2016), Wade Wilson/Deadpool in *Deadpool* (Tim Miller, USA, 2016), and Jillian Holtzmann in *Ghostbusters* (Paul Feig, USA, 2016). Lee has nothing to say about the ratio of men to women (four films, five men: one woman), but instead concentrates on what he calls "a strong whiff of studio cowardice" and the "stale reminder of the tiresome heteronormativity that continues to stifle change within blockbusters" (Lee). Asking why blockbusters still seem to conform to the strictures of the Hays Code, Lee suggests that the root of the problem is based in two assumptions about the potential audience. The first assumption is that the bar should be set to that lowest common denominator, which means films need to have characters and storylines that studio executives assume will have the broadest appeal, and are pitched at achieving PG-13/12A ratings. Since survey data indicates that more than a third of U.S. movie tickets are bought by people over 50, and less than half of Americans aged 50 to 64 think same-sex marriage is acceptable, then the lazy assumption is made that this section of the audience must not be antagonized. Furthermore, Lee argues, movies rely on international sales, and exporting to even more conservative nations such as China which exercise high levels of censorship means that studios try to play safe. What has sold before (both internationally and at the box office) is assumed to be what will sell again.

Lee's points about the context in which these films were made—the role of studios, markets, and assumptions about which audience segments must be placated—help to explain why simply drawing attention to the problematic deaths of lesbian characters will have little effect unless much wider structural problems within the entertainment industry are acknowledged and addressed. The concept of "box office poison" alludes to the idea that no one wants to see certain storylines or actors: that their presence will actively deter viewers and a film will consequently fail at the box office. This idea applies equally to television audience viewing figures. In this chapter we consider what is actually poisoning the box office and suggest that there has been a damaging shift towards an ideology of postfeminism and high individualism for characters and women industry workers alike. The shift depoliticizes lesbians on screen, making them largely indistinguishable from heterosexual characters. Behind the scenes it puts pressure on women to act like "one of the boys" in order to succeed in a male-dominated industry.

How Lesbians Became Chic

The first kisses between women on prime-time television took place in 1974 in two shows at opposite ends of the earth: the Australian soap opera *The Box* and a BBC drama called *Girl* in the UK (Beirne, "Screening," 26; Ellis-Petersen). These kisses did not mark the start of a surge in on-screen clinches between women. It took years for the American legal drama *L.A. Law* to follow their lead, in 1991, and no more British women locked lips before the watershed (a 9pm a cut-off time after which content that is considered not suitable for children can be shown) until 1994 when Beth Jordache kissed her friend Margaret Clemence in the evening soap opera *Brookside*. This latter kiss took on a special significance nearly twenty years later, when a brief clip of it made it into the video montage at the opening ceremony of the London Olympics in 2012. As AfterEllen.com reported, because the opening ceremonies were not censored in most countries where they were screened, this footage became the first (albeit very fleeting) same-sex kiss shown in 76 countries where homosexuality is illegal (The Linster).

Although kisses may have been few and far between, since the 1970s there has been an increase in the numbers of characters who express same-sex love and desire. Several scholars, including Judith Mayne and Sasha Torres, agree that initially the increase was a calculated response to the massive impact of the second-wave feminist movement in the USA. Torres argues that advertising executives were excited by the potentially lucrative market of white, middle-class urban women who wanted to consume images of strong women. As a result studios looked for projects containing such characters, and so from the late 1970s into the late 1980s more television programs included white, financially independent professionals espousing the most reductive and non-challenging version of feminism: the idea that women are competent human beings and have strong bonds with each other. However, shows with too many women working together and supporting each other could conjure the specter of lesbianism, so occasional lesbian characters would be introduced with finite storylines, sometimes contained to just one episode. Their presence was supposed to demonstrate that "lesbians" were a different group of creatures from the main cluster of heterosexual characters. The rare regular lesbian characters, such as Marilyn on the American series *HeartBeat* (1988–1989), might have storylines that acknowledged their sexuality, but these were not integrated into the overall narrative arcs of the shows in the same way as they were for the heterosexual characters (Torres 182). The increasing numbers of lesbians on the television screen in the 1980s did have an overall effect of making lesbianism more visible in mainstream culture, but primarily worked to confirm that lesbians marked the outer limits of acceptable feminist sisterhood.

The 1990s, by contrast, were the period of "lesbian chic," a phrase that graced the cover of *New York* magazine in 1993 when it featured k. d. lang. In August of the same year lang also appeared lounging in a barber's chair on the cover of *Vanity Fair* while the model Cindy Crawford, in a bathing suit and high heels, "shaved" her foam-lathered face. From that point on "lesbians seem[ed] to be everywhere—in mainstream magazines ranging from *People* to *Cosmopolitan*, in movies like *Chasing Amy* and *Set It Off*, on television shows like *Friends, Mad About You*, and, of course, *Ellen*—saturating the cultural imagination" (Ciasullo 577). The UK saw a similar burst of visibility. In addition to the *Brookside* kiss, there was the television adaptation of Jeanette Winterson's novel *Oranges are Not the Only Fruit* (BBC, 1990); the adaptation of Nigel Nicholson's book about his mother Vita Sackville-West's relationship with Violet Keppel, *Portrait of a Marriage* (BBC, 1990); *A Village Affair* (Moira Armstrong, UK, 1995); the prison drama *Bad Girls* (ITV, 1999–2006); a talk show called *Gaytime TV* (BBC, 1995–1997); and, spilling over into the 2000s, *Tipping the Velvet* (BBC, 2002), based on the novel by Sarah Waters.

At the time this level of saturation seemed to signal that lesbian characters would become commonplace, even if the chic version of lesbianism made available (with the rare exceptions of lang and characters such as

Corky in the film *Bound* or Cleo in the film *Set It Off*) tended towards something that looked remarkably like "conventionally attractive straight women," who were white, young, thin, and affluent (Ciasullo 578). The problem with this version of lesbianism is not that it is inaccurate (many lesbians are all of these things), but that is both partial (many lesbians are none of these things) and, because of the way that representations of heterosexual women work, it is desexualized. With the exception of Gillian Anderson's Scully on *The X-Files* and of course Xena and Gabrielle, the "conventionally attractive straight women," at least in the 1990s before more complex women's roles regularly made it onto the screen, tended to be the *objects* of (men's) desire. It was therefore hard to place two supposedly lesbian versions of this figure together and expect sexual sparks to fly.

The lesbian chic phenomenon, in effect, made lesbians simultaneously visible and invisible. Danae Clark, in her influential 1991 essay on "Commodity Lesbianism," saw the potential impact of lesbian chic just as it began to appear on the advertising horizon. For advertisers, lesbian chic was an idea that made it possible to highlight an untapped source of style. Since the 1980s "gay window advertising" had been popular as a technique used to appeal to both heterosexual men and gay men who were presumed to be affluent. Advertisements used solo models or single-sex groups and subcultural cues in order to avoid alienating either group by directly referring to neither. The effect of such gay window advertising was to link sexuality "to a particular mode of fashion for self-expression" (Clark 197). It implied that sexuality was nothing more than a lifestyle choice enjoyed by those able to consume the right products and certainly had nothing to do with identity politics. This dual marketing strategy then extended from men to women and lesbian chic was able to make its own stylish appearance as a commodified version of lesbian urban subculture.

Urban lesbians, sporting shorn heads or short dreads, leather biker jackets, blazers, vests, mini-skirts, and Dr. Martin boots were highly visible at anti-establishment protests in the UK and USA. As members of groups such as Lesbians and Gays Support the Miners, recently fictionalized in the film *Pride* (Matthew Warchus, UK, 2014), Stop the Clause (formed in response to the piece of repressive government legislation that became Section 28 of the Local Authorities Act of 1988) as well as OutRage! and Stonewall, lesbians engaged in lively political theatre in Britain. One group of them rappelled into the House of Lords, while another invaded the set of the *Six O'Clock News* on the BBC. On city streets in North America as members of the Lesbian Avengers they staged fire-eating spectacles in order to show that they could consume the fires set against them and make themselves more powerful (Sommella 432). With ACT-UP and Queer Nation in New York or Aids Action Now in Toronto they invaded establishment meetings, held media savvy demonstrations and performed as part of mass "die-ins," trying to raise awareness of the impact of government health policies around HIV on gay men. To the extent that the world of fashion seeks to co-opt subcultural styles, these lesbians seemed edgy, confident, and cool. Their public solidarity with gay men was a departure from previous decades, when lesbian politics had focused largely on developing feminist analysis. Since certain gay men were advancing a claim to political legitimacy based on their consumer status as "DINKS" (Dual Income No Kids), the increased association between gay men and lesbians made the latter seem attractive as a potentially lucrative market. Taken together, these factors influenced the rise of lesbian chic.

While the fashion for lesbian styles is long gone, the impact of lesbian chic on representations remains. Clark explains that at the time it offered "lesbians the opportunity to solve the 'problem' of lesbianism: by choosing to clothe oneself in fashionable ambiguity, one can pass as 'straight' (in certain milieu) while still choosing lesbianism as a sexual preference; by wearing the privilege of straight culture, one can avoid political oppression" (Clark 197). Heterosexual women too, she argues, could adopt these styles in order to signal non-conformity, because the subtleties of such "lesbian" style were no longer distinctively (or exclusively) lesbian. Evacuating the meaning and politics of lesbianism from lesbian styles, and given that straight women could now look "gay" tended to make lesbians disappear altogether by making them indistinguishable from their straight sisters. Martha Gever makes the point that "this new form of visibility may produce a new form of invisibility. It can be conscripted for a program of normalization whereby women who have been regarded as unnatural perverts will be newly perceived and accepted as ordinary and inoffensive, therefore indistinguishable from heterosexual women" (Gever 26). Or, as Sherrie Inness succinctly puts it, "homosexual = heterosexual" (Inness, *Lesbian* 67).

One outcome of this visibility/invisibility conundrum for lesbian characters is that their tales seem no different from those of heterosexual women characters who have fairly limited storylines anyway: "homosexual = heterosexual" indeed. Kelly Kessler points out that "yes, lesbian representations are permeating the prime-time schedule; however, the automatic association of lesbians with the three Ms (marriage, money and motherhood) becomes problematic" (Kessler 138). In her study of lesbian representation on television in New Zealand, Alison Hopkins found that most of her focus-group participants "agreed that lesbian characters were appearing more often on prime-time television" but that the "quality or verisimilitude of these characters had not improved significantly" (Hopkins 105). Women characters became interchangeable—except that the lesbian and bisexual ones are more likely to die, of course. This means that simply substituting lesbians for straight characters in existing storylines would make little difference because if, for example, "one of Charlie's Angels were a lesbian, this would probably not change the blatant sexism or bourgeois ideology of the show, or its emphasis on individual solutions to social problems" (Becker et al. 27). The technique of individualizing characters (to refuse to signal that they belong to a social group) is a postfeminist strategy.

I'll Be Postfeminist in the Post-Patriarchy

Contemporary attitudes to feminism in the Western, post-industrial context are captured by the term "postfeminism." In this context women's lives are entangled with an ideology of liberalization, one of the planks in the neoliberal platform of globalization. Liberalization promises more access to choice. The idea is that everyone is a unique individual (not marked by race, class, gender, or sexuality) who should be able to enjoy a diverse range of personal relations, including cohabitation, same-sex marriage, and other options made possible by liberal divorce and adoption laws, for example (McRobbie 28). This liberalization assumes feminism is taken for granted but simultaneously undermines it as outmoded and irrelevant for young women today. Thus popular culture refers positively to feminism (usually represented as a perfectly reasonable desire for equality, access to jobs and education, and sexual liberation) to show that its goals have been achieved. Claims that young women now have personal freedom and absolute choice as individuals (because of liberalization) means that there is no longer any need for them to see themselves as part of a group (women) who experience oppression *as women*, let alone as members of other groups that are discriminated against.

This mainstream, consumer-based set of claims pits groups of women against each other. Old-fashioned strident feminism is for older women or those from "developing" countries where "traditional" values artificially hold women back, while younger Western women are under pressure to carefully self-monitor (increasingly, by using self-tracking and goal-setting apps on their smartphones) in order to strive for individual "female success" irrespective of race, class, or sexuality, rather than "feminist success" (McRobbie 30). Martha Lauren, David Dozier and Nora Horan provide an example of how this focus on "female success" plays out on television, where the mainstream press insists that there has been a "rapid evolution of the portrayals of gender in prime time." Such accounts distort reality by drawing attention to examples of powerful women characters to claim that "a new, more progressive type of female character [is] becoming commonplace" but do not acknowledge how rare they are in terms of overall numbers of women characters (Lauren, Dozier and Horan 203). Nor do the accounts acknowledge that the tactic of frequently placing women characters in senior management roles in police, legal, or hospital dramas, or as the CEOs of major corporations, misrepresents their actual numbers in these roles in real life, thus subtly communicating the message that feminist goals (assumed therefore to be parity with selected powerful men) have been achieved. Adrienne Rich calls this "the decoy of the upwardly mobile token woman" (Rich 639).

Overall, this combination of individualization and liberalization affects all women, but has a number of specific effects on lesbian and bisexual characters. Most striking is that it depoliticizes sexuality. Eva Krainitzki neatly summarizes the problem, stating that "postfeminist cultural representations seem to combine ageist tendencies, the commodification of gay culture, and a generalized de-politicization of the figure of the lesbian" (Krainitzki 15). It removes any suggestion that lesbian and bisexual women are part of a collective group that is oppressed. Discrimination at work, or in accessing services, unequal treatment in marriage or adoption laws, and personal experiences of homophobic violence are typically missing from lesbian or bisexual storylines. Homophobic characters are individualized too, depicted as simply ignorant or bigoted unlike the tolerant main (heterosexual) characters. This limits perceptions of community and the kinds of stories that can be told about women's relationships. Furthermore, if lesbians are not considered part of a *group*, then each of their deaths is just an isolated storyline which is individual to the requirements of the specific film or show, not part of a wider pattern, especially not one with any relationship to real life.

Kissing Doesn't Kill (Ratings)

Just before lesbian chic hit the newsstands, one of the most inventive campaigns around HIV proclaimed that "Kissing Doesn't Kill: Greed and Indifference Do" a message that came from the artists' collective Gran Fury. Plastered over blown-up photographs of three couples kissing (two same-sex and one opposite-sex, all from different races) as a pastiche of the contemporaneous United Colors of Benetton clothing advertisements, the slogan appeared in 1989 on buses in New York City and San Francisco as part of the "Art Against AIDS on the Road" project. Another equally powerful and ultimately more famous one was "Silence = Death" designed by the Silence = Death Project and taken up by ACT-UP as, in effect, their logo. The point of these slogans was to increase visibility, capture the urgency of the AIDS crisis and to provoke the public into understanding that real people's lives were at stake (Crimp 28–29). "Kissing Doesn't Kill" specifically challenged the fearful assumption that HIV could be transmitted by simply touching someone who was sick. Ironically, this slogan now appears remarkably apt for a discussion of the various levels of on-screen intimacy between women. On the one hand, it is as if showrunners believe that to allow their characters to kiss would sound their death knell in terms of ratings by invoking the "Ellen effect." On the other hand, if the characters do kiss then they are likely to speedily join the ranks of all the dead lesbians—possibly even in the very same episode. Yet showrunners also seem enamored with the so-called "Sweeps Week" kiss as a way to boost ratings. This kiss can only happen if one of the characters involved is a heterosexual main character and the woman she kisses is neither referred to nor appears ever again.

Perhaps one of the most noticeable (and remarkable) oddities in the lives of fictional lesbians is the lack of intimacy that is shown between them. Cragin points out this tension at the heart of television representations: the fact that many same-sex couples (whose defining characteristic is supposed to be the sex they have) are shown without depicting any actual erotic activity. There is a clear double standard around showing same-sex kissing or sex scenes, when compared to opposite-sex scenes. *Buffy the Vampire Slayer* is an excellent example of this: while Buffy writhed naked in bed with her male lovers Angel, Riley, and Spike, Willow and her lover Tara had to touch foreheads, hold hands, sing, and use magic as a metaphor for sex. They did not kiss until just before Tara died. Equally, in *Pretty Little Liars* all of the heterosexual Liars are shown having sex with their male partners, but the audience has to infer that Emily, the lesbian, is doing the same when she lies down almost fully clothed and shares relatively chaste kisses with her female partners. In fact, the "sex scene" with Paige, Emily's longest-running girlfriend, actually takes place in a black-and-white fantasy sequence that wittily pays homage to film noir and is located entirely in the drug-altered mind of one of the other Liars, Spencer. On the daytime soap opera *Guiding Light* the characters of Olivia and Natalia live together, fall in love, and navigate a series of relationship challenges without ever kissing. They have to communicate their erotic desire by doing what seems to have become a new stand-in for lesbian intimacy: placing their foreheads together. The one kiss they do have is a truly bizarre one. Before they have even expressed any interest in each other Olivia grabs Natalia and kisses her, in order to show her that other people assume they are already a couple.

The former lovers Sara and Nyssa kiss when they first encounter each other after a long separation on the fantasy show *Arrow*. After Sara has died, been resurrected, and left to become one of the *Legends of Tomorrow* she visits Nyssa in prison during a dream sequence. The women hug tightly and clasp hands, but touch their foreheads together when logic dictates they should have shared a farewell kiss. Sara does kiss another woman goodbye. Over the course of just one episode, Sara becomes interested in a nurse, Lindsey, who is a closeted lesbian living in the 1950s (the *Legends of Tomorrow* team travel through time). The women kiss twice, once when they are flirting with each other and then again when Sara takes her leave. Because they are not in an established, loving relationship, their kisses fall more under the "Sweeps Week Lesbian Kiss" umbrella which we discuss below.

This remarkable level of discrepancy has remained consistent over time and in both television and film. Sophia Davidson Gluyas points out that in Australian films of the 1970s, "lesbian desire is sanctioned by these texts but lesbian sex is not" (101). Her description of the 1970s film *Don's Party* (Bruce Beresford, Australia, 1976) could equally apply now: "There is plenty of heterosexual sex in the film. However, despite there being two female characters attracted to each other, there is no lesbian sex" (Gluyas 101). Torres too identifies what she calls "TV's refusal to represent lesbian erotic life" (Torres 179). Paradoxically, then, lesbians and bisexual women, who in heteronormative culture are so often reduced to *only* being sexual, do not have that sexuality confirmed on screen if they are in a loving relationship with each other. Vicki Eaklor speculates that American audiences may be "more afraid of lesbian love than sex, but more averse to gay sex than love" ("Kids," 167). The problem of not letting women kiss is that the audience becomes unable to see them as erotically involved, the very fate that makes it so easy to dismiss Ruth and Idgie in *Fried Green Tomatoes* as being friends rather than lovers.

Two Women Kissed On Screen ... You Won't Believe What They Did Next

If, on the one hand, lesbians' relationships seem to be strangely platonic, on the other hand when same-sex desire *is* shown it frequently lacks other contextualizing elements and takes place between women who are *not* in a loving relationship. In part this can be attributed to the effects of "Sweeps Week." This is a selected period of time repeated four times a year (February, May, July and November) when audience survey companies collect viewing figures in order to provide studios with ratings for their shows. This information is then used to sell spots to advertisers who naturally want lots of people to be watching: thus the higher the ratings, the more expensive the advertising slots. Television producers have long attempted to increase viewership during these predictable periods through much-hyped events on their shows. Since the 1990s a kiss between two women appears to have been considered the perfect choice for this type of event. Judith Mayne suggests that the (in)famous 1991 same-sex kiss on *L.A. Law* was perhaps the first example of this phenomenon. The legal drama was highly praised and considered innovative during its first seasons but was losing its shine by the time of the kiss. Mayne suggests that "it is tempting, then, to see the lesbian kiss—like an interracial romance that occurred during the same season—less as an innovation and more as desperate maneuvering to acquire attention and viewership" (Mayne, *Framed*, 97). Although the website TV Tropes.org acknowledges that the "Sweeps Week Lesbian Kiss" has steadily lost its power to boost ratings, it has contributed to the intertextual fabric of women's on-screen intimacy.

The Sweeps Week kiss had become such a dominant practice by the mid–1990s that, like the response to Lexa's death on *The 100*, it garnered mainstream attention. Writing in *The New York Times* Virginia Heffernan explained why the kisses worked so well to bring eyeballs to shows. They were highly visual, cheap, controversial, and reversible, with no long-term implications for the characters because "sweeps lesbians typically vanish or go straight when the week's over." In *Bitch Magazine* Diane Anderson-Minshall provided the context for the Madonna–Britney Spears kiss at the 2003 MTV Video Music Awards: "if you've turned on the TV during sweeps month in any recent year, you may well have wondered whether all the girls have gone gay" (27). Anderson-Minshall argues that these kisses occur in fairly complex territory where longer-term relationships also appear, but overall "these single-episode storylines and ratings ploys keep the subject firmly in novelty territory" (29). A potentially problematic impact, she goes on to note, is that "this new proliferation of girl-girl kisses on television imprints popular culture with a false sense of social—and political—acceptance" that does not mirror real life for many people (Anderson-Minshall 87).

A study of New Zealand high school students found that they could see through these kinds of novelty stunts, noting that the lack of explicit sex scenes or the "depiction of lesbianism as 'experimental' and constructed within norms of heterosexualized attractiveness" were cynically "designed to attract an audience while simultaneously meeting requirements of palatability" (Jackson, 158). The long-term impact of the Sweeps Week kiss, when coupled with the intertextuality of all mainstream lesbian representation, helps to explain why the high school students can argue that "in looking like all of the other pretty straight women on television, the 'lesbian' becomes unrecognizable, and even explicitly sexual acts may be understood as experimental displays between women who are 'really' heterosexual" (Jackson, "(Un)recognizable" 164). The Sweeps Week lesbian kiss can both normalize same-sex desire and simultaneously depoliticize it.

The refusal to show complex stories and the tendency to depoliticize women's desire can be traced back to the early days of Hollywood and the belief that the audience had a low level of comprehension and a high level of intolerance. For example, novels that were adapted for film had storylines changed in order to simplify and de-gay them. This was a strategy "for creating mass culture that would offend as few as possible [...] The film industry's role was to reach the American market with stories that conformed to expectations, whether those expectations were about genre or the moral compensation that was spelled out in the [Hays] Code" (White 22). Decades later, the approach taken by GLAAD seems to indicate that conformist expectations remained at the center of representations. The early intention of GLAAD was to support and approve of "images of gays and lesbians that corresponded to what the presumably heterosexual mainstream would most readily embrace and find least objectionable," which translated into "representations that would not offend white, middle-class, conventionally gendered, mainstream norms of respectable behaviour" (Doyle 15–17). The logic for this position came from an article by two psychologists, Marshall Kirk and Hunter Madsen, on the future of the lesbian and gay movement published in the gay men's magazine *Christopher Street* in 1984. The gist of their article was that the movement needed to draw on public relations and advertising strategies, and should emphasize respectability, law and justice. It should avoid any focus on sexual activity, seek out celebrity endorsements, and should "cast gays and lesbians as victims in need of protection" (Doyle 16).

That suggestion—to present lesbians and gay as victims—has often been coupled with the individualizing tactics of postfeminism to evacuate not just sexuality but community from the lesbians and bisexual women found on screen. Same-sex love is individualized and rendered either effortless or tragic, removing serious engagement with institutional and structural factors or community responses to them. To provide an explanation for this pattern of isolation, Moss and Simić examine the trends in post-communist Croatian cinema. They find:

> not only is lesbianism not presented as a political problem, but the whole political (as well as private) Croatian context of real lesbians is completely effaced in order to victimize our heroines further. Paradoxically, to "protect" the heroines in the eyes of the audience, to keep their metaphorical quality "virginal," the politics of queerness and queer politics must disappear completely from the film [Moss and Simić 277].

In other words, women feeling love for their own sex can be sympathetic characters only if they are not connected to any wider political group nor inclined to express any sense that they experience oppression.

One way to individualize lesbianism is to suggest that a same-sex attracted woman does not need a lesbian community because every woman she meets is a potential partner. For example, the fantasy show *Supernatural* had a recurring lesbian character, the hacker and cosplayer Charlie. Until she was murdered, Charlie seemed able to pick up women effortlessly, without ever having to visit a lesbian or gay bar or even (in spite of her extensive online skills) use a dating site or app. This stock character had earlier appeared in *The Jane Austen Book Club* (Robin Swicord, USA, 2007) in the form of Allegra, a lesbian in her twenties who picks up women not in a gay bar or at a political meeting, but while engaging (perhaps ironically) in death-defying activities. In the final scene she sits alone, surrounded by all the heterosexual couples who have worked through their issues over the course of the film. Eva Krainitzki's study of films featuring older lesbians did not find that these characters were able to pick up women (presumably because older women are supposed to be sexless), but did find that they were "generally depicted alone, no friendships with other lesbian women are established, no intergenerational encounters are allowed and the concept of lesbian community is absent" (Krainitzki 16). In *The Kids Are All Right* (Lisa Cholodenko, USA, 2010) Jules and Nic and their two children "seem to live in a domestic bubble within an apolitical world" although "this cocoon-like life does facilitate [Jules'] bizarre hetero affair, however, since there are no other lesbians in sight to whom Jules can turn for a fling" (Eaklor, "Kids" 163–164). So while young women have no community but are able to pick up chicks with well-placed eye contact, older lesbians are simply alone. Perhaps most significant is the fact that women who love women are highly unlikely to espouse political viewpoints or a sense of solidarity with each other.

There are some bright spots. Stef and Lena are a lesbian couple raising a large brood of teenagers on the television series *The Fosters* (2013–). Not only do they have a number of lesbian friends and tend to hire lesbian contractors for work on their house, but one of Lena's work colleagues, the formerly straight Monte, is attracted to Lena, begins to consider she may be bisexual, and starts to date one of the Fosters' friends. *Pretty Little Liars* also toys with themes of the singular lesbian versus the reality of lesbian community. It is already an unusual show because it has a major lesbian character in Emily Fields, who is one of the five main Liars at the heart of the show. From the very first episode of season one onward Emily works her way through a series of girlfriends. Fancifully, the show suggests that a teenage lesbian can be out (once her homophobic mother Pam comes round to the idea) and live a full life where basically every woman she meets is also a lesbian, bisexual, or even nominally straight woman who is interested in getting together with her. This conceit might carry more weight if Emily was more butch or had more sexual swagger and women would therefore have a reasonable basis for assuming she would welcome their advances. Arguably this lack of realism is in keeping with the rest of the show which wittily plays on every filmic convention as the plots—involving ever-expanding webs of deceit—spin out. Emily's ability to captivate women by batting her eyelashes is no more absurd than any other activity in the show, and is certainly in keeping with the conventional depiction of every on-screen lesbian being free from identity politics.

Pretty Little Liars does complicate this picture (as it does so many others) by including one character, Samara, who runs an LGBT group (and of course wishes to date Emily). Through her role in the LGBT group Samara is supposed to provide the community support that will help the self-loathing Paige to come to terms with her internalized homophobia, although instead Paige just becomes jealous of the time that Emily and Samara spend together. In later seasons the show extends its subversive message that there is a wider queer women's network beyond individual relationships (in real life, to rely solely on one's partner is very isolating and likely to be detrimental to mental health). In season three *Pretty Little Liars* takes another Liar, Hanna, to a lesbian bar while she is shadowing the suspiciously acting Paige (who is there on a date with Shana, another lesbian who dies on the show). Season seven goes even further and uses a highly energetic lesbian bridal party to both normalize same-sex marriage and show how far Emily's formerly homophobic mother Pam has come: she joins in with the party and starts making plans to socialize with the women in it.

Another exception to the idea that lesbianism is an individual lifestyle choice devoid of community is *Call the Midwife*. The series is set in the 1960s when both the nurse Delia and midwife Patsy could be fired if their relationship was discovered. The two women express ambivalence over their desire for and fear of a wider lesbian community. Delia, for example, enunciates the need to find more "women like us" and suggests that they could go to the Gateways Club, a real lesbian club that existed in London at this time. Patsy responds with a classically closeted statement: "I don't want be with other women like us. I just want to be with you." Although the show does not explain how Delia is able to overcome Patsy's reluctance, by the end of the episode they have made their first foray into this world-famous lesbian underworld and are shown dancing together at the Gateways.

In spite of these promising exceptions, generally women who love women on screen are used more like removable background coloring than as central movers and shakers in the plots. They are not the only group whose stories are seriously underrepresented. In this sense, how different are lesbian or bisexual characters from other women on screen? In her often-quoted 1982 essay Monique Wittig wrote that "lesbians are not women" by which she meant that lesbians are distinct from the social class of "women" because the latter are defined through their exploited relationship to the social class "men" in a patriarchal system. While she may have made an incisive political point that much-despised lesbians were in fact at the vanguard of a movement for human liberation, in everyday terms lesbians are only too clearly part of the group "women," especially when it comes to their storylines. As people of color they also intersect with a group of actors and characters who tend to have a remarkably limited range of roles available to them. More and more voices are beginning to challenge this status quo, making it obvious that the only way to change what appears on screen is to change what is happening behind the scenes. The most common suggestion is to simply increase the diversity among writers, producers, directors, actors, crew, and reviewers, which means tackling the bigger structural problems in the industry.

Behind the Scenes

Because they are artistic and creative media, the film and television industries as a whole frequently make the suspect claim that they reward merit. Thus, the tale goes, if there are more white straight men's stories on screen than those of black lesbians that is because they are "objectively" better stories written and directed by those with superior skills and performed by more talented actors. An increasing number of industry workers have begun to question such assertions and to openly criticize the major Hollywood studios for their lack of diversity and openly discriminatory practices—paying women stars significantly less than their male co-stars, for example. The perception that white men unfairly dominate screen roles is supported by the fact that the Academy of Motion Pictures Arts and Sciences membership—that is the people who determine nominations and cast ballots for the Oscars—are, in fact, old (median age 62), white (94 percent), men (77 percent). Trying to respond to the anger over this level of bias, Academy President Cheryl Boone Isaacs has called for broader inclusion "in all of its facets: gender, race, ethnicity and sexual orientation." She announced that of 683 new invitations to join the Academy of Motion Pictures Arts and Sciences, 46 percent went to women and 41 percent to people of color. Under her leadership there has also been a move to change the old guard of the board membership so that those members who are no longer working cannot vote (Gray). This type of initiative demonstrates what one determined woman can do, but it will take many different approaches to tackle decades of symbolic annihilation.

Started in 2015 in response to the complete absence of black actors in the Academy Awards nominations for 2014 films, the hashtag #Oscars SoWhite (#OSW) drew attention to the ongoing problems in the Hollywood studio system. The hashtag was resurrected when nominations for the 2015 films once again failed to include any black actors. April Reign, the creator of that hashtag, has called on Hollywood to address its long history of exclusion. She argues that the economic excuses which are typically trotted out are simply not credible when a film like *Star Wars: Episode VII—The Force Awakens* (J.J. Abrams, USA, 2015) which has lead actors who are both female and black has crossed the $2 billion mark in box office earnings. Remarking "Don't tell me that people of color, women cannot fill seats" in an interview with *The LA Times* Reign challenged the industry to examine "who makes the decisions with regard to greenlighting films so that we see more people of color and more LGBTQ people and more people who are differently abled up on the screen telling their stories as well" (Tre'vell Anderson). In Britain the Act for Change Project was launched in 2014 with the goal of increasing diversity in the live and recorded performance arts (defined as television drama, film, audio, and live theatre). The Project also intends to eliminate discrimination in these fields on the basis of race, gender, disability, sexual orientation, age, socio-economic background, nationality or religion through education, research, and advocacy (www.act-for-change.com). Project Diamond, meanwhile, is a new initiative designed to monitor who is working on television in the UK by asking workers in confidence to report their gender, gender identity, age, ethnicity, disability and sexual orientation in order to try and compile an accurate picture of where the problems lie, although it is not clear how commissioning editors or advertising executives will use this information to increase diversity in the industry (Conlan).

These initiatives to increase diversity are all based on the idea that not only should a range of people be employed in a multibillion dollar industry, but that diverse voices reflect reality. The limited numbers of women and people of color in key roles, as studio bosses, producers, directors, writers or advertising executives has the effect of reproducing a narrow perspective, which assumes that diverse and more challenging depictions of lesbians (or women in general) and complex storylines involving them cannot succeed. Part of the problem in challenging this image is women's lack of power within an industry which devotes millions of dollars to its ongoing promotion of comfortingly familiar patriarchal imagery.

Just looking at gender, it is useful to compare the arguments in support of increasing women's presence in other male-dominated fields. In the wider corporate world, evidence is accumulating that having women in positions of leadership influences the "bottom line." In a 2016 report by the Peterson Institute for International Economics, Washington, D.C., a survey of almost 22,000 firms in 91 countries demonstrated a positive correlation between firm performance and women in executive leadership positions, but not board membership. The authors suggest that "policies that facilitate women rising through the corporate ranks more broadly could be significant" (Noland, Moran and Kotschwar 1). In science, gender mainstreaming practices lead to the inclusion of women in positions of influence in science, technology and engineering fields. It is essential to both scientific practice and scientific knowledge that scientists recognize and are responsive to the outcomes of gender inequality and bias in their work. A whole host of major social problems, including climate change, health disparities, poverty rates, violence, food security and the impact of transportation, are better addressed by attending to gender relations, the condition of women and the innovative ideas coming from them. The entertainment industries are no different. Lisa French confirms that "there is a business case that links diversity to innovation" and that "women are frequently *the* pivotal agents of change through initiating and driving reforms that may not otherwise occur" (French 190, emphasis in original).

Martha Lauzen of the Center for the Study of Women in Television & Film at San Diego State University has been keeping track of the numbers of women employed in the industry since 1998. Each year she publishes two useful analyses of behind-the-scenes employment of women in the top grossing films (*The Celluloid Ceiling*) and in prime-time television (*Boxed In*). In 2015 the overall employment data for men and women in major behind-the-scenes positions on the top films (as writer, producer, executive producer, director, editor, cinematographer) indicated massive disparities. Overall, women made up only 19 percent of these key roles, with a minuscule one percent of the top 250 films employing more than ten women in any of these major roles (compared to 61 percent employing more than ten men). A third employed no women or only a single woman in a major off-screen role, whereas only one percent employed no men or only a one man in a major off-screen role. A full 91 percent had no women directors at all (Lauzen, "Celluloid" 2). This matters not just in terms of income for the women occupying these specific roles, but because increasing the numbers of women in major roles has a knock-on impact on other women's employment. For the top 500 films of 2015, there was a noticeable distinction between the numbers of women and men employed in major roles if a woman held a significant position on a film. For example, more than half of the writers on films with at least one woman director were women, compared to only 10 percent of writers on films that only had men directors.

Television continues this pattern. For the 2014–2015 prime-time television season on the broadcast networks, 27 percent of the major roles (in this case, creators, directors, writers, producers, executive producers, editors, and directors of photography) were held by women. As is the case for film, when women hold these major roles it makes a difference to the chances that women will also be working in other major roles. Women made up 32 percent of writers on programs that had at least one woman executive producer, but only 6 percent of writers if all of the executive producers were men, and if a program had at least one creator who was a woman then half of its writers were also women, compared to 15 percent on shows with no women creators. Women made up nearly a quarter of directors on programs that had at least one woman creator, but only a tenth if the show had only men in the creator role (Lauzen, "Boxed" 1; 5). In terms of characters, although the contrast was not so dramatic, having women working behind the scenes did make a slight difference to what appeared on screen. For example, if a broadcast program had at least one executive producer who was a woman, then women made up 43 percent of major characters, but only 37 percent if all the executive producers were men.

The discrepancies between women and men characters overall are quite striking, particularly between television and film. To start with, on broadcast networks, 42 percent of speaking characters and the same percentage of major characters are women, up only three percentage points since the 1997–1998 television season. Women are consistently younger than men, with most women in their 20s and 30s and most men in their 30s and 40s. Only 18 percent of women characters are in their 40s, compared to 25 percent of men. In addition, on broadcast networks, cable and Netflix programs men were more often seen at work (55 percent versus only 43 percent of women) (Lauren, "Boxed" 2; 5). In the top 100 domestic grossing films of 2015 women were much worse off than they were on television, even though the year was an historical high for women in film. They made up just 22 percent of protagonists, 34 percent of major characters, and 33 percent of all speaking characters, and so women are clearly better off on the small screen. However, just as on television, men were older (54 percent of all male and 34 percent of all female characters were over 40) and more likely to be shown working (64 percent of men compared to 44 percent of women).

Film and television also mimicked each other around race: white women made up 76 percent of all female characters, in comparison to 13 percent black, 4 percent Latina and 3 percent Asian women in films, while 77 percent were white, 15 percent black, 4 percent Asian, and 3 percent Latina in television (Lauzen, "Man's" 1–3; Lauren, "Boxed" 2). Since women of color were also less likely to be major characters, and supporting characters are more likely to die, a fairly obvious set of patterns emerges. However, just as was the case with television, more women working behind the scenes translate into better roles for women on the big screen. Women made up fully *half* of all protagonists in films which had at least one women director or writer, compared to a slim 13 percent when those positions were exclusively held by men. The percentage of speaking parts increased too, from 30 percent when only men were employed as directors and writers to 40 percent when at least one woman occupied one of those roles (Lauzen, "Man's" 4).

Martha Lauzen is not the only scholar to have found this pattern of discrimination based on who is working behind the scenes. The research by Stacy Smith and colleagues at the University of Southern California, Annenberg, for the Media, Diversity & Social Change Initiative also reveals that the proportion of female characters has not changed in any meaningful way for half a century. Their series of reports examine the sexualization of female characters, their age and social status, and the likelihood of being shown in their workplace. This analysis of female characters in films from eleven countries suggests that female filmmakers were more likely to create roles for female characters. Lyle Friedman, Matt Daniels and Ilia Blinderman have used the Bechdel Test to explore the ways in which the outcome of the test (pass/fail) is correlated with the presence of women in the critical off-screen, decision-making roles. The importance of having women in the significant off-screen jobs of writer, producer and director is made evident in the analyses of 4000 films from 1995–2015. When writing and production teams were all men, over 40 percent of films failed the test; when at least one woman writer was in the team, only 17 percent failed. They noted that "what is on screen reflects behind-the-scenes brotopia." Perhaps surprisingly, there has barely been any difference in nearly a generation in the proportions of women in these positions and therefore in the fates of women characters. In 1995 women represented 18 percent of writers/producers/directors and 37 percent of films failed the Bechdel test. Twenty years later, in 2015, women represented 17 percent of writers/producers/directors and 38 percent of films failed the Bechdel Test.

Digging down even further, Hanah Anderson and Matt Daniels (Polygraph.cool) have examined in greater detail some 2000 screen plays in order to determine who speaks by age and gender. The analysis included only characters that had at least 100 words of dialogue. The study linked the screen play analysis with IMDb (Internet Movie Database) information about the actor who played the character. The data indicated a striking increase with age in dialogue for male characters and a corresponding decrease with age in dialogue for female characters. The picture is not uniform, although while North American studios seem unwilling or unable to increase the diversity of stories they tell, there are some better results in the international film industry with films from France and the United Kingdom having higher pass rates than those from the U.S. or Canada.

One of the Boys

All of the numbers that have been crunched show that women get more work and better roles when other women are calling the shots. However, they still have to negotiate the delicate balance of power and control between groups behind the scenes and this affects what the audience ends up seeing. Judith Mayne compares the experiences of two Hollywood directors of the 1930s: George Cukor, a gay man, and Dorothy Arzner, a lesbian. As she explains, "Cukor's homosexuality may have threatened his status as a Hollywood director, but he was still able to take risks and to make decisions that were available only to men" (Mayne, *Directed* 64). Critiquing the idea that Arzner was accepted by her male peers because her lesbianism made her "one of the boys," Mayne argues instead that attempts to define her in this way "can offer only a completely distorted view of the obstacles she encountered as a peripheral member of the boys' club" (Mayne, *Directed* 64). Since the early days of Hollywood and continuing into the present day, with very few exceptions, women who take on major behind-the-scenes roles are remarkably outnumbered by men and therefore use "gender management strategies" in order to navigate their workplace experiences (Lauren, Dozier and Horan 204). A quarter of women working in Australian audiovisual industries reported feeling pressure to try and fit in as "one of the boys," for example (French 194). By "blending in" and not drawing attention to their gender women hope to be taken seriously and considered for future projects, because the business is very much organized around networks of contacts. Therefore "people hire others they like and with whom they are comfortable working," which usually translates into others who share their world view (Lauzen, Dozier and Horan 205). Studying television production in Ireland, Anne O'Brien found that "women were positioned as outliers who had to adapt and conform to the male-dominated practices that remained normative and unquestioned" (O'Brien 265). The paradox here is that women are expected to adapt themselves to a masculine mold in order to fit in, but that does not mean they are treated in the same way as men.

Like other workplaces, television and film production remains a highly gendered space, all the claims about meritocracy notwithstanding. The idea of "risk" plays out differently for men and women, for example, with men holding more decision-making roles and handing out more opportunities to take risks on new projects to other men. When projects fail men's mistakes are more often forgiven but women's career progression is slowed down (O'Brien 265). In Australia women report slow promotion rates, discrimination, stereotyped assumptions about their abilities, sexual harassment, and experiences of being excluded from groups and tasks (French 194). In Ireland women find themselves "caught in a bind of being expected to do indispensable [emotional] labor that was simultaneously unvalued or invisible and which served to free men from the requirement to do that part of production work" (O'Brien 268).

These layers of discrimination are nothing new, but the context in which they occur has shifted in recent decades. With the ascent of post-feminism, women are less likely to see themselves as part of a group and therefore unlikely to agitate for structural change in the way the industry works. In this worldview, "the primacy of the individual to generate successful work and career outcomes is paramount. Therefore, any issues with 'failure' at work become the responsibility of the individual worker rather than that of the organization" or of the wider society (O'Brien 260). Women are therefore likely to refuse to see gender as a relevant factor in their workplaces, blame themselves for stalled careers, do not seek support on the basis of group solidarity, and do not want to risk their professional reputations by questioning whether there is an underlying problem in the way things are done.

Adulterating the Box Office

All of this behind-the-scenes information is useful for understanding the limits on what makes it onto the screen. In the current system, scripts and series ideas must be pitched to studio executives who are already primed to prefer stories about themselves. Additionally, the assumption is that what advertisers are interested in (and what networks will therefore purchase) is what they in turn assume will appeal to the desired demographic (supported, of course, by numerous statistical projections). The demographic is typically boys and young men, a group that, if marketing claims are to be believed, is—disturbingly—apparently either deeply misogynist or profoundly narcissistic. They will not, we are repeatedly told, watch anything that isn't about them (oddly, enough, this seems to echo the idea that the men behind the scenes prefer projects and co-workers who are comfortably familiar, or just like them). At some point the boys and men must come to believe this claim about themselves, and the rest of the world is expected to swallow and capitulate to this narrow view as well. Since only what is perceived to be highly marketable will receive support, then the assumption seems to be made that films which will "appeal" to these young men are marketable, whereas all other types of films are box office poison.

And yet women make up more than half of cinema audiences, outnumber men in film school attendance, and heavily subscribe to screenwriting workshops. The young men do not, actually, dominate in these areas. To claim that they do and that their limited ability to pay attention must be catered to is belied by the active processes by which other stories (and other groups) are silenced. Women report that in the film school or workshop setting their ideas for women-centered storylines or interesting female characters are actively discouraged. In her post on *The Hathor Legacy* entitled "Why film schools teach screenwriters not to pass the Bechdel test," Jennifer Kesler outlined the numerous ways in which her writing instructors and professors discredited her efforts to bring female characters' stories forward in her scripts. "According to Hollywood, if two women came on screen and started talking, the target male audience's brain would glaze over…. By having women talk to each other about something other than men, I was 'losing the audience'" (Kesler).

If films and television programs transparently reflected reality then claims made about audiences and what they can stomach might make sense. But commercial moving images are advertising vehicles designed—ultimately—to manipulate the audience into consuming ideologies, products, and a sense of where they belong in the world. For example, in post-soviet films which either kill lesbians or banish them so that women cannot be together at the conclusion of the story, "the jettisoning of lesbian characters beyond the cinematic text reifies the dominant national and patriarchal narratives. As cultural products these films represent the staunchly essentialising attitudes of their producers and of the societies in which they were produced, casting into doubt the possibility of 'real' lesbian representation in cinema" (Laćan 231). In such films two processes are simultaneously at work. One caters to a narrow and limiting vision of the nation that is attributed to the audience, and the other produces that vision through the film which is then treated as if it merely reflects the "essence" of the nation that is already there.

Similar processes are at work in the USA. Shirley MacLaine, who played Martha in *The Children's Hour*, noted how the director removed the intimacy between the two women that had been present in Lillian Hellman's original play. MacLaine recalled that Hellman "had written a slow examination of one woman's personal growth in the area of falling in love with another woman. But Willie Wyler didn't want that," and he cut the scenes (that were in the play) which depicted this growth. According to MacLaine, Wyler "thought they would be too much for middle America to take. I thought he was wrong, and I told him so, and Audrey Hepburn was right behind me. But he was the director, and there was nothing we could do. Even so, I conceived my part as if those scenes were still there" (qtd. in Vito Russo 140). In other words, while the two women actors felt that the woman playwright's version of women's emotional lives was compelling and truthful, the male director exercised his greater institutional power to justify his decision to deny their sense of reality and to deliberately oversimplify the women represented in the film.

Women themselves, working in the industry, can also find themselves making the same kinds of alterations that Wyler made, because "network executives assert control over creative decisions taken by new or relatively inexperienced writers and creators," and the latter "expand their sphere of influence by producing programming that generates ratings and, to a lesser extent, critical acclaim" (Lauren, Dozier and Horan 203). Since "current and recent television content influences the type of content writers and creators produce," then writers and creators tend towards reproducing recognizable work which reflects work already being done, at least until they have established enough power to take more creative control. For women, given their slower career progression, this might take a very long time (Lauzen, Dozier and Horan 210). When television shows attempt to break the gender mold for their characters, they become:

> consumed with explaining how a female or male could possibly fill such a role, how the character came to find herself or himself in this role, how they navigate this less-traveled road, and other characters' reactions to this role reversal [...] This type of premise can lead to overly repetitive and thus often unsuccessful series [Lauzen, Dozier and Horan 211].

Racism is another ideology which violently limits which stories are regarded as valuable, as the #OSW debacle demonstrates. In terms of producing ideas about race, women, and sexuality which are then made to seem natural and truthful, on-screen black lesbians are more likely to be butch than are white women. As Ciasullo summarizes it, "the mainstream edict: the femme body is necessarily a white body, so a Black lesbian cannot be a femme. What she can be, however, is an amalgam of mythologies of Black lesbianism" (Ciasullo 597). This state of affairs arises because the dominant ideology of femininity that stretches all the way back to the era of slavery equates femininity with whiteness. Blackness, therefore, cannot communicate femininity and so black characters are written to ensure that they don't.

None of this is to suggest that audience members and all the people working behind the scenes are automatons simply obeying ideological and marketing imperatives. There is plenty of room for messy incoherence at transmission and reception stages, as Stuart Hall explained and as MacLaine's decision to conceive her role "as if those scenes were still there" (qtd. in Russo 140) demonstrates. However, the endless repetition of particular messages can start to affect people's perceptions. Romantic comedies that present stalking behavior by the male protagonist as evidence of his true love for the woman who repeatedly rejects him, for example, can influence women viewers to endorse stalking myths if they found the films realistic or became immersed in them (Lippman 20–21). Equally, lack of exposure to complex tales about lesbian and bisexual women's lives can negatively affect how some audience members feel about *any* such content. A report commissioned by the BBC on audience perception found that 17 percent of heterosexual respondents felt that there was "too much" portrayal of lesbians (with 16 percent thinking there was "too much" of bisexual people and 21 percent of gay men). In contrast, other minority groups (defined in the report as British Asians, black people, and disabled people) did not raise the same degree of resistance in the audience, with only 11 percent, 9 percent and 5 percent respectively of the audience feeling that there was "too much" portrayal of these groups (BBC, *Research* 47).

Conclusion

In her slightly jaded analysis of the current state of lesbians in film, Vicki Eaklor concludes that it is highly unlikely that "less exploitative plots and characters will even be possible within present power structures" (Eaklor, "Kids," 166). These structures, formed from a combination of patriarchal interests, racist assumptions, postfeminist claims about individual female success, and assertions about market imperatives, are very powerful and effective at obscuring whose interests they serve. After all, if audiences can be persuaded through the relentless repetition of seductive advertising messages to put aside commonsense and take on insupportable levels of personal debt in order to possess the latest "must-have" item, why must their supposed prejudices around lesbian love and community be catered to? Are those prejudices and dismissals of lesbian existence not, in fact, at least partially generated by the strategies of using the Sweeps Week kiss, lesbian chic, or dead lesbian to maintain a clear and often-repeated message of lesbian impossibility?

Becca Cragin argues that there are effective ways to make a character recognizably lesbian or bisexual without resorting to these dominant strategies. By "representing lesbian-specific cultural and political history, by depicting homophobia and heterosexism, or by not replicating heterosexism in the structure of the show" (Cragin 195), and repeating these fresh techniques across many shows, the dominant ideas could be replaced. However, if writers and creators "write not only what they know but also what they have been rewarded for producing within the creative sphere" (Lauzen, Dozier and Horan 212), and women struggle to get and then maintain a foothold within the industry, then it will continue to be a challenge to mount a meaningful assault on this tired old set of stories.

4

ALL THE DEAD
LESBIANS (IRL)

No one wishes to draw a causal line from a lesbian character dying on screen to a lesbian who dies In Real Life (IRL). As Jo Chiang asserted in an opinion piece in *The New York Times*, "women who love women aren't tragic" and the real-life stories of these women can be as full of joy and despair as anyone else's. Furthermore, the impact of the media on real people's lives is complex and multi-layered. There are cases of people watching something and then going out and copying it in real life, but that type of direct cause-and-effect is very rare. Usually there is a complicated and messy relationship between family, school, work, friends, political or faith communities, and both mainstream and subcultural worlds. The media is just one spoke in this wheel, but it is an influential one at individual and societal levels. It translates and communicates information and messages about the correct alignment of all the other spokes, socializing youth and producing culture (Craig et al. 257–258). As Sue Jackson points out, "in a culture where heterosexuality is normative and alternative expressions of sexuality are marginalized and regulated, media may, for some, provide the primary or only informational sources about queer possibilities for oneself" (Sue Jackson 152).

Although of course the lives of real people are the ones that actually matter, characters' lives are important because of the impact they have on those real lives. They can hold out promise for a different world. They can disgust or please viewers, they can persuade viewers to hold their own lives up to scrutiny, and they may provide the catalyst for change. Shared love of characters and shows can promote community building. For some viewers stories are undoubtedly just pure entertainment, forgotten as soon as the screen goes dark, whereas for others they are a lifeline. But whatever characters may mean to any given viewer, they do not exist in a vacuum. Viewers watch them from the circumstances of their own lives, within racial, legal, economic, social and cultural webs, family dynamics, religious narratives, and in school, workplace and national contexts. For some people, seeing a character on-screen whose life somehow approximates their own or their dream of what their life could be like can be incredibly inspiring. Equally, if that character dies they can experience the death as very painful, even desolating. And while Chiang is right to question the fundamental message that women + woman = tragedy, the lives of some young lesbian and bisexual women are in reality marked by loss in ways that are not the same for their heterosexual sisters. Homosexual ≠ heterosexual, in fact. In this chapter we interrupt our program to take a brief detour to reflect on "real life."

Not Yet Equal

First comes the bad news. Although being lesbian or bisexual does not *cause* death in real life, the combination of isolation, violence, harassment, and symbolic annihilation that can be meted out to them can have a significant negative impact on the mental and physical health of young women in these groups. There is a reason why the fans who mobilized after Lexa's death on *The 100* chose to raise money for The Trevor Project, whose mission is to end LGBTQ youth suicide through crisis intervention, suicide prevention, education, advocacy, and policy change (www.thetrevorproject. org). Rob Cover argues that the mainstream media provides four rationales for LGBT suicide in order to link sexuality with (inevitable?) death. One is the rationale of non-heterosexuality, in which sexuality is blamed for suicide and the claim is backed up with statistics. A second is the rationale of shame and guilt, where LGBT people kill themselves due to the "unbearable" shame of their sexuality or the guilt of having disgraced their families. The third rationale is heterosexism: because they cannot lead satisfying lives in a heterosexual world, LGBT people kill themselves. Finally, there is the rationale of individual peer behavior, in which LGBT people kill themselves as a consequence of rejection or teasing from their peers (Cover, "Mediating" 1175). Simultaneously portraying the lesbian as psychotic or emotionally unstable, the story of the suicidal or self-destructive lesbian is one of the oldest and most common lesbian death tropes. These insane women's "violent passions" lead them to irrational behaviors where they cannot bear to face life without the objects of their affection and so they resolve to end their lives (Duggan 124–155). This act of suicide—sometimes murder-suicide—is interpreted as the last resort of a lonely lesbian contemplating insufferable heartbreak.

While these neat explanations work to maintain a comfortable sense of distance and pity for the presumed-to-be heterosexual reading and watching public, it is true that at any age the condition of lesbian and bisexual women "IRL" is haunted by violence. In a national survey Catherine Taylor and Tracy Peter found that homophobia remains rampant in Canadian schools, while Gail Mason in Australia and Douglas Janoff in Canada show that lesbians are targeted for murder because of their sexuality. Mason explains that men often viciously respond to women who reject their advances. In the case where the woman rejecting him is a lesbian, the man's response may be even more vicious as her very existence threatens the heterosexual and patriarchal order which tells men they have the rights to women's bodies.

Against this background it is not surprising that the Center for Disease Control (CDC) in the USA and McCreary Centre Society in Canada both sound the same alarm. Lesbian and bisexual young women are not doing well compared to their peers. In their analysis of the material produced by the Youth Risk Behavior Surveillance System (YRBSS) for the CDC, Laura Kann and her colleagues use the phrase "sexual minority youth" which they define as those youth who "identify as gay, lesbian, and bisexual and those who are not sure about their sexual identity as well as those who have sexual contact with only the same sex or with both sexes." In her study of the ways young women cope with homophobia Diane Pendragon uses the similarly awkward phrase "sexual minority female youth" because the women she interviews define their sexuality in a number of different ways: as lesbian, bisexual, queer, bisexual lesbian, uncertain or refusing to any particular label (6). Regardless of how they define themselves, many of these women (although not all, it should be noted) tend to struggle more than both their heterosexual peers and sexual minority male youth.

The McCreary Centre Society in British Columbia, Canada, spent more than a decade studying the physical and mental health of lesbian, gay and bisexual youth in schools across the province. In 2007 it released *Not Yet Equal: The Health of Lesbian, Gay, & Bisexual Youth in BC*. This study noticed some sharp differences in their experiences between groups of women. For example, lesbians and bisexual adolescents were more likely to be living alone or in foster care. While only 9 percent of heterosexual girls had run away from home in the past year, 40 percent of lesbians and 28 percent of bisexual girls had (Saewyc et al., 13). Rates of sexual and physical abuse were also quite different as the following table shows.

	Lesbian	Bisexual female	Heterosexual female
Sexually abused	29%	36%	11%
Forced to have sex	15%	23%	5%
Physically abused	45%	35%	17%
Physically hurt by boy/girlfriend	24%	14%	5%

(All figures taken from Saewyc et al. 14).

In terms of feeling sad, discouraged or hopeless in the past month, lesbians were far more likely than anyone else to feel this way: a shocking 61 percent compared to 50 percent of bisexual girls, 22 percent of heterosexual girls, 35 percent of gay boys and 13 percent of heterosexual boys (Saewyc et al. 29). The report points out that most lesbian, gay and bisexual youth did not attempt suicide, but lesbians were five times as likely as heterosexuals to think about doing it, and 38 percent of them had attempted to kill themselves in the past year, as had 30 percent of bisexual women compared to only 8 percent of heterosexual girls (Saewyc et al. 31). For both lesbians and bisexual girls rates of suicidal thoughts and attempts have been steadily increasing over the years, whereas they have been significantly declining for gay men (Saewyc et al. 32).

The disturbing findings from the *Not Yet Equal* study are not isolated to one Canadian province. In August 2016 the CDC released its report on "Sexual Identity, Sex of Sexual Contacts, and Health-Related Behaviors Among Students in Grades 9–12" in the USA (Kann et al.). This study is much larger and covers a wider range of practices than the Canadian one. The CDC collapses lesbians and bisexual women together, so the different experiences of those two groups cannot be separated out. Overall, however, the two studies mirror each other. For example, 66.5 percent of lesbian and bisexual girls felt sad or hopeless compared to 35.5 percent of heterosexual girls. Lesbian and bisexual girls had seriously considered attempting suicide at more than double the rate of heterosexuals (46.6 percent compared to 19.6 percent). The differences between the groups got even wider in terms of making a suicide plan (42 percent of lesbian and bisexual girls, 15.7 percent of heterosexual girls) and attempting suicide, which 32.8 percent of lesbian and bisexual girls had done compared to only 8.4 percent of heterosexuals (Kann et al.).

Such stark numbers cannot get at the nuance in people's lives, the various elements that intersect to make one young woman find her life unbearable when another one who ostensibly has the same sexuality might not. Details about race, class, immigrant status, experiences of colonialism, rural living, family dynamics including the peculiar strains of military service among other factors would all sharpen the picture. Overall, though, the broad image is striking. Young lesbians and bisexual women are doing worse than all other groups.

This is a very important point, because there is a widespread belief that lesbianism is more socially acceptable than being gay and so lesbians are supposed to have an easier time of it than their gay brothers. General statements about the "LGBT community" or assumptions that improvements for gay men will lead to improvements for lesbians can very easily obscure the different challenges that women face. It is therefore crucial to consider how women can be affected by practices such as the Sweeps Week kiss with its corresponding implication that lesbian desire is never real, is very transitory (by the next week everything has gone back to normal), or is only done to attract an audience. The kind of invisibility which is the outcome of lesbian chic and lifestyle individualism, coupled with the emphasis on the "real" heterosexuality of an actor during interviews about their non-heterosexual roles mean that on-screen lesbians slide towards the category of performative bisexuality.

"Performative bisexuality" is defined as "engaging in homoerotic acts with other women, usually in front of men and most often in the context of social settings like fraternity parties, bars, clubs and other crowded sexualized spaces" (Fahs 432). This is not a form of bisexuality as sexual identity: it is an act undertaken by usually heterosexual women feeling pressured to please the men who are assumed to be their audience. Fahs points out that "women's sexuality shifts in response to changing social trends and pressures more readily than men's sexuality, which can be particularly dangerous in a patriarchal climate" where patriarchal fantasies are dominant and unquestioned (Fahs 435). Fahs suggests that the pressures to engage in performative bisexuality are beginning to feel more compulsory for young women, in part because of the influence of reality television shows which include the obligatory "girls making out together" scene. This type of activity becomes more and more a form of entertainment directed at pleasing men (who increasingly demand and expect it) which then "leaves little room for explorations of same-sex desire in a multifaceted way" (Fahs 446).

The fallout from "performative bisexuality" is threefold. First, men as a group appropriate women's sexuality. Second, the heterosexual women performing bisexuality retain strongly homophobic attitudes and, perhaps because of its compulsory element, do not feel open toward women who are bisexual or lesbian nor develop any kind of political consciousness about how women's sexuality may be exploited (Fahs 446). Finally, lesbianism is assumed to be more acceptable than gay men's sexuality because it is regarded as a performance that already belongs in the realm of heterosexual men's sexuality and is therefore not a real sexuality at all. Diane Pendragon reports that sexual minority female youth overall tend to experience isolation, lack of access to knowledge and role models, lack of acceptance (including a struggle to accept themselves), pressure to conform, and harassment and violence (7–9). It is no wonder that young lesbian and bisexual women are not thriving in a world which does not take them seriously.

Kann and her colleagues point out that "because many health-related behaviors initiated during adolescence often extend into adulthood, they can potentially have a life-long negative effect on health outcomes, educational attainment, employment, housing, and overall quality of life" (Kann et al.). Equally, although showrunners insist on treating each death of a character as an individual incident necessary to their story, for viewers drawing on their intertextual knowledge, as we have already argued, the deaths form part of an Ur-text. The effect of this Ur-text is cumulative over the lifetime. Here, then, are two interconnected elements which may influence each other over many decades of a woman's life: feeling worthless in adolescence can be compounded by watching a television screen covered in dead lesbians, and becoming attached to characters that inevitably die can reinforce poor health.

Resilience

The bad news is grim, but there is also good news. While negative media representations make lesbian, gay and bisexual people as a whole "feel excluded from society and limited their identity expression" (Gomillion and Giuliano 343), lesbians and bisexual women (at any age) can be remarkably resilient, using a variety of tactics to minimize the impact of oppression and to find supportive community. In reviewing the data from the Youth Risk Behavior Survey, Kann et al. note that "most sexual minority students cope with the transition from childhood though adolescence to adulthood successfully and become healthy and productive adults" (Kann et al.). Pendragon adds that sexual minority female youth develop a range of coping strategies to develop a healthy, confident sense of themselves. These included deferment and avoidance (putting off dealing with coming out to family members when it did not feel safe, for example), re-defining and re-inventing themselves, resisting other people's definitions of them, persevering in the face of setbacks, and engaging in education and activism (Pendragon 10–12). Many of these tactics involve an active and critical engagement with a sense of future possibility and one way to reach that—in the absence of real-life role models—is to latch on to fictional characters and connect with the community (online) that shares their enjoyment of them.

Characters in television shows and in films can inspire women to change their lives in many very positive ways. This was one of the unassailable impacts of *XWP*. In her interviews with participants in XenaSubtextTalk, for example, Rosalind Hanmer remarked that in addition to wanting to see Xena and Gabrielle get together, "they also wanted their own sexual/love desire to become a reality." A participant who was unemployed, under-educated and lived in an economically deprived area in England "gained self-esteem and personal empowerment" from her experiences participating in the fandom (Hanmer, "Internet," 154–155). Both characters and celebrities can act as important role models who inspire pride and provide sources of comfort and examples of strength. Lesbian film viewers, for example, "identified most with female characters who did not conform to traditional feminine roles" and they were particularly positive about "actresses who were rumored to be lesbian and to films featuring close friendships between women" (Gomillion and Giullian 333). Positive role models, such as out lesbians like Ellen DeGeneres, are sources of strength and figures to emulate, as well as influences which help women feel that their lesbian identities are socially acceptable or to feel pride in their own resilience.

Given their typical isolation from real life role models, the media is an important source of information for youth as well as other groups who are extremely isolated. Young people constantly consume media, both offline sources such as television and film and online material through websites and social media. They are also producers of media, especially blogs, sources like Facebook and Tumblr, shorter posts on Twitter and Instagram, and videos on YouTube. All these different types of media can provide useful supports for LGBTQ youth (and the newly out) in developing the resilience they need to develop their selfhood. This works in different ways depending on the type of media. Offline media can be useful for escapism and can also generate feelings of empowerment. One eighteen-year-old Asian lesbian high school student in Toronto, for example, watched *XWP* and incorporated its messages about developing inner strength in order to foster her own sense of perseverance (Craig et al. 264). Online media, on the other hand, can work as both a site of activism against homophobia and a way to find and sustain a feeling of community and connection.

In the aftermath of the debacle over Lexa's death several producers of online media have used it in exactly this way. In her *IndieWire* blog Dorothy Snarker provides some suggested responses that viewers can use when trying to discuss, with family and friends who may not see that there is a problem at all, why it matters to real-life lesbians that fictional lesbians are dying in alarming numbers. She addresses the most frequent dismissive comments that such viewers have to contend with, including the old chestnut "Well, characters die all the time on TV" (Snarker, "Why"). In a very creative intervention BuzzFeed has posted a series of short videos in the style and format of a Public Service Announcement. They show lesbian youth repeatedly stating "I am affected" (www.buzzfeed.com). The clever use of the PSA format challenges viewers to see the deaths of queer women on television as a public health concern that all citizens must acknowledge and fight to end.

This sort of engaged use of online media typically includes a space for comments, so that people can not only respond to the content but see what others think about it too. Overall, participation in online discussion groups tends to improve self-acceptance and offers "their members a sense of community and belonging that is often unattainable in the real world" (Gomillion and Giuliano 338). Shelley Craig and her colleagues, studying the way that LGBTQ youth use media, conclude that especially in its online versions, media can provide an important catalyst for resilience IRL.

We now return to our regularly scheduled program.

5

IT GETS BETTER

When she was thirteen, Shameen Kabir saw *The Children's Hour* on television. She later wrote that while it demonstrated to her that there were other women who also desired women, she "was devastated when the character played by Shirley MacLaine hangs herself because she realizes she desires the woman played by Audrey Hepburn. I desperately wanted to see a reworking of this lesbian desire. I needed images that would rewrite the lesbian without the tragedy" (Kabir 3). To find them she initially looked for other performances by the same actors. This experience is telling. It draws attention to the major role that characters play in helping young women realize they are not alone. It captures the dreadful impact of those characters' deaths. It suggests that the actors matter immensely as a first point of connection, and it emphasizes the longing for new and different stories.

The opportunities to do the re-writing that Kabir longed for have expanded dramatically in recent years. *The Children's Hour* is now more than fifty years old. Although it continues to be shown on television, and therefore could potentially still have the same devastating effect on an unsuspecting viewer, there are many other stories which have rewritten such dire old tales. Vicki Eaklor goes so far as to suggest that "the 'victim' of one's own sexuality has all but disappeared" ("Kids" 156). To find fresh stories all a viewer needs to do is change the channel, turn to Netflix and other streaming services such as One More Lesbian, or buy or rent a DVD from a distribution service such as Wolfe Video (or, of course, Amazon). And there is plenty to choose from: after all, the *L Word* in the USA, *Lip Service* in the UK, and *Lost Girl* in Canada all ushered in the brave new world of television drama centered on women who loved women, didn't they? This shift would imply that the dead lesbians, bisexuals and subtextual pairs scattered across television and film screens no longer matter because they are outnumbered by living, cheerful characters who get married, have babies, and are just as banal as their straight screen-mates (Kessler).

In 2010 the syndicated columnist Dan Savage launched the "It Gets Better" Project. Its purpose was to reassure suicidal or depressed young LGBT people who were being bullied or harassed that their lives would improve over time. This promise seems to be mirrored in the media. It is certainly true that there have been improvements in representations of women's same-sex desire and some shifts in the way that the entertainment industry functions, suggesting that not only do personal lives get better but so do symbolic ones. However, the phrase "it gets better" can also be used ironically to stand in for the phrase "it gets even worse," as, for example, when a person recounts a series of barriers and then, to emphasize the immensity of the challenge facing them, tells their listeners "wait! It gets better!" before describing an even greater problem. This chapter discusses how, for lesbian and bisexual women on screen, "it gets better" in both of these senses.

Improving the Picture: By the Numbers

Over the last ten years, GLAAD has been publishing data on the numbers of LGBT characters on TV in the USA in its annual *Where we are on TV* reports. In 2012 it added an annual *Studio Responsibility Index* to analyze both the numbers and quality of LGBT characters in films from the major Hollywood studios. For the 2015–2016 TV season in the USA GLAAD studied 881 series regulars on 118 primetime scripted TV shows on the five broadcast (free to air) channels. Compared to the previous season, the number of regular lesbian characters (as opposed to either recurring or one-off characters) had increased from 28 percent to 33 percent of all LGBT characters. In other words, there were now 23 regular lesbian characters on scripted TV shows, out of 881 regular characters, although several of these had died by the end of the season. On cable (pay for view) channels, there were 31 lesbian regular or recurring characters, or 22 percent of the total number of LGBT characters, a proportion that was down from the previous year. Streaming services (Netflix, Hulu, and Amazon) had a higher proportion of lesbians (36 percent of LGBT characters) than either of the other two formats.

Films did much more poorly than scripted television and streaming series, mirroring the generally poor showing for women in the film industry that we discussed in Chapter 3. GLAAD looked at the 126 films released by the seven studios with the top grossing films in 2015, which were 20th

Century–Fox, Lionsgate Entertainment, Paramount Pictures, Sony Columbia Pictures, Universal Pictures, Walt Disney Studios, and Warner Brothers,
as well as the 46 films from the "art house" studios, namely Focus Features,
Fox Searchlight, Roadside Attractions, and Sony Pictures Classics. For the
seven major studios, 17.5 percent of the films (mostly comedies) had LGBT
characters, with men outnumbering women by three to one. The proportion
of these characters who were people of color had decreased from the previous year, with 25.5 percent in total (in the 17.5 percent of films) compared
to 32.1 percent in the 2014 release year. The "art house" releases had a
slightly greater proportion of LGBT characters: 22 percent in 2015, which
had doubled from the previous year. With a few exceptions, such as the
film *Freeheld*, almost all of the characters had supporting roles: they are
"included as the setup of a punchline or exist as an isolated token character
who never gets the chance to bloom into a fully formed personality"
(GLAAD, *Studio* 4).

GLAAD's figures give the most up-to-date details and, because of
the global reach of American popular culture, can stand in as a snapshot
for what is happening on screens elsewhere. Other studies which do exist
tend to support the general findings of the GLAAD reports. For example,
Brigette Rollet's study found only twenty fictional lesbian characters on
French TV over a ten-year period, although she did notice a trend of more
lesbians appearing on talk shows and in documentaries. Of the fictional
characters, however, as she argues, "being regularly victimized, or seen only
by others, they are not potential role models for a gay and lesbian audience"
and are only supposed to be "reassuring straight viewers in their sexual
preferences" (Rollet 97). In her study of lesbian representation on TV in
New Zealand between 2004 and 2006, Hopkins combined an analysis of
the content—how many lesbians, how did they fare, particularly in terms
of intimacy, compared to heterosexual characters—with an analysis of audience responses to the characters and their storylines. Lesbian characters
overall represented only 1.2 percent of the total of 1192 characters during
Hopkins's study period.

As we discussed in Chapter 2, the effect of such sparse numbers was
made worse by the poor quality of the representation: characters that were
supposed to be lesbians (not bisexual women) were hard for viewers to read
as such because their sexual and emotional relationships appeared to be
primarily with men. Hopkins found that lesbian audience members were
frustrated by this, because they valued realism or authenticity in characters.
Interestingly, even though this was a study of New Zealand, viewers there
perceived lesbians as an international category, so that the characters did

not need to have authentic "Kiwi" traits, they just had to appear to be "authentically" lesbian. This raises the question of what makes a representation seem authentic, which comes from a combination of the actors themselves, the nature of the roles, the types of stories told.

The Women Who Play Women Who Love Women Whom We Love to Love

Historically, actors have been skittish about playing women who loved women. Their doubt may have partially come from the sense that many lesbian roles are truncated. How demoralizing for an actor who has finally landed a role with a corresponding paycheck to open the script and see that her character will be disposed of in short order. Equally significant was their concern over several potential sources of fallout: typecasting (which would severely limit potential roles given how few lesbians appeared on screen); assumptions that they must be a lesbian because they played one on TV; the hate mail—including death threats—that they could expect to receive; and homophobia, both internalized and that coming from other people.

The pattern of concern can mostly be discerned from the very first appearance of an identifiably Sapphic character. Vito Russo argues that Countess Geschwitz in *Pandora's Box* (George Wilhelm Pabst, Germany, 1929) is "probably the first explicitly drawn lesbian character on film" (24). Geschwitz was played by Alice Roberts, a Belgian actor who was apparently horrified that she would have to communicate desire for Lulu, the character played by Louise Brooks. Brooks later recalled that she initially thought that Roberts was foolish to be so worried about the potential impact of this role, but then realized that fans of the film assumed that she herself was a lesbian. Brooks allowed "the rumors to spread, to shock people and because she was truly attracted to women and to the upper class gay life" (Weiss 24), and she typically embraced many opportunities to flirt with scandal anyway.

Brooks' response was rare, however. Over the years women who play lesbians or bisexuals have consistently discovered that their own sexuality is immediately called into question. On the one hand, it is as if their professional skills are assumed to fail them in this specific area of performance. On the other hand, all the questions about their sexuality reveal a deeply held heteronormative anxiety over potential contamination between fictional and real lives. The questions communicate a subtle message that actors should perform in such a way that the audience can be reassured in the end that it is all just an act. In 1967, for example, Anne Heywood discovered that "after playing Ellen March in *The Fox*, [she] found it necessary to tell the press, 'I've played murderers, but I've never killed anyone'" (Vito Russo 212). The following year *The Killing of Sister George* (Robert Aldrich, UK) was released. The film is remarkable for three reasons: it depicts a love triangle between three women (as opposed to the more frequent pornography-lite storyline of two women and a man); it has quite possibly the most uncomfortable (both to watch and surely to perform) sex scene in lesbian cinematic history; and it includes scenes filmed with real lesbians at a real lesbian club, The Gateways in London. All three main actors (Beryl Reid, Susannah York and Coral Browne) had different reactions to their roles but certainly the press was interested in the link between the actors and the sexuality of their characters. According to Vito Russo, "when Beryl Reid appeared on the Johnny Carson show to publicize *The Killing of Sister George*, she was compelled to reiterate that she was not in fact a lesbian, for the press had been focusing its questions on her sexuality rather than on the film" (211), whereas in Britain press reports about the film "were careful to suggest that all three actresses felt uncomfortable about playing lesbians" (Gardiner 150).

The relentless focus on actors' sexuality is not unique to the USA or UK—the same dynamic is at play in New Zealand. Sue Jackson notes that the "heterosexual audience is generally more aware of 'lesbian' sex displays as acts of performance than they are of heterosexual portrayals is perhaps, at least in part, influenced by the knowledge that the actors portraying them are (often) 'really' heterosexuals" (Sue Jackson 154–155). Hopkins explains why the audience is so aware of the actors' sexuality. As she points out, "when actors who play lesbian characters are interviewed they are required to reiterate their heterosexuality by discussing their (male) partner, their wedding plans, or their baby plans. In restoring heterosexuality, these texts juxtapose the real with the fictional" (Hopkins 46). The emphasis in these examples is on heterosexual actors having to explain that they are not their characters, but lesbian actors can also find themselves scrutinized.

The Oscar-nominated Canadian actor Ellen Page came out publicly during a speech she gave at a Human Rights Campaign event in 2014. She later drew attention to the absurdity of actors being asked about the connection between their on- and off-screen sexuality and being expected to show concern over the potential damage to her career of both taking on lesbian roles and being out personally. She reported encountering assumptions that she would now be typecast as *only* able to play gay characters. In an interview with *The Guardian* in 2016, she noted that having taken on several lesbian roles, "she had been asked if she feared becoming pigeon-holed," but that "no one asks: 'Ellen, you've done seven straight roles in a row—shouldn't you shake it up and do something queer?'" (Child). Although Page's frustration reveals that the question is preposterous—after all, acting is based precisely on the ability to convince an audience that one is not playing oneself—typecasting remains a concern for actors.

In 2013 SAG-AFTRA (Screen Actors Guild–American Federation of Television and Radio Artists) produced a report about the experiences and perspectives of their members around sexual orientation and gender identity. The report was based on a survey of 5,692 respondents, of which 61 were lesbians and 301 were bisexual women and men (the total number in the bisexual category was not split up to distinguish between women and men). SAG-AFTRA wanted to get a sense of "the progress toward full inclusion of LGBT performers in the entertainment industry" (Badgett and Herman 10). Although the report suggested that, on the whole, it is getting better for these performers, barriers and challenges remained. The picture it paints is of the power of the fictional and real worlds to alter each other, whether through fears over contamination or via dreams coming true.

The perils of typecasting and homophobia have to be negotiated. Vito Russo argued that "actors have always resisted playing homosexual roles lest they be typed—especially those actors who are gay in private life" (211). Of respondents who had never played a lesbian, gay or bisexual character, 17 percent of straight ones said that they did not want to play such a role. A total of an additional 12 percent reported fear of typecasting, fear of the role's impact on their ability to get other roles, and worry that they would be presumed lesbian, gay or bisexual themselves (Badgett and Herman 23). At least since the era of classic Hollywood cinema characters have been typed in order to be recognizable. White notes that "casting and perform-ance" are already a reading of type; the audience performs a reading on another level, informed by cultural and subcultural codes, spectatorial experience of the star in other roles, and subsidiary discourses (149). That is to say, the choice to cast a particular performer in a lesbian or bisexual role is in part dependent on how closely she matches assumptions about types, and there may be a link to the actor's own sexuality. SAG-AFTRA found that 71 percent of their lesbian respondents had played a lesbian or bisexual role compared to 33 percent of the heterosexual women surveyed (Badgett and Herman 22).

Audience members may also be inclined to read Sapphic tendencies into a character if the actor has previously played a lesbian. This has a knock-on effect: more than a quarter of lesbian and gay and a fifth of bisexual respondents believed that their LGB roles had affected whether they were hired for subsequent straight roles, whereas only 3 percent of straight actors held the same belief (Badgett and Herman 23). The boundary between real and fictional life seemed to be porous in other ways too. Amanda Barrie, an 80-year-old British actress famous for her work on the long-running soap opera *Coronation Street*, recalled that for decades she feared coming out as bisexual in case it ruined her career (Lyell, "Amanda"). More than half of LGBT and over a third of heterosexual performers believed that directors, producers and casting directors were biased in their choices of who to hire, while over the previous five years 9 percent of lesbian and gay performers had been turned down for a role because of their sexuality.

Other forms of homophobia create additional challenges. Before the film version was made, Beryl Reid performed the role of George in the stage version of *The Killing of Sister George*. The play did very poorly in provincial theaters, with audience members either walking out or maintaining what Reid described as a "stony silence." She said that "the people of Hull would barely serve us in the shops, they were so horrified" (qtd. in Gardiner 137). During the filming of scenes at the Gateways club for the film version, the extras comprised both professional actors and real club members. The professional extras were uncomfortable, and Gateways members put this discomfort down to three reasons: they were annoyed that amateurs were being paid; they were too hot in the claustrophobic space; and they did not like having to dance with real lesbians (Gardiner 141). It was unusual at the time for the professionals to know that they were on a set with lesbians, and certainly the Gateways members attributed only part of the problem to homophobia.

By the time of the SAG-AFTRA survey it was far more likely than it had been in the 1960s that actors would be out at least to their peers, with nearly 80 percent of lesbians (but only around half of bisexual women) out to some degree in their professional lives. All the lesbian, gay and bisexual actors tended to become more closeted with personnel working higher up the decision-making ladder, though, with only 13 percent of lesbian and gay and 2 percent of bisexual actors being out to industry executives (Badgett and Herman 32–33). Workplaces could be quite hostile, with on-set discrimination, such as "anti-gay slurs and less respectful treatment directed at LGBT performers" by crew members, directors and producers, being commonplace. More than half of lesbian and gay and more than a quarter of heterosexual respondents to the SAG-AFTRA survey had heard such comments. Furthermore, lesbian and gay actors tended to have lower daily earnings than their peers (Badgett and Herman 29–31). Taken together, lesbian actors (and perhaps those perceived to be) are likely to face a hostile set, bias against being hired anyway, typecasting, and truncated roles.

The SAG-AFTRA survey, which confirmed that lesbians were far more likely than heterosexual women to have played lesbian or bisexual roles, also revealed actors' assumptions about the potential slippage between real and fictional worlds in the minds of their colleagues. While 40 percent did not believe that playing a lesbian or bisexual woman would make others in the industry believe that an actor was one in real life nearly the same proportion (35 percent) thought that they would (Badgett and Herman 23). As if determined to prevent any slippage and to insist that lesbians are only ever characters and are never real, and that women who do not look like stereotypical "dykes" cannot possibly be lesbians, actors are asked to comment on how different, odd, or challenging it is to play gay. Interviewers, for example, make the assumption that "the heterosexual actors who play gay characters found same-sex intimacy difficult" (Hopkins 46). Women are very rarely asked if they find kissing men a challenge because this is assumed to be their natural behavior. Although actors increasingly dismiss questions that insist on such assumptions, the repetitive nature of these questions reinforces the perspective that heterosexuality is something that is found in the real world, while lesbianism is a fiction which only occurs on screen.

Intertwined Lives

All of the above examples point to challenges within the industry, but characters and the actors who portray them can spill into and out beyond each other in other ways as well. Viewers' avid consumption of almost any representation of same-sex desire, regardless of whether it includes symbolic annihilation, frequently goes together with a fascination with the actors who portray women who love women. This can lead to a complicated inter-textuality. As White puts it:

> our relationships to stars go beyond identification. The same-sex star crush narrative, with its complex negotiation of identification and desire, idealization and recognition, is particularly revelatory for queer subjects. Simply put, when you recognize your lesbianism through movies and movie stars, you identify your desire. Stories about stars facilitate the construction of lesbian identity through identification with others who share one's preferences [36].

Fans follow the careers of actors who portray lesbians or bisexual women, and are sometimes rewarded with the desired-for outcome: the actor herself is lesbian or bisexual. "One source of pleasure has been the rare scene of an actress with a cult reputation acting out that rumored sexuality on screen, such as Marlene Dietrich kissing another woman in *Morocco* (1930)" (Becker et al. 29). This pleasure is rooted in the era when subtext (based on extra-textual knowledge about actors' personal lives) added a layer of delight rather than dismay at this exploitation of the audience's yearning.

In more recent years, after decades of activism mitigated many of the more devastating legal, economic and social consequences of coming out, more actors have not only come out but have also talked about the impact of playing lesbian or bisexual roles on their decision to do so. In 1996, for example, the English actor Sophie Ward came out as a lesbian after por-traying an ostensibly heterosexual mother who fell in love with a lesbian in *A Village Affair* (Moira Armstrong, UK, 1995). Because Ward was a for-mer model, had a classic "English rose" appearance, and was the daughter of a famous British establishment actor (Simon Ward), the mainstream media professed fascination with her but she chose to give her first public interview about coming out to Rhona Cameron, the lesbian co-host of *Gaytime TV*. During this interview Ward explained that one of the reasons she wanted to do the film was that she felt there would be other people in her situation—a married mother who falls for a lesbian, which described both her character and her own life—and she wanted to talk about the experience while giving press interviews to promote the film. Advised against doing this, she waited to come out publicly and noted with humor that in this instance (perhaps because she did not meet stereotypical expec-tations) no-one seemed to be "confusing" her with her role even though she wanted them to draw the parallel.

Another woman whose life mirrored that of one of the characters in her film was Josefine Tengblad. She explained that the storyline of *Kiss Me (Kyss Mig)* (Alexandra Therese Keining, Sweden, 2011) in which Mia, who is about to marry her long-term boyfriend, falls in love with her soon-to-be stepsister, Frida, largely reflected her own life. In fact, she suggested that making the film (she produced it and also played the role of Frida's betrayed girlfriend) was personally very significant. "What would have happened if I hadn't made this journey? If I hadn't done this film? I think I'd still be with my ex-husband, because I don't think I would have had that strength" (Minero, n.p.). Similarly, Ellen Page commented on the rela-tionship between her involvement in the drama *Freeheld* (Peter Sollett, USA, 2015) and coming out publicly herself. *Freeheld* is based on the true story of terminally ill New Jersey police officer Laurel Hester's attempt to get her pension passed on to her partner Stacie Andree (played by Page).

Page explained that "what blows my mind is how my own personal journey paralleled the development of that movie. It felt wildly inappropriate to be playing this character as a closeted person" (Child). This experience of real life mirroring fiction, or the idea that playing a fictional role can precipitate real emotions is even examined in Marina Rice Bader's film *Anatomy of a Love Seen* (USA, 2014). It explores the idea that through an intense on-set dynamic two actors could fall in love which each other while playing characters who fall in love. The action of the film deals with the director's attempt to re-create that connection some months after the film-within-the film was shot, because the two women have since broken up.

In sharp contrast to the era of *The Children's Hour* (or even to the relatively recent late 1990s before the true impact of the neoliberal flood which had swept through the political, cultural, and economic landscape could be seen) there are now "out" lesbians and bisexual women owning the screen. Ellen DeGeneres with her eponymous daily talk show is the most high profile and mainstream example, but there are others. In addition to Portia De Rossi (DeGeneres' spouse) there are also Lea Delaria and (until her character was killed in season four) Samira Wiley on *Orange Is the New Black*, the comedians and actors Wanda Sykes and Kate McKinnon, the Canadian Ellen Page, the Venezuelan actor and former supermodel Patricia Velásquez, the Australian Ruby Rose who has convincingly moved from modeling and DJing to acting, and two successful British examples: singer/songwriter and actor Heather Peace and the comedian Sue Perkins. There are women whose careers have spanned decades: Lily Tomlin, Jodie Foster, Jane Lynch, Sara Gilbert, Leisha Hailey, Clea DuVall and Rosie O'Donnell. There are otherwise very private actors such as Kristen Stewart who decide to talk about dating women because they do not want their reticence about their private lives to be misconstrued as shame or deliberate concealment when their partner is a woman.

This list suggests patterns in both the American and British industries around who can risk being out. The majority of the women listed are professional comedians in addition to being actors, while several of the rest combine acting with other forms of professional performance, as musicians, models, and talk show hosts. In terms of who could take the risk, one participant in the SAG-AFTRA survey remarked that "if he or she was a drop dead gorgeous male or female romantic lead, I'd suggest staying in the closet—I think it's easier for character actors to 'come out'" (Badgett and Herman 37). This comment gets at the idea that "the industry's economic imperative—to provide entertainment to a broad market—seems to some industry observers to create potential risks for casting LGBT actors in roles that the viewing public may not accept," raising the question of whether LGBT performers could be marketed to the public and whether assumptions about their marketability would be likely to affect whether they were hired in the first place (Badgett and Herman 10).

Interestingly, while many performers believed that the public could still be sold on out lesbian, gay or bisexual actors as romantic leads, they asserted that producers and studio executives did not share that view. The figures are quite striking. For example, when asked if they thought that "the public WILL NOT want to see actors known to be LGB in heterosexual romantic leads," 26 percent of lesbian, gay, bisexual and transgender respondents agreed that this would be true for lesbian, gay and bisexual actors in films, with slightly fewer concerned that it would be true for lesbian or gay actors on television (23 percent). A mere 16 percent of them thought that bisexual actors on television would be affected by a public unwilling to see them in those roles (Badgett and Herman 19). The non–LGBT respondents were less optimistic: for film, 33 percent believed the public would not want to see lesbian or gay actors in the roles, and 30 percent feeling the same held for bisexual actors. The numbers dropped slightly for television, but not to the levels maintained by the LGBT respondents: 31 percent for lesbian or gay actors, and 27 percent for bisexual actors. Of course, these percentages indicate that the vast majority of respondents believed that the public would be prepared to see lesbian, gay or bisexual actors playing heterosexual romantic leads on film and television, but it is noticeable that the lesbians, gay men and bisexuals seem more optimistic than their straight colleagues.

All of the actors are concerned that industry decision makers, such as producers and studio executives, are less likely than their other colleagues to risk believing in the capacity of the public to be convinced by the acting ability of the LGB performers. Conversely, in a neat reversal, some viewers find *heterosexual* actors unconvincing when they are performing a lesbian romantic role. High school students in New Zealand, for example, felt uncomfortable watching straight actors playing lesbian characters because they perceived the actors themselves to be "uncomfortable with kissing and touching" and that they tended to perform their roles as if they were playing teenage girls at a slumber party rather than women who were genuinely attracted to each other or in a long-term relationship (Sue Jackson 158).

In spite of the complex limits on who feels they are able to risk being out and why, it matters immensely that some women are open about their lesbianism or bisexuality. In 2010 the BBC published a report on the *Portrayal of Lesbian, Gay and Bisexual People on the BBC*. The study, which combined audience research, public consultations, and meetings with community groups, was conducted on behalf of the BBC Working Group on the Portrayal and Inclusion of Lesbian, Gay and Bisexual Audiences as part of the corporation's overall diversity strategy. The BBC is publicly funded and is expected to "portray and celebrate the range of cultures and communities across the UK," come up with original and engaging content, and give "an accurate picture of the many communities that make up the UK" in order to promote understanding and discussion among them (BBC, *Executive* 5). What is so interesting about this study is that, rather than simply count the numbers of characters in a given year (an approach which does not reveal how many of them will live) it examines how lesbian, gay, bisexual and heterosexual people perceive portrayals of LGB people.

The BBC report suggests that it is "incredibly important" to people who had either recently come out or were not yet out to most friends and family members to see performers (the study uses the catch-all term "talent") who are open about their sexuality (BBC, *Research* 22). For viewers who have little access to a community, or who feel that they do not or cannot belong to one, it really matters that performers are out and unapologetic about their sexuality. Role models are therefore important to lesbian, gay and bisexual adolescents in particular, as they can help them develop a strong and healthy sense of self (Gomillion and Giuliano 332). Just being exposed to lesbian characters was significant in these terms (although traumatic material or negative role models could have a detrimental effect), and the experiences of out celebrities could have a direct and positive impact on lesbians' lives. In one study, a bisexual woman and a lesbian both commented on how important it was that Ellen DeGeneres not only came out but that her process of coming out received a lot of media attention, which made them feel good about coming out too (Gomillion and Giuliano 344).

Perhaps even more significant than their being out is the fact that some of these women have also portrayed characters who love other women, which supports the findings of SAG-AFTRA about lesbians being likely to play lesbians and also raises the question of what makes a performance seem authentic. Thus Heather Peace appears as a lesbian in *Lip Service*, in the British medical soap opera *Holby City*, and in *Waterloo Road* which is set in a British high school. Lea Delaria, Samira Wiley, and Ruby Rose all played lesbians in *Orange Is the New Black*. Sue Perkins (better known as one of the co-hosts of *The Great British Bake Off* television show) wrote and starred in her own short-lived comedy about a closeted veterinarian in *Heading Out* in 2013. Clea DuVall, who played a lesbian in the comedy *But I'm a Cheerleader!* (Jamie Babbit, USA, 1999), plays the girlfriend of the President's daughter in the TV show *Veep* as well as a lesbian in the film that is her own directorial debut, *The Intervention* (Clea DuVall, USA, 2016). In other films, Lily Tomlin was an older lesbian in *Grandma* and Ellen Page a younger one in *Freeheld*.

In 2016 the *Ghostbusters* director Paul Feig affirmed that the character of Jillian Holtzmann, played by Kate McKinnon, was gay, although the film contains no explicit acknowledgment of her sexuality. Interestingly, being able to see Holtzmann as gay suggests that the techniques for seeing extra-textual and intertextual cues required under the Hays Code remain in play. Writing about the summer blockbusters which hint that some of their characters are queer, Benjamin Lee asks "why are we conforming to a Hays Code sensibility when violence and straight sex are up on screen for all to see?" After all, a negotiated decoding of Holtzmann is primarily accessible to those who know that McKinnon is a lesbian (she is typically described as the first openly gay cast member on the long-running NBC comedy show *Saturday Night Live*) and can read the intertextual clues in her performance. These include her costume, her flirtation with fellow Ghostbuster Erin, and her speech at the end of the film about having no family until she found Abby and the rest of the team who meet her need for love. Her reference to the love provided by a chosen family clearly resonates with women in the queer community across the globe who have found this kind of love and support after their traditional family rejects them (Gomillion and Giuliano 347).

The support provided by a chosen family is at the heart of *Liz in September* (Fina Torres, Venezuela, 2014) which stars another out lesbian, Patricia Velásquez, who also produced this women-centered film about a group of lesbians dealing with love and (unfortunately) loss. Incorporating footage of her personal history as a model, Velásquez plays Liz, a former model who is now dying of cancer. She and her friends and former lovers gather annually at a lesbian-run guest house where they are able to be open and supportive of each other. The closed group is accidently joined by a straight woman, Eva, whose marriage is failing because neither she nor her husband can move on from the impact of their son's death from cancer. The story, which is adapted from a play by Jane Chambers, deals with the healing power of love and the importance of letting loved ones go—Eva and Liz fall in love and Eva assists when Liz is ready to terminate her life rather than undergo dehumanizing and agonizing treatments. *Liz in September*, which has been described as the first Spanish-language lesbian film, is distinctly lesbian-centered with themes that will be familiar to many networks of lesbians in, for example, the group of friends who are all former and current lovers, the emotional pain of the famous author Dolores who is closeted, the alcoholism of the woman who let her one true love get away, and the annual visit to a secluded safe space where the women all feel free to be themselves. The final scenes of the film show Eva, along with her young daughter named after Liz, fully integrated into the group. This level of authenticity and lesbian-centeredness, coupled with high production values and performances by well-established actors, demonstrates what can be done to tell lesbian stories effectively. It is doubly hard in this context, then, to have to watch Liz die and see Eva, although now belonging with her chosen family, nevertheless remaining single.

"Not at all like any lesbians we had ever met"

Overall the anxiety about and yearning for any possible slippage between actors and their characters (or should that be characters and their actors?) can be traced back to a concern over "authenticity," and here lies a core problem in addition to the larger industry ones discussed in Chapter 3. What is an "authentic" depiction? Very little of what is shown in film or on television is realistic or authentic, given the imperative to sell products by associating them with something attractive, modish, or wealthy and trying to generate dissatisfaction with their own lives in viewers' minds. Tinseltown, Bollywood and other national film industries sell dreams, and television jumped on the same bandwagon as soon as it could. A non-commercial public broadcaster such as the BBC, which commissions its own content, is not so dependent on peddling promises, but it does have to compete in an increasingly crowded marketplace not just on home territory but also in selling its shows to overseas purchasers (which show commercials when airing BBC content and therefore need to satisfy advertising executives). It is questionable, then, whether anyone would feel that their specific group was represented authentically, but given their long history of tragic stereotyping, lesbians and bisexuals are highly concerned over what does get shown.

In the early days of GLAAD activist protesters demanded more authentic portrayals of lesbians and gay men on screen. They were fighting back against the tired and damaging stereotypes of limp-wristed queens, butch dykes, and sexually voracious bisexual women. The message seemed clear: these caricatures are offensive and real lesbian, gay and bisexual people are as varied as are straight people, so studios should put some effort into depicting realistic lives. In spite of decades of activism and very real changes in what is now shown, these audience members still seem to want what they wanted 40 years ago, which are "authentic" images. The difference is that now many heterosexual viewers expect this too, and large proportions of the audience are concerned at the potentially negative impact of tenacious stereotypes.

The BBC report, for example, found that half of the UK population was comfortable with LGB portrayal, with only 19 percent feeling uncomfortable (BBC, *Research* 14). All audiences "evaluated LGB portrayal in the light of how they perceived others might relate to it, as well as their own immediate emotional response" to it (BBC, *Research* 13). In terms of LGB audiences specifically, they wanted more diversity in the portrayals, more lesbians, more bisexual people, and fewer stereotypes of gay men (BBC, *Research* 8). In particular, lesbians and gay men alike felt that there were fewer lesbians portrayed, than gay men, and in terms of genre, they wanted authentic portrayals that felt "real and true to life" (rather than stereotypes) as well as more diversity, not just of lesbian characters, but of other forms of diversity too such as disabled, black and ethnic minority groups (BBC, *Research* 21; 15). Populating the screen with fewer stereotypes is not the same as telling "authentic" stories, however, whatever those may be in any given context.

In spite of its scenes with real lesbians filmed at The Gateways club, *The Killing of Sister George* seemed inauthentic to many of the lesbians who went to see it in 1968. Reviewers for both the British lesbian magazine *Arena 3* and *The Ladder* published by the Daughters of Bilitis in the USA agreed that the film was unpleasant and primarily a heterosexual male fantasy flick (Gardiner 151), and Mary McIntosh remarked that the "main characters were not at all like any lesbians we had ever met" (qtd. in Gardiner 152). Women were very disappointed by the sex scene, complaining that it seemed clinical and, unlike the sex they had, did not include any kissing. According to Gardiner, kissing was cut by censors, but the scene as a whole communicated on screen the extraordinary level of discomfort that both Coral Browne and Susannah York felt while filming it. They took days to leave their respective trailers, feeling deeply uncomfortable about performing the scene, and when it had to be re-filmed York suggested that a body double was used so that they did not have to be in the same studio as each other. Now that both women have died it is impossible to know the root of their anxiety: but given the evidence of the more recent SAG-AFTRA study, York's recollection that it was difficult "being undressed in front of a lot of technicians" it is highly likely that the almost certainly all-male set itself was a very hostile space in which they had to try and work (qtd. in Gardiner 151).

Whatever the truth of the matter, as the first lesbian sex scene shown in mainstream commercial cinemas (Gardiner 148) *The Killing of Sister George* provides something of a template for many subsequent depictions that fluctuate between the gruesome, the strangely passionless, and the highly unlikely. The sex scenes in *La Vie d'Adèle (Blue Is the Warmest Colour)* (Abdellatif Kechiche, France/Belgium/Spain, 2013), *Carol* (Todd Haynes, UK/USA, 2015), and *Black Swan* (Darren Aronofsky, USA, 2010) respectively illustrate the point. Same-sex sex scenes in general (if these are even shown, given the discrepancy between levels of same- and opposite-sex intimacy) are a constant source of frustration. Their inauthenticity seems to stem from several sources: intertextuality influencing ideas about what a lesbian sex scene "looks like"; lack of imagination on the parts of directors and actors; lack of consultation with women who might actually *know* something about lesbian sexuality; and censorship. This dissatisfying state of affairs only seems to improve when it is tackled head on as a serious issue. The directors of *Bound*, for example, hired Susie Bright (a feminist sex-positive writer and performer) to choreograph the much-lauded sex scene and the producers of *The L Word* brought in consultants to do the same.

Square Pegs

Such a simple solution to the problem of representation—hiring a consultant—cannot work for other barriers to telling authentic lesbian stories, because these are based in the limited number of narratives in circulation. The Dead Lesbian may be a powerful cliché but other narrative clichés abound: for men, there is the damaged hero, the maverick, and the lone wolf, and, for women, the supportive girlfriend/wife/woman colleague. As Stacey explains, different genres provide the narrative framework or "enduring patterns" within which stories are told (Stacey 71). One of the first questions, then, is whether same-sex love between women can fit into these existing patterns, or whether it requires a completely new perspective. Here the contrast between storylines featuring lesbians and those that center heterosexual men is extraordinarily distinct. In heteronormative narratives, when a man's wife/girlfriend/family dies he turns into a vengeful lone wolf or a damaged hero. When a lesbian's girlfriend dies, she kills herself, becomes so destroyed by the loss that she goes on a killing spree (as Willow does on *Buffy the Vampire Slayer*), she remains single (because lesbians can only ever find one partner in life), or she disappears from the show she was on.

Perhaps the fact that, on the whole, lesbian and bisexual women tend to be supporting characters without their own distinct storylines is also what makes their tales seem so unconvincing. With the exception of the black bisexual protagonist Annalise Keating in *How to Get Away with Murder*, the lesbian's or bisexual's story is never advanced through the death of a white man character. Becca Cragin confirms that even as the numbers of lesbians (and gay men) appearing on screen has increased, they are still highly unlikely to be the main characters. Thus "fleeting and subordinate representations may increase marginality however much they may aim (or claim) to reduce it. Routinely framing lesbianism as an issue, situation, or event increases the likelihood that it will not be included more extensively as an ongoing part of the narrative" (Cragin 194). But what about films or shows that do focus on lesbian and bisexual women's culture and experience? The characters may not be secure (think Liz in *Liz in September*, Dana in *The L Word*, Cat in *Lip Service* or Poussey in *Orange Is the New Black*) but are their settings at least convincing while they are still alive?

Until recently the efforts over the last thirty-odd years to make lesbian-centered mainstream work all seem to have faltered at the same hurdle: genre. The first lesbian romance film that has a tentatively happy ending (Cay agrees to ride on the train with Vivian to the next station) is *Desert Hearts* (Donna Deitch, USA, 1985). Adapted from Jane Rule's 1964 novel *Desert of the Heart*, the film was produced and directed by a lesbian, Donna Deitch. The adaptation is more resolutely cheerful and less profound than the book, and deals with the growing romance between Vivian, a university professor, and Cay, a casino worker in Reno, Nevada, where Vivian is temporarily resident in order to qualify for a divorce from her husband. The challenge for Deitch was how to create a film that could cross the divide between the conventions of romance film (overcoming external obstacles) and the types of obstacles which a woman must overcome in order to find romance with another woman. These include "heterosexual men, suicide, murder, neurosis, isolation, depression, homophobia and fear of discovery" (Stacey 71–72). Since none of these obstacles belong in conventional romance which is usually the site of more light-hearted fare, "the symbolic barriers to lesbian desire have typically not been overcome through forms of closure. Lesbian romance, then, has been defeated by problems too great to resolve in narrative terms" (Stacey 72). Stacey concludes that the film, while enjoyed by many lesbians, fails as a *romance*. It is a story about lesbian love and desire, but does not quite work to tell that tale in the comfortable, familiar and enjoyable manner expected from this genre.

Similarly, the sitcom *Ellen* no longer made sense as a *sitcom* once it aired its famous "Puppy" episode in which Ellen comes out, just after Ellen DeGeneres, who played her, confirmed "Yep, I'm Gay" on the cover of *Time* magazine on April 14, 1997. Chapter 2 noted the curse of the "Ellen effect," which refers to a spike in viewing figures around a lesbian storyline followed by a precipitous decline. Over the last twenty years cultural commentators and academic scholars alike have spilled a lot of ink over *Ellen*, DeGeneres, and the on-going consequences of the show including its cancellation, effect on DeGeneres' mental health, and impact on her subsequent reinvention as the massively popular and successful host of the syndicated *Ellen DeGeneres Show* which first aired in 2003. What is relevant here is the mix of factors which Cragin argues made it impossible for *Ellen* to continue on air after the character of Ellen Morgan came out. These included the shifting politics of DeGeneres herself, but perhaps more important were "the ideological and generic expectations and constraints of the sitcom form, of *Ellen*'s producers, and its audience; and the contentious understandings of the role sexuality plays in defining and marketing lesbianism" (Cragin 193). The latter two factors meant that a lesbian Ellen Morgan could no longer be funny: "lesbians" were decontextualized and over-sexualized ciphers that simply did not belong in a sitcom.

It Can Get Better

In her analysis of lesbian intertextuality, Elaine Marks points out that "a major thematic transformation takes place when women begin to write about women loving women. The experience of loving a woman is, for the narrative voice, the experience of awakening, the revelation of an unknown, unsuspected world which, once glimpsed, can never be ignored" (Marks 361–362). Although Chapter 3 noted that just having more women in major roles behind the scenes does not automatically lead to improved outcomes on screen, it does have the potential to do so. The director Dorothy Arzner's films are focused on women and women's communities and her "Lesbianism affects her films in diffuse ways. There are no lesbian plots, no lesbian characters in her films; but there is constant and deliberate attention to how women dress and act and perform, as much for each other as for the male figures in their lives" (Mayne *Directed* 63). By the 2000s there were increasing opportunities for women directors and showrunners to engage in this kind of detailed attention in new types of women-centered films and ensemble shows. Independent filmmakers such as the American Marina Rice Bader or the Australian Louise Wadley produced high quality films that reached a wide audience through streaming services such as Netflix or Vimeo, while others such as the American TV producer Irene Chaiken have achieved success in the world of commercial television. New funding models, in particular crowdsourcing, make access to finances easier than in the era when studio executives greenlit what they felt were recognizable products.

Louise Wadley's 2015 Australian feature, *All About E*, is a perfect example of a film which combines all of the new opportunities. Made through Wadley's production company, Girls' Own Pictures, the film was largely funded through crowdsourcing. It made the circuit of LGBTTQ film festivals before arriving on the on-demand streaming services Netflix and Vimeo, and could also be purchased or rented through the lesbian film distribution company Wolfe Video (WolfeVideo.com). On television the success of black female-led dramas such as *Scandal* (2012–), *How to Get Away with Murder* (2014–) and *Empire* (2015–) as well as shows with mostly Latina women in the cast such as *Devious Maids* (2013–) and *Jane the Virgin* (2014–) indicate that there is a substantial audience for these women's stories. Several of these shows include lesbian and bisexual characters, but it was the Showtime series *The L Word* (2004–2009) that really seemed to herald a sea change.

A series about a group of lesbian and bisexual women living in West Hollywood, *The L Word* initially presented their lives through the perspective of Jenny Schechter, a writer who became fascinated by her lesbian neighbors, had an affair with a woman, and subsequently plunged headfirst into the lesbian world she found all around her. Although she was eventually found dead in a swimming pool, adding her body to the overall Dead Lesbian count, on the way to that inevitable fate she (and the audience) was treated to six extraordinary seasons of lesbian and bisexual women's storylines. While the show was very heavily criticized by some vocal members of the LGBT community (in particular for not representing the whole community), it dealt with issues that are central to many lesbians' lives, including how to get pregnant, how to deal with homophobia, being closeted, being a player versus being monogamous, cheating, domestic abuse, heteronormative assumptions, men's voyeurism about lesbians, being left for a man, interracial and inter-class dynamics, the drag king scene, transgender experiences, the scene itself, and so on. The show also included a lot of sex scenes (presumably one of the ways Ilene Chaiken, the showrunner, was able to sell the idea to a network?) which, having been choreographed by lesbians, were striking for their authenticity. The show even incorporated a sort of meta-commentary on the ways in which lesbian representation is typically only on-screen for men's pleasure by having a male voyeur spy on Shane, the most sexually active character on the show. The series was ground-breaking and generated both a lot of scholarship and commentary and a feeling that now there could be shows that revolved around lesbians and bisexual women.

For a short period of time lesbian-led dramas seemed to be the order of the day. The BBC responded both to the success of *The L Word* and to its own audience survey with *Lip Service* (BBC 2010–2012), created by Harriet Braun, a series about a group of lesbians set in Glasgow, Scotland. This show enjoyed only two very brief seasons of six episodes each before it was unceremoniously cancelled, but it generated a lot of interest as a landmark. In addition to the mini-series based on the Sarah Waters novel *Tipping the Velvet*, three more of the lesbian novelist's works, with central lesbian characters, were adapted for the small screen: *Fingersmith* in 2005, *Affinity* in 2008, and *The Night Watch* in 2011. The ABC Family network drama *The Fosters* (2013–) is about an interracial lesbian couple, Stef and Lena, who are raising a large family. Although it is primarily a teen drama and so the couple competes for storylines with the other characters, nevertheless it is another ground-breaking series that includes multiple lesbian characters and shows the dynamics of lesbian parenting.

Bisexual women also began to make it to the pivotal roles in television shows. In Canada the plots of the supernatural series *Lost Girl* (2010–2015) revolved around the central character of Bo, a bisexual succubus in a love triangle with a lesbian called Lauren and a shapeshifter/wolf called Dyson. Dealing with questions of oppression, loyalty, chosen family, and non-monogamy, the show, like others that were designed around women's stories, covered many themes that were familiar to lesbian and bisexual women. Although *Lost Girl* managed to kill Lauren's girlfriend Nadia as well as the bisexual Valkyrie Tamsin along the way, a substantial portion of fans were thrilled that when the series ended Bo had chosen to be with Lauren rather than Dyson, reinforcing the rarely seen message that women can choose long-term relationships with each other even when an appropriate male mate is available. As a final example of this new crop of shows, *How to Get Away with Murder* (2014–) features Annalise Keating, the bisexual lawyer who skillfully manipulates her lovers, colleagues, staff and students as she deals with the fallout from her husband's death. This last show is produced by Shonda Rhimes as part of her Shondaland production company, an example of how much innovation is possible when a woman of color with a keen sense of politics is in a major decision-making role. Rhimes's impact supports Lisa French's study of women in Australian audiovisual industries, which demonstrated that women in a variety of roles (writers, director, producers, editors, screenwriters, cinematographers and costume designers) have "made important contributions to global cinema through telling stories from female perspectives, often with central female protagonists. Their success is significant because it indicates that stories featuring female characters, brought to the screen by women in key creative roles, have strong business value" (French 191).

This Has to Be a Joke, Right?

The above examples indicate that shows and films about lesbians and bisexual women can be highly successful, but most of them have gone off the air and in their absence one of the only remaining sources of women-centered stories are prison dramas because they are set in institutions housing a wide range of different types of women. From the 1950s to the 1970s they tended to fall into the titillating B-movie or Blaxploitation genres, but from the 1980s onwards *Prisoner Cell Block H* (which ran from 1979–1986) and *Bad Girls* began to tell more complicated and gritty stories, laying the groundwork for *Orange Is the New Black* and *Wentworth*. These newer shows took a more feminist, intersectional approach, telling stories of women from diverse backgrounds and attempting to critique the prison-industrial complex. Both shows acknowledge that while there are lesbians in prison, the setting also provides opportunities for otherwise straight women to have sexual and emotional relationships with other women. The shows also highlight the powerlessness and violence women in prison experience, the fundamentally corrupt nature of the institution, and women's attempts to exercise agency and control over their lives. In their fourth seasons both shows killed off main characters: Poussey Washington on *Orange Is the New Black* and Bea Smith on the season finale of *Wentworth*. As though black lesbian deaths were the punch line to a sick joke, Poussey's death came after the spate of dead lesbian characters during the first half of 2016 had raised mainstream awareness of how precarious their fictional lives were. Barely weeks later, Bea died in an episode called, incredibly, "Seeing Red," the very title of the episode of *Buffy the Vampire Slayer* in which Tara is killed. It really seemed as if showrunners were not only aware of the Dead Lesbian Trope, but on these particularly popular and successful shows they were determined to use it to undermine any sense that these women-centered stories provided a safe space for same-sex love.

Bea's death seemed to be a gratuitous example of the Lesbian Sex = Death component of the trope. *Wentworth* is a reworking of the original Australian soap opera *Prisoner Cell Block H* which had also been enormously popular (and a focus for rowdy lesbian viewing parties, just as *XWP* and *The L Word* would be a few years later). Both shows therefore contain many of the same characters and storylines. Bea Smith is a pivotal main character and is written out in both versions around the fourth season mark. Just as being heterosexual made a difference to the fate of Martha in the Hays Code-era version of *The Children's Hour*, so Bea's sexuality altered the way she met her end. In *Prisoner Cell Block H* she is transferred to another prison, Barnhurst, by the sadistic lesbian prison officer Joan "The Freak" Ferguson, the final outcome of several plots (by both women) to rid Wentworth Prison of the other. She is eventually reported to have died off-screen in Barnhurst. This version of Bea is completely heterosexual: in *Wentworth* she is not. Here, she begins an intense and loving relationship with fellow inmate Allie Novak, and the prison psychologist reassures her that if she has found love she does not need to worry about labels such as gay or bisexual. Bea's hard-won happiness is particularly poignant: first, because she came from an abusive marriage and this is her first loving relationship, and, second, because these unfamiliar feelings of love are transformative—she relinquishes her position as prison top dog because she no longer wants or needs that feeling of power over others.

The morning after they have sex for the first time, Allie is attacked in the shower and deliberately injected with a drug overdose by Joan Ferguson (who in this version is still known as "The Freak" but is an inmate). When Bea learns that Allie is unlikely to survive she confronts Ferguson and deliberately impales herself on the screwdriver that Ferguson wrests from her as they struggle. Holding Ferguson's hand she forces her to stab her multiple times and Bea expires on the ground gazing up at the clouds and, presumably, fondly imagining that she is about to join Allie in death. At that point the show cuts to a scene of Allie waking up in the intensive care unit. This is a by-the-book version of the Lesbian Death Trope: a woman must die after having sex, preferably driven to despair and therefore suicide on learning that her lover is dying and/or dead. The lover, if she survives, must also experience loneliness and despair because her partner is now gone.

White People Politics: Orange Is the New Black-ish

If Bea's death is an alarming example of how the full Dead Lesbian Trope is still being deployed, Poussey's death is even more disturbing because she is explicitly sacrificed in an attempt to make white viewers care about the politics of racialized violence in the contemporary USA.

The penultimate episode of season four of *Orange Is the New Black* shows two Litchfield Prison inmates, the lovers Poussey Washington and Brook Soso, holding each other in their arms, slowly dancing in a cardboard box lined with aluminum foil. In this last moment of intimacy between the two women, Poussey tells Soso that she is worried about Suzanne "Crazy Eyes" Warren, traumatized after being forced by a sadistic correctional officer to fight her ex-girlfriend, Kukudio. Soso responds "It's like we are in a horror movie" referring to all the violence the Litchfield inmates had recently suffered at the hands of abusive and negligent prison staff. Soso's statement should have fired a warning shot across Poussey's consciousness: in horror movies the black characters are always expendable. However, in this tender moment the warm-hearted black woman appears oblivious and secure as she replies "the kind you'd watch at sleepovers when you were a kid and then you'd have to run to your mum at the end—[she'd] hug you, tell you it was all made up." At this moment a discursive trade-off has happened to this normally witty character. The writers forego Poussey's penchant for funny yet critical one-liners, and instead pick a response fitting for the white middle-class blonde-haired main character, Piper Chapman. Poussey's well-established pop cultural savoir-faire, her black cosmopolitanism, and her comical racial consciousness remain off-screen. In effect, Poussey momentarily "turns white."

At the end of this episode Poussey, who is a small, slight woman, is suffocated to death by an incompetent prison guard who kneels on her during the poorly executed removal of the inmates who are staging a peaceful protest. The showrunners scripted Poussey's death as an homage to Eric Garner, a black man who had been suffocated to death by a New York City police officer, Daniel Pantaleo. Garner's death was similarly banal: his infraction was that he had been selling loose cigarettes. They also wanted to honor the activist movements Say Her Name and Black Lives Matter. On the surface this homage seems necessary: there has to be some way to pause the entertainment and acknowledge the real-world horror of state-sanctioned violence and the seemingly relentless elimination of LGBT people and people of color, especially in a show that aims to reveal the structural injustices by which disproportionate numbers of people of color and poor white people are incarcerated. But it is important to ask why the producers, writers and showrunners of *OITNB* would think that, given the highly saturated "repertoire of imagery" (Hall 232) of suffering black people, the image of *yet another* suffering black lesbian person would be a fitting tribute, when it seems merely to add to an already insufferable burden.

In a *Vulture* interview Samira Wiley, who played Poussey, addresses the spectators who were the potential targets for her character's death and contextualizes *Orange Is the New Black*'s use of white liberal representational practices. Wiley explains that "some people who love *Orange Is the New Black* don't know what 'Black Lives Matter' is. They don't have a black friend and they don't have a gay friend, but they know Poussey from TV and they feel just like you said—you feel like you knew her" (qtd. in Fernandez). Wiley's statement clearly indicates the mobilization of white liberal politics and its regime of representation to draw empathy from a white and heterosexual audience for a black cause. This practice has a long pedigree. According to Elizabeth Alexander, writing about the video footage of Rodney King being beaten by police officers in Los Angeles in 1991:

> Black bodies in pain for public consumption have been an American national spectacle for centuries. This history moves from public rapes, beatings and lynchings to the gladiatorial arenas of basketball and boxing. In the 1990s African American bodies on videotape have been the site on which national trauma—sexual harassment, date rape, drug abuse, AIDS, racial and economic urban conflict—has been dramatized [Alexander 78–79].

During the American Civil War the wounded black body was objectified and used as evidence to support progressive white politics—that is to say, white people drew each other to their cause by deploying the image of the brutalized black man. *The Scourged Back,* a 1863 photograph which was reproduced as a carte de visite was mobilized by abolitionists during the civil war to illicit "empathy and activism" (Jackson 12) and show the cruel reality of slavery. This image depicts a black slave called Gordon (in some cases, Peter) with his back horrendously scarred from vicious whiplashes. White abolitionists shared this image of the half-dressed Gordon, providing accompanying captions with statements on his good manners and intellect to counteract any tendency to believe that he may have been a brute and therefore have deserved such a beating. Making its way into *Harper's Weekly,* this image was reprinted alongside the image of Gordon as a U.S. soldier, thereby representing his transformation from slave to civilized man. Cassandra Jackson argues that the "realist and sentimental aesthetics" deployed in the representation of the wounded black male body fetishize it "as an object of white desire" (12), and so the fetishization or objectification of Gordon's scarred body depended on the brutality of slavery: the frisson of pleasure came from the thrill of horror.

Poussey fits into this familiar aesthetic which uses the spectacle of the premature death of black lesbians to bring pleasure and a sense of security to other groups. As bell hooks notes, "there is a collective cultural agreement that black death is inevitable, meaningless, not worth much. That there is nothing to mourn" (hooks 45). To that extent that both the audience and the characters themselves are often aware that black and lesbian characters are marked out to die, death has become such a code for race and sexuality that it is not clear whether characters die because they are black or lesbian or if it is their death that identifies them as black or lesbian. However, *Orange Is the New Black* has a number of significant black characters. Why, then, is it Poussey rather than one of these others who is selected for death?

For most of season one the other black lesbians, Suzanne "Crazy Eyes" Warren, defends Piper. Her blackness is played up to accentuate how foreign prison is for Piper and how out of place she is there. Although, like Piper, Suzanne also grew up in a respectable middle-class white family, in flashbacks she is shown as not "fitting" into it: she has a mental illness which jeopardizes all of her relationships. In Litchfield she can be excessively attached to certain people and very violent: she beats up Poussey while she is working as a henchman for Vee, another black woman who is an abusive master manipulator and battles to take the top dog position among the inmates. Vee dies at the end of season two, so the show cannot use her to draw attention to the Black Lives Matter movement. In fact, Vee's competition with Poussey serves to highlight the latter's worth as a respectable black woman, because while Vee draws women to her by exploiting their need for a maternal figure, Poussey sees through to the self-serving motivation behind her actions, calling her "a pedophile without the sex." Another major black character, whom Vee has been controlling for years is Tasha "Taystee" Jefferson, Poussey's friend and a woman who reluctantly rises through the prison hierarchy through her intelligence and sense of justice. Once she rejects Vee she moves into a central position of power in Litchfield. There are also "Black Cindy" Hayes, a con artist and thief who converts to Judaism, and Janae Watson, a gifted athlete who has problems controlling her anger.

These examples show that there are several potential candidates to fulfill the role given to Poussey: black women characters with whom the audience is familiar and in whose lives they have become invested. None of these others, however, have achieved "transtextuality." This is a term used by Manthia Diawara to describe the ability to transcend imposed stereotypes and to achieve recognition as individuals (255). The "controlling images" described by Patricia Hill Collins typically trap black characters into specific cultural roles (Diawara 271), but through "transtextuality" they can break free of those controlling images and be seen as individuals rather than as representatives of their group. This is a privilege typically reserved for white men characters. For all of its excellent intentions to bring a variety of women's stories to the screen, *Orange Is the New Black* centers the white, blonde, middle-class lead, Piper Chapman, and thereby delineates the remaining cast into the role of supporting characters. This centering was intentional: during a 2013 interview on NPR's *Fresh Air* Jenji Kohan, the creator of the show said that:

> You're not going to go into a network and sell a show on really fascinating tales of black women, and Latina women, and old women and criminals. But if you take this white girl, this sort of fish out of water, and you follow her in, you can then expand your world and tell all of those other stories ["Orange"].

Through Piper the show therefore presents the world of Litchfield through a middle-class white gaze which reduces the other women to "types," in this case to fertile Latinas, quiet Asians, loud-mouthed sassy black girls, big Pacific Islander women and no indigenous Americans at all. The paradoxical assumption (rightly or wrongly) is that for Piper/the audience for whom she stands in as proxy to actually *care* about the fate of one of these women (and therefore about all the other women in that grouping) she has to transcend her group, become less true to "type." And yet the distancing pleasure of objectification only works if she remains wholly different from Piper.

To negotiate this paradox the show decides that Poussey can achieve "transtextuality" through her middle-class mobility and cosmopolitanism. She is coded as the "black lady" through her middle-class upbringing, drawing on the politics of respectability (like the soldier-citizen Gordon with his scourged back, she was an upright citizen who therefore did not deserve her death). Flashbacks show Poussey as adventurous, making her cosmopolitan, fleshing out her mobility and playing out her innocence, removing any sense of criminality from her life. She is the only black woman who is able to cross racial lines and leave the group of black women through her relationship with another woman of color, the isolated, lonely and suicidal middle-class idealist Brook Soso. The two of them imagine a future after Litchfield where they can live together and travel the world, not constrained by race, sexuality, gender, or ex-convict status: a truly individualized dream of unfettered possibility.

In these ways Poussey symbolically "transcends race" but this does not guarantee her safety. In fact, this kind of "race-neutral" depiction of black lesbians that transcends controlling images adds another problematic layer in its color-blind killing of underrepresented lesbians of color. In the show's most dehumanizing season, with the white characters becoming ever more self-centered and enthusiastically flexing their white privilege against their Latina and black counterparts, Poussey's death is depicted an insidious triumph of white supremacy. The black lesbian can achieve transtextuality but she can never be equivalent to the other middle-class lesbians on the show, Alex Vause or Nicky Nichols. Within all of this ambivalence about what Poussey Washington means there is one point of certainty: Poussey's life had a radical possibility of representing black lives mattering in a way that her death, no matter how politicized, can ever achieve.

Conclusion

On the one hand, given all of these dramatic changes, concerns over the rising body count and persistence of the Dead Lesbian component of the "Bury Your Gays" trope may seem misplaced, when actors can come out and continue to work, alternative revenue streams and a wide array of distribution sites exist, and lesbian directors can call the shots. On the other hand, the fact that lesbians continue to die on screen in order to tell other characters' stories or to draw attention to a "real life" movement indicates how much further there is still to go.

The slippage between characters and actors raises questions about the impact of fiction on real life. This can be very positive and sometimes encourages actors to come out, which may still negatively impact their careers but will almost certainly be personally beneficial to them. The slippage also demonstrates that audience members need to feel that what they are watching is "authentic," believable, and reflects diversity. To meet that need genres themselves have to adapt to be able to tell different types of stories. Entertainment journalists and industry professionals also need to stop insisting that when an actor performs heterosexuality she is not really acting, but when she plays a woman who desires another woman she is.

Overall, then, it can be argued that things have been getting better for actors, stories, and audiences. The challenge for people both inside and outside the industry is to maintain this momentum, to tell women-centered stories, and to recognize that progress is not inevitable.

6

FANS DEMAND BETTER

New York Post entertainment critic Elisabeth Vincentilli rewrote the tag line of M. Night Shyamalan's 1999 supernatural thriller *The Sixth Sense* in order to capture the television viewing landscape not just in the spring of 2016 but over the past three years: "I see dead lesbians." Lexa's death on *The 100* clearly struck massive chord. The fan community's reaction was swift, voluminous and completely negative. The showrunners had been interacting with fans through social media, and queer fans had been assured that the Clarke/Lexa relationship would be explored rather than exploited for men's titillation. When Lexa expired in Clarke's arms their sense of betrayal was palpable. Damage control by the show's creative team resorted to the increasingly familiar excuse that the "story" led them there and that they had never heard of the Dead Lesbian Trope anyway. Many fans identified this as a defensive and inadequate response.

Within hours of the episode being aired fans had rushed to social media to protest and on Twitter they started circulating the message "Lesbian fans deserve better." This was adapted to "#LGBTfansdeservebetter," a hashtag which subsequently formed the basis of the LGBTfansdeservebetter.com website. Weeks after the initial shockwave had passed Jason Rothenberg, the creator behind *The 100*, acknowledged at a fan convention that the significance of lesbian representation was beyond his level of understanding. He remarked that the death "touched a nerve; it activated something in people who, their whole lives, have had to deal with things that me as a straight, white guy obviously couldn't relate to" (Prudom). The rapid and explosive reaction by the show's fans and weak or dismissive responses such as Rothenberg's (and Sally Wainwright's the previous year) generated heated debates over the responsibilities of showrunners, the impact of particular types of representations on communities, and the politicizing effect of symbolic annihilation.

This death was not, however, the first time that fan communities had responded to the representations that moved or infuriated them and had attempted to engage in dialogue with studios and showrunners, a group that has often been collectively referred to using the phrase "The Powers That Be" or TPTB, about the direction shows were going in or the use of stereotypes in films. Over the years, in the process of attempting to speak back to TPTB, viewers found each other and discovered their collective voice. They generated a sense of community, created and sustained lesbian spaces, and affirmed lesbian sexuality.

The determination to influence the decisions taken by TPTB through viewer activism and to actively foster a feeling of community has a long history starting, in the USA, with actions undertaken by the National Gay Task Force (NGTF) in 1973 and followed by the increasingly corporatized efforts of GLAAD. These groups tried to create a mechanism for lesbians and gays to demand less deeply offensive portrayals on film and television and for lesbians and gays to have input to improve their representation. GLAAD, in particular, took an industry insider approach as a way to get executive producers on their side. The fans who occupied the Xenaverse in the 1990s, by contrast, used the internet in innovative ways to take control of copyrighted material and refashion it. In dialogue with writers, producers, and studio executives they hoped to get their demands for more complex, interesting, and lesbian material on screen, and to get industry insiders to recognize not only the huge demand but the potential benefits of telling different stories.

Fan "elders," such as Mary D. Brooks, Kym Taborn and Destini among others, as well as many beta readers, who provided editing services to fan fiction writers, honed their skills in order to practice productive gatekeeping and to enhance overall feelings of belonging for members of the fan community. These women had an early foothold in relevant technology. They were instrumental in setting up internet chat rooms, hosting fan fiction on sites such as Archive of Our Own/AO3 (archiveofourown.org) and Passion and Perfection (www.ralst.com), and creating websites such as the Australian Xena Information Page (ausxip.com) which provided the capacity and technological skill to manage Subtext Virtual Seasons before YouTube had been invented.

The Xenaverse also created a rich and sustaining sense of community. The "Otalia" fan community that developed around the characters of Olivia Spencer and Natalia Rivera on *Guiding Light* similarly provided its members with a sense of belonging to a chosen family. Both the more formal and the community-based approaches remain relevant as audiences continue to try and hold studios to account through initiatives such as "The Lexa Pledge" and to extend the stories (and lives) of the women characters they love.

GLAAD Puts on a Show

Quite apart from the relentless diet of dead or evil queers, the twentieth-century history of media representations of lesbians and gay men had been fairly grim. The most common stereotypes were the butch dyke and screaming queen, played for laughs but without any reference to the camp sensibility present in the real-life versions of these cardboard cutouts. News media coverage of political protests or community issues tended to be either sensationalist or non-existent. The NGTF (now the National LGBTQ Task Force) set itself up New York City in 1973 in order to intervene in this landscape and decided to take a public relations approach to improving the visibility, rights, and representations of gay men and lesbians.

Ronald Gold took on the media component of the NGTF's actions and, influenced by his background as a reporter for *Variety*, was more interested in working with the entertainment industry to improve representations rather than take a revolutionary approach and attempt to dismantle the whole edifice. His timing was propitious: in his study of GLAAD Vincent Doyle notes that in the 1970s television networks were responding to the demands of the new social movements by creating a mechanism through which a moderate organization would be allowed to speak for an entire constituency. The networks' prime concern was to avoid any kind of damaging controversy, not to meet the demands of under- and misrepresented groups who were starting to agitate for change. The advantage to NGTF of this new mechanism was that because Gold was taking a reformist approach the networks were willing to work with him and so the group did have some success in moderating the "overtly hostile and pathologizing" depictions that had been commonplace until then (Doyle 36–37). By the 1980s the NGTF re-directed its attention towards the impact of HIV and AIDS, and GLAAD formed (again in New York City) to fill the void.

GLAAD initially adopted militant tactics, such as zaps, rallies and protests, but within two years of its founding had begun to shift towards utilizing media industry insider knowledge to try and encourage change. By 1988, for example, the Los Angeles branch of the group "hoped to quickly establish a reputation as a legitimate and professional media advocacy organization" (Doyle 50). It worked to speak directly to decision makers within the industry, both through behind-the-scenes meetings and through targeted media campaigns. In fact, one campaign it ran in 1990 indicates that TPTB have for a very long time known that there is an on-going problem with the symbolic annihilation of lesbians and gay men, all of their recent denials notwithstanding. In fall 1990, to coincide with the publication of one weekend's box office receipts and the release of a set of television ratings, GLAAD ran one advertisement stating that "Hollywood Images Fuel Gay/Lesbian Bashing" in *Daily Variety* and another asking "Where Are the Lesbian and Gay Characters This Season?" in the *Hollywood Reporter* (Doyle 52). Twenty-five years after GLAAD asked that question in the *Hollywood Reporter* Jacquie Lawrence, the author of the novel *Different for Girls*, had to ask an almost identical one in *The Guardian* newspaper. "Where have all the lesbians gone in TV and film?" she queried in March 2015. She addressed the reason for only asking about lesbians in her accompanying article. If gay men were missing in 1990, the same could not be said in 2015. As she explains, the British Film Institute found that over a three-year period there had been 29 films about gay men but only nine with "significant lesbian content" (Lawrence). Whatever improvements in representation had been achieved over the intervening quarter century had not been evenly distributed.

Throughout the 1990s ongoing restructuring and careful branding, leveraging of major media events such as Ellen DeGeneres' coming out in 1997, and interest in attracting media professionals to work for GLAAD meant that by the end of the decade "traditional activist strategies like direct action came to be minimized in favour of the imperative to engage constructively, wherein being constructive signified avoiding confrontation whenever possible" (Doyle 79). Furthermore, in keeping with its desire to be seen as an insider organization, GLAAD began to work on strategies that would show it was part of the media business. One of the most high profile ways in which GLAAD developed a reputation for being a good media team player has been through its Media Awards.

According to the GLAAD website, the GLAAD Media Awards "recognize and honor media for their fair, accurate and inclusive representations of the lesbian, gay, bisexual and transgender community and the issues that affect their lives" (www.glaad.org/mediaawards). Various types of media are nominated for the annual awards and voting on the material is undertaken by three different groups, which are made up of GLAAD staff and board members, GLAAD Shareholders Circle members, and GLAAD volunteers and allies. That final group, which by including volunteers seems to have the most grassroots element, also includes (as "allies") previous Special Honorees, key media industry allies, and Event Production teams. As Doyle found in his analysis of the Awards, there was substantial difference in the weight given by each of these groups to the material they voted on. Thus the volunteers "tended to value texts for their originality and complexity," whereas for staff and board members "perceived impact on heterosexual audiences was the most important criterion" (Doyle 96). In other words, the Awards are not set up, in any sense, to reward media based on what the LGBT "community" (itself very hard to pin down) might consider has merit.

GLAAD itself emphasizes that nominees for the Awards are judged on four criteria. First, the representation must be "Fair," meaning that it does not resort to stereotypes, "Accurate," and "Inclusive," by which they mean that the representation should (ideally) reflect the diversity that exists within the LGBT community. Second, the work should demonstrate "Boldness and Originality," a requirement that GLAAD suggests could be met by "non-traditional" approaches to the content (although whose traditions could be broken in this way is not made clear). The third measure is "Impact." This refers to work that "dramatically increases the cultural dialogue about LGBT issues, or reaches an audience that is not regularly exposed to LGBT images and issues," although again no means to measure such impact is provided. The fourth and final criterion is "Overall Quality," a concern because "fair, accurate, and inclusive images may be weakened when they are part of a poor-quality project" (www.glaad.org/mediaawards). GLAAD is primarily concerned with mainstream media, working on the assumption that the media created by and for the LGBT community itself is unlikely to be defamatory, and so the sort of crowd-sourced films made by women about same-sex relationships are highly unlikely to ever make it onto the list of nominees.

As the voting groups and criteria suggest, the Media Awards are fundamentally fundraising events designed to increase GLAAD's profile. They were first presented in 1990 at a dinner held by the GLAAD New York chapter, followed the next year by another one in Los Angeles and have been held every year since then. The initial ambitious goal was to attract celebrities and therefore raise visibility and money for the organization, and the strategy worked. Seating plans, the role of corporate donors and sponsors, a media line with a background showing the relevant logos, and strategic placement of celebrity attendees are all designed to maximize the impact of the event. Reviewing his own involvement in one of the Awards shows, Doyle draws attention to a fundamental paradox at the heart not only of the GLAAD Media Awards but of the organization as a whole. This is the assumption that to be successful the Awards shows need to juxtapose "images of queer vulnerability" against more positive ones emphasizing mainstream inclusion (achieved in part thanks to GLAAD's work). Thus GLAAD "had a (financial) interest in maintaining and even heightening the polarity inherent in longstanding patterns of media representations that portray LGBT people either as victims to be pitied or as beacons of mainstream conformity and normalcy" (Doyle 111).

Although GLAAD's corporate role as arbiter of mainstream representations has been diluted through the effects of sponsorship scandals and the rise of social media (through which audience members can target industry insiders directly), the central paradox remains. Should studios be held to account for depictions of weak or doomed victims? After all, "assumptions are made based on heteronormative stereotypes of gay loneliness and isolation" (Krainitzki 15). Given this paradox, it is not surprising that the recipients of the Media Awards should be outraged, rude, dismissive or hurt when women express anger over the decisions of TPTB to kill off the lesbian or bisexual characters (Atwell, "Last"). The whole recognition process is set up to reassure them that queer women are sad victims (read: dehumanized) who should be grateful for any non-stereotypical (read: villainous butch) representation. Those viewers should certainly not consider themselves qualified to question or criticize the decisions taken by TPTB.

The Media Awards are not the only "measure" used by GLAAD to assess what is coming out of television and film studios. Based on the popular Bechdel Test, GLAAD has developed the "Vito Russo Test." This Test assesses a film against three criteria: whether the film has "a character that is identifiably lesbian, gay, bisexual, and/or transgender" who is not "solely or predominantly defined by their sexual orientation or gender identity," and who "matters" to the plot (GLAAD, *Studio* 7). While this is a valuable tool (like the Bechdel Test) to generate discussion and provide a ready yardstick, the Vito Russo Test does have its flaws. The Dead Lesbian Trope frequently kills off the lesbian or bisexual character in order for a main (typically but not always male) character to develop. In this sense, her *death* can matter to the plot, and so a show or film can kill off its lesbian and still pass the Vito Russo Test. In addition, unlike the Bechdel Test, the Vito Russo Test has not made the transition into popular consciousness and so the fact that the *Studio Responsibility Index* for 2016 shows that only 36 percent of the inclusive studio films (or eight out of twenty-two) passed the Test did not lead to much thoughtful analysis in the mainstream media.

More useful than this test are the annual state of the industry reports. As we discussed in Chapter 3, GLAAD has been publishing data on the numbers of LGBT characters on TV and in film in the USA in its annual *Where We Are on TV* reports and *Studio Responsibility Index*. The benefit of these reports is that they provide data which can trace patterns in the numbers and quality of LGBT characters on television and in film. In common with a general trend towards acknowledging the striking dominance of white characters on television, GLAAD emphasizes the need for diverse representations. The overall demand, however, remains the same as it always has: writers "must reject harmful, outdated stereotypes and avoid token characters that are burdened with representing an entire community through the view of one person" (GLAAD, *Where* 3). A disadvantage with the television report in particular is that it lists the characters who are slated to appear in upcoming shows and therefore does not review the fate of those who were covered in previous reports. However, the reports are useful snapshots that do track changes over time, and note that positive representations can trend downwards as well as upwards.

GLAAD's highly polished and professional style has increased awareness about the importance of responsible representation, even if the organization has been criticized for seeming to be primarily concerned with affluent white gay men's interests at the expense of other, more marginalized sections of the queer community. As Doyle puts it, GLAAD executives have long been challenged by the division between activists and professionals and to manage this and be able to claim that GLAAD has the necessary credentials to be taken seriously as the voice of the LGBT movement, senior staff "redefine activism as an insider game that required the professional skills and values they already possessed" (91). What GLAAD has always done, moreover, is largely collapse lesbians (and women generally) into the category of gay, so that improvements (however measured) in the on-screen presence of men are assumed to have a beneficial knock-on effect for women. Yet, as the GLAAD reports themselves—along with Jacqui Lawrence's article in *The Guardian*—show, representations of gay men and lesbians are not increasing (or improving) as the same pace. GLAAD's lack of grassroots engagement can also leave audience members frustrated if they want to have a significant impact on TPTB, because the various tools that GLAAD uses tend to reward showrunners and actors after the fact for images and storylines (usually about men) that did not offend.

GLAAD's approach of drawing on insider knowledge and connections to influence the decisions taken by showrunners now competes with much more direct action (or at least with much more noise) via social media.

That change was precipitated by the internet which "lowered the threshold for effective action in the movement field, making it possible for agents with the right kinds of social, cultural, and symbolic capital to challenge the dominance of powerful players even in the absence of large amounts of economic capital" (Doyle 243). Using these techniques some fan communities are motivated to create and sustain lesbian space both on- and off-screen, and to engage with writers, actors and producers more directly.

Hardcore Nutballs

In a retrospective written ten years after *Xena: Warrior Princess* began, Cathy Young provided a synopsis of "What We Owe Xena" and emphasized not just the subtext but the role of the internet, because "other than 'The X-Files,' 'Xena' was the first cult hit of the Internet age: the face that launched a thousand Web sites" (Young). A common story told by people reflecting on how they became involved in the Xenaverse and everything that it opened up for them is that, having watched just a few episodes or during the period when reruns of season one were showing during 1996, they became desperate to find more material on the series and they searched on the newly minted web in order to do so. In an article in *The New York Times* in March 1998, J.D. Biersdorfer noted that the show debuted at the "same time the popularity of the Internet began to explode across America, and the two entities have been intertwined ever since" (Biersdorfer). The new possibilities generated by the internet (and the excitement of finding like-minded fans around the globe), the relatively large number of online participants, the high level of engagement between the show's writers, producers, actors and the fans which the internet made possible, and the widespread fascination with the show propelled *XWP* and its now recognizable subtext into the mainstream. Although Facebook (and MySpace), YouTube, Twitter, Instagram, Tumblr and other social media platforms had not yet been invented, and accessing the world wide web required an extremely slow dial-up modem connection to the telephone network (severely limiting the use of graphics or any form of streamed material), fans found each other through Usenet Groups, on message boards and in Chat Rooms.

Xena: Warrior Princess did not air in Australia until more than a year after its first appearance in North America. That lengthy delay gave Mary D. Brooks time to hear about the show and decide she could not be less interested in something that she assumed would be as trite as the earlier fantasy show *Wonder Woman* which aired from 1975–1979. However, having been asked by a friend to tape (on VCR of course) the first episode when it aired in Australia on December 12, 1996, Brooks was instantly hooked. Like others before her, she immediately searched the web for information about *XWP* and found Tom's Xena Page (www.xenafan.com). By the end of that first night she had decided to create her own Xena fan page. Although she was unclear on exactly what it would contain she wanted an Australian perspective and somewhere to put her own artwork, which consisted of "montages based on each episode that could tell the story using screen grabs." As she explains, "on my travels through the 'Net I discovered that this medium was relatively new, so I embraced it and ran with it" (qtd. in Stafford 144). The show seemed to precipitate a sort of urgent creativity in many of its (however initially reluctant) viewers, and just three days after seeing that first episode Brooks had set up her fan site. Limited by tiny amounts of data storage she soon had to migrate to a larger site, www.ausxip.com (hereafter AUSXIP). In addition to using AUSXIP to host information about the show, fan fiction and artwork, for a while Brooks took on the volunteer job of fan fiction editor for Tom's Xena Page. This task became too much for her because as AUSXIP grew in popularity so did the amount of work involved in dealing with news and articles about the show and its cast that people were sending in from everywhere around the globe.

Brooks' influence has been extensive because of AUSXIP, but she was not the only person performing an intensive labor of love to build community through the Xenaverse. Early members of the Xenaverse, like Brooks, were frequently women and men who had a lot of technical or computer competence (that is, they were "geeks") who could assist others in posting stories, images, screen-captures, and videos. They were also able to construct websites, webrings, and fan fiction and image archives. In 1996 Kym Masera Taborn, a tax lawyer, established a website for the "International Association of Xena Studies" (initially the International Association of Xenoid Studies) called *Whoosh!* (whoosh.org). The website became enormously popular: as late as 2009 it was still receiving 3,000 visits each day, or about one million per year. It was the repository of episode guides (eventually of many different shows), interviews with cast members and producers, fan fiction writers and even characters, in-depth articles on various aspects of the show and the history it raided, reports from fan conventions, a message board and chat room, and an FAQ guide to the show as a whole. Over the course of the site's prime years, from 1996 to 2005 (when Taborn's husband Wesley died unexpectedly), a total of 66 people worked for *Whoosh!* in various capacities including several who also held major roles in other parts of the Xenaverse, such as Debbie Cassetta who founded the Sword and Staff charity, Tom Simpson who ran Tom's Xena Page, and Tory Moore who co-hosted the famous Xena nights at Meow Mix, a lesbian bar in New York City.

All of this determined and collaborative effort to set up the architecture and supportive environment through which the Xenaverse was created and maintained was crucial to the development of online and real world spaces which still remain active and dynamic, although fans who experienced the development of the Xenaverse while it was actually happening refer to periods of intense immersion in it that cannot be replicated today. Petra de Jong, who was President of the Dutch Association of Herculeans and Xenites, for example, recalls that having discovered *XWP* in 1996, she was in a Xena chatroom called The Pub when a Xenite in New York City invited her to come and visit. Several women report similar experiences of chatting online with other fans and then going to stay with them, often traveling outside their home country for the first time, and forming lasting bonds with the other fans as a result. De Jong did go to NYC and had such a good time she decided to return to the city a few months later en route to visit a different Xenite in Texas. While in New York she went to see Lucy Lawless performing in the musical *Grease!* as well as Renee O'Connor at a convention. "Those were wild weeks with an overdose of *Xena* [...] It is hard to describe the atmosphere. It was like one big party: *Xena* fandom was pretty new, everyone was excited, there were no egos or politics yet, and it was all fresh" (qtd. in Stafford 107). Christine Boese, meanwhile, refers to a period when she "gave up all pretense of interacting in the real world and went on night-for-day and day-for-night reading binges, consuming whole [fan fiction] novels onscreen in a single sitting" (Boese, "Spinning," para. 14). These types of deep engagement with the Xenaverse that many early fans went through speak to the powerful need for and impact of feeling connected to a community sharing complex and detailed stories about lesbian lives and affirming each other in their alternate readings of the relationships depicted on television.

Christine Boese's 1998 doctoral dissertation, "The Ballad of the Internet Nutball: Chaining Rhetorical Visions from the Margins of the Margins to the Mainstream in the Xenaverse," provides a sense of how immense the Xenaverse was, thanks to the creative energy of people like Brooks, Taborn, and many others. The people who were intense *XWP* fans and highly active in creating and sustaining the Xenaverse came to be known as "Hardcore Nutballs," the term that was given to them by Lucy Lawless (Stafford 137), and Boese's title acknowledges this. Boese's work teases out the strands in the intricate web that formed the Xenaverse. Produced in

both CD-ROM format and online (www.nutball.com), it deliberately mimics the form of the Xenaverse itself and is an early example of a scholarly
work trying to both utilize and demonstrate the way that hyperlinks create
the illusion (?) of endless possibility.

In her dissertation Boese attempted to map the various sites of the
Xenaverse that were active in 1998 when she was writing, which she roughly
divided into non-commercial and commercial types. There were Resources/
Links Sites, under which she included Tom's Xena Page, Whoosh.org, and
AUSXIP (then known as Mary D's Xena Information Page) among others;
web rings (sets of sites linked together on a topic) for Xena, Gabrielle, Callisto, and the Subtext; international fan clubs; collector's items; community
sites; personal sites; Usenet; and fan fiction. On the more commercial side
were Listservs; web chat rooms; web bulletin boards; the Official Xena site
on the MCA/Universal Studios website; merchandise sites; America
Online; Internet Relay Chat; ICQ (an instant messaging system); games;
and parody sites. What was particularly crucial to making this enormous
architecture work for a lot of fans was that the "entwined commercialization
and domestication of the Internet normalized everyday access to the technology required to participate in such communities" (Driscoll and Gregg,
570). Because the internet was anonymous and easy to access the number
of people who actively participated in the Xenaverse was much higher than
would ever had been involved in more traditional fandoms (Gwenllian
Jones 407). From the privacy of their homes, sitting in the dark into the
early hours looking at a green cursor blinking away on a black background,
women (and men) could visit another world entirely, one where anything
seemed possible.

The Xenaverse created lesbian space that could be visited daily even
though it could not be mapped to a physical location and contained no
actual lesbian bodies. Indeed, several of the people working so hard to
maintain this space were not lesbians at all. The Official Xena Conventions
brought writers, cast members and fans together in hotel conference rooms
where, sometimes, cast members performed femslash narratives. For most
participants the Xenaverse was and remains a virtual space, but nevertheless
a place of pilgrimage that could be transformative (Millward, "New" 431–
436).

Access to the fandom and their own online activities led to a "variety
of life-changing situations" for fans (Hanmer, "Internet," 154). Fans started
by surfing the internet looking for information about *XWP*, using the internet in order to involve themselves in fan activities, and writing fan fiction.
Hanmer found that "some fans decided to move house, or leave their jobs

and start new lives with their new friends or lovers found through their online fan activities" ("Internet," 154). To provide a sense of just how powerful the impact of the fan community could be on people's real lives, Hanmer gives the example of a woman who left an abusive marriage with the support of friends she had made on a Xena list. She had come across this list because there were only reruns playing of the show and, feeling the urgent need for new Xena material, she had searched the web to find it (Hanmer, "Internet," 155). Nikki Stafford's book entitled *How Xena Changed Our Lives* provides numerous examples of women and men undertaking dramatic shifts in their life courses because of their encounters in the Xenaverse. Boese recalls that in May 1997 when her "real life took a downturn" she "entered the Xenaverse completely and wholeheartedly, never looking back. I have heard others report this total immersion as well, and many describe how *Xena* and the online Xenaverse literally saved their lives during health crises or other extreme circumstances" (Boese, "Spinning," para. 12). Having been thoroughly immersed in reading Xena fan fiction during a difficult period in her life, Boese emerged into what she called "real life" in "a distinctly Xenite form," in which she visited Xena Conventions, went to see Lucy Lawless perform, continued to read fan fiction, and worked on her doctoral dissertation on the Xenaverse.

The significance of this interconnected web of engagement was a sense of agency for the fans. In a meditation on the impossible-to-quantify "authentic" Xena experience, Carolyn Bremer argued that online fans "have seized the means of production in a very political power move," writing fan fiction, sharing interpretations on message boards, and influencing the decisions taken by TPTB (Bremer and Boese para. 21). Jamie Stuart suggests that "for some audience members, what is on the screen is how they wish their own world looked and how their own lives worked. [Henry] Jenkins discusses how fans of particular works can take that wishful landscape and try to make their own world look more like it" (Stuart 20). One way they do this is to take action in their personal lives, trying to embody the values of their favorite characters, traveling abroad, and trying new activities, for example. Another tactic is to try and enact change at a larger scale, by influencing studios and networks to tell new stories and throw money behind women-centered shows.

Fans were able "to communicate their desire for alternative narratives directly to producers in an era in which new technologies allowed for 'queer hacks' of mainstream entertainment content" (Maris 124). As Andrew Leonard found in 1997, examining the question of "Who Owns Xena?," producers, writers, editors and actors in the show were not only very aware of all of the online fan activity around *XWP*, many participated in it through mailing lists and chat rooms (2). Cathy Young pointed out that various people involved in the series, including the writer and producer Steven Sears, actively participated on message boards or lurked around them. Rather than reining in this online activity by threatening lawsuits, the general sense was that it was a crucial factor in boosting the show's popularity (Leonard 6). Because "power in these communities is about intimate networking" (Driscoll and Gregg, 575), through their networks fans were able to "significantly influence the show's narrative arc to an unprecedented extent" (Maris 124), including the decision by Steven Sears to hire the fan fiction writer Melissa Good to write two scripts for the show. Thus for Hardcore Nutballs and other Xenites the power of their immersive and transformative experience prompted feelings of shared ownership which urged them to try and influence the show itself.

After *XWP* ended so brutally many fans felt horribly betrayed, needed to grieve deeply, and latched on to any pronouncements by TPTB that there might be a "Fix-It" *XWP* movie that could resurrect not just Xena but the relationship between her and Gabrielle. In addition they turned to fan fiction and virtual subtext seasons and continued to go to the Official Xena Conventions (not without their critiques of the naked commercialism of these events) in order to maintain their sense of connection to the wider Xenaverse. They searched for other female pairs into which they could pour their energy and interest, such as Olivia and Natalia on *Guiding Light* and Jane and Maura on *Rizzoli & Isles*. They also put time and effort into fundraising, particularly through the "Sword and Staff" charity which was set up in 1997 by Debbie Cassetta. After an organization refused the proffered $4,500 that had been raised at the New York City Xenafest that year, Cassetta founded Sword and Staff to direct the efforts of fans who wanted to donate to "the greater good" (Stafford xi–xiv).

This creativity, energy and decades-long commitment to lesbian fandoms—which, it is important to note, were maintained by heterosexual women and men as well as by lesbians—is important for two reasons. First, it shows how profoundly women feel the need for more complex and satisfying representations of lesbians (and women in general) on-screen and the labor that they are willing to perform to ensure that spaces for such representations exist. Second, it has a recursive effect "IRL": arguably, not only do these fandoms connect women to lesbian communities, but they also feed back into media representations that do try to respond to this demand, whether through actors who engage with fandoms or producers who develop web series for specific fan communities. Coupled to these outwards-directed efforts are community-building practices. *Whoosh!* set a high standard for engaged research into the components of the Xenaverse, but now social media has largely taken over the space where community responses to troubling stories—as well as advice and support for those who are troubled by those stories—can be found. In all of these ways, members of the Xenaverse both consolidated the power of the community they had built up over time and extended it outwards into new fandoms where they could meet new people with whom they could share some of their many organizing skills.

Big Purple Dreams

A later (although sometimes overlapping) group of fans who were dedicated to a different on-screen pairing were the "Otaliafans." These were women who became enraptured with the relationship that began to develop between Oliva and Natalia in 2008 on the soap opera *Guiding Light.* This venerable show had been a staple of the American cultural landscape for 72 years when it was finally cancelled in 2009. Before it departed from the airwaves it brought the two former sworn enemies together in a romantic relationship. When Olivia was unwell after she suffered from problems associated a her heart transplant Natalia moved in with her and her daughter Emma in order to assist her (in true soap opera fashion, Olivia's new heart had formerly been beating inside Natalia's now-dead husband). As the two women went about their everyday lives together (which involved a lot of folding laundry and eating at the kitchen table) they became each other's primary source of emotional support and began to act like a married couple sharing the care of Emma. Through this process they fell in love although, as befits the genre, they had a large number of serious barriers to overcome before they could settle down as an actual couple. The barriers included both women's internalized homophobia, the offer of marriage from a heterosexual man called Frank who was in love with Natalia, her narrowly missed wedding to him, the Catholic Natalia's religious beliefs and her son's hostility, and both women's need to process their shift from opposite-sex to same-sex focused sexuality.

The Otalia fan community coalesced rapidly and were brought together in particular by Destini, who started a YouTube channel to which she uploaded all the scenes showing Olivia and Natalia together so that others could watch the romance unfold. The "Otaliafans" community also communicated under the umbrella of the forum on LiveJournal called "Big Purple Dreams," a phrase which referenced comments made in one episode by Olivia and Emma about their New Year's wishes. Three of the women who maintained the Big Purple Dreams sites, Destini, Mel and Christi, also held a weekly podcast in which they discussed each episode of the show in great detail. The Big Purple Dreams community was a space for women to air their enthusiasm for Otalia and their pleasure in watching a romance that developed slowly, rather than the more typical storyline where a couple's relationship is rushed so that it felt like a forced ratings grab. Like the relationship between Xena and Gabrielle, it was the subtle interactions and level of comfort with each other rather than spectacular declarations of love that many viewers found authentic.

Big Purple Dreams was also somewhere for women to share their own experiences when they mirrored those of the women on the show. In an interview with Tiffany D'Emidio for *Eclipse Magazine* in 2009 Destini, Mel and Christi explained what it was about both Otalia's storyline and the feeling of community that made Big Purple Dreams so important to them. Mel, for example, explained that she had met a woman through another campaign around a different show and had discussed labels such as "gay" with her. Because Otalia's relationship was depicted as growing organically rather than something based in the organized lesbian movement it really spoke to this woman, who was in a same-sex relationship and did not see herself as "gay" but simply as a "mom." Destini, meanwhile, commented that the fictional couple's challenges were almost too close to home for comfort. Her own partner had been straight and married when they met, and they, like Otalia, had to work their way through ideas about sexual identity labels, religion, and the expectations of heterosexual men like the character of Frank (D'Emidio, "Conversation").

American daytime soap operas are not syndicated internationally the way that shows like *XWP* are, nor are they available through streaming services, so the fact that there were women around the world who belonged to the Big Purple Dreams community indicates how powerful the Otalia storyline was. According to D'Emidio, by May 2009 fans were following the romance from at least 28 other countries. While many relied on Destini's YouTube channel to watch clips, some wanted to watch *Guiding Light* in its entirety. These fans' determination to see the show could be quite inventive: one woman in Ireland reported that she had a friend in the USA who recorded the show and then, when she played back each episode after work, she would point her webcam on her laptop at the screen so that the two women on opposite sides of the Atlantic could watch it "together" (D'Emidio, "Guiding").

On LiveJournal Big Purple Dreams ended up with 7,215 registered users who made a total of more than half a million posts, and the most users ever online, at 1,018, were active on June 24, 2009. These were impressive figures. In April 2009, when CBS announced that the show would be cancelled, the community rallied and attempted to lobby to save it, either on its current network or through another one. One woman, Crystal Collins, posted a list of the addresses of relevant industry executives and her own model letter that others could adapt to send to them in order to facilitate lobbying. Noting—using a tactic drawn on by other fans as well—that with her good level of education and disposable income she belonged in a desirable demographic, her letter pointed out that Otalia was creating a huge amount of interest in the show, as measured by increased ratings and news articles in mainstream publications such as *Entertainment Weekly* and LGBT magazines such as *The Advocate* (D'Emidio, "Fans"). Here, then, was an active, engaged and international community of women inspired to reach out and connect because of their shared love of Otalia and their own experiences which were reflected in the couple's storylines.

Venice the Series

Fans were not the only people trying to save Otalia. Once she heard that *Guiding Light* was cancelled Crystal Chappell, who played Olivia, approached Procter & Gamble (who owned the characters) to see if they would consider moving them across to another daytime soap opera (*As the World Turns*) or create a web series featuring them. Although Procter & Gamble were not interested Chappell was aware of the enormous commitment that fans had to Otalia. Destini had encouraged her to start using social media in order to connect with them and Chappell joined forces with one of her lesbian friends, the writer Kim Turrisi, with a view to making a webseries to meet the fans' demands for more lesbian content. They set up a production company, Open Book Productions, and together with a number of other women who brought with them social media and web design skills, they launched *Venice the Series*. The series was a web soap opera based (and filmed) in Venice Beach in California and initially dealt with the love triangle between Gina (played by Chappell), Ani (played by Jessica Leccia who played Natalia on *Guiding Light*) and Lara, played by another daytime soap actor, Nadia Bjorlin. Chappell used her network of contacts in the world of daytime soaps, built up over her twenty-year career, to bring in a large number of recognizable soap stars to act in the show. Although initially the episodes were very short (a mere six minutes), Open Book Productions was able to eventually increase their length to a more substantial 15–20 minutes. Unlike other webseries designed for a queer women's audience, which were usually free, to watch *Venice the Series* viewers had to pay a subscription of $9.99 for twelve episodes. Although the crew and cast acted for free the subscriptions were needed to pay for server space to stream the episodes. The show won Emmy Awards in 2011 and 2014 in new categories that were created to acknowledge the shift to web-based formats.

At the same time that Open Book Productions were developing *Venice the Series* they were also producing merchandise to promote the show, such as calendars as well as underwear and other types of clothing carrying the show's logo. Other productions followed, including *The Grove, Beacon Hill* and a film *A Million Happy Nows*, although funding challenges led to delays and gaps in the rate of work coming out of the company. Almost all of it, however, featured Chappell and Leccia together in one form of relationship or another, which made sense given that their original chemistry as Otalia is what had drawn the Big Purple Dreams community over to the Open Book Productions sites to pay to watch them in these new roles. Certainly Chappell was aware of this, explaining that she decided to launch the production company because she had been interested in creating web content generally and wanted to "give the Otalia fans a new home" (qtd. in Fairman).

One wide-ranging interview with Chappell and Turrisi dealt with their views on Otalia as well as the motivations behind their online work. They both drew attention to the fact that same-sex storylines on daytime soap operas were being cut at that time. Chappell also commented about the two women on *Guiding Light* not being permitted an on-screen kiss once they were in a romantic relationship with each other. Chappell remarked that "the lack of a kiss was disgusting and dangerous" and that while she was on the soap she "realized we were touching foreheads. I understand building suspense and longing, but then the realization hit me that they are never going to let these two women kiss" (qtd. in Fairman). However, she also reflected that, for Otalia and the couple's fans, perhaps the show's cancellation had a positive side to it: at least they got a happy ending, when in soapland no couple is ever truly safe.

Shipping Their Own Characters

Both the Hardcore Nutballs and Big Purple Dreams community have been particularly successful in influencing shows and creating new series and spaces for discussion. Another source of support for subtextual readings and the communities that develop around them comes directly from the actors portraying the characters. This is a relatively new level of engagement. When the large studios controlled the messages that actors should communicate about their shows and films, audiences members had to dig deep to uncover any hint of a lesbian interpretation offered by a particular actor. As Weiss notes, "the studios went to great lengths to keep the star's image open to erotic contemplation by both men and women, not only requiring lesbian and gay stars to remain in the closet for the sake of their careers, but also desperately creating the impression of heterosexual romance" (Weiss, "Queer Feeling," 290). Access to actors has dramatically changed in recent years. Studios and production companies have proliferated and they exert less of a stranglehold over publicity for their products. There has been an almost exponential growth in social media outlets which permit close, immediate and sustained links between actors and fans. Furthermore, the multi-million dollar business of fan and industry conventions creates opportunities during panel discussions and interviews for fans and journalists to directly ask actors about their characters. Footage of panelists' replies is almost immediately uploaded to the internet for the entertainment of people who could not—or never would—attend such events.

Whereas studios and official fan clubs had channeled communications in the past, now (in addition to those pre-existing avenues) these newer forms of connection have made it possible for fans and actors to have some direct dialogue about what the characters mean. This is another area where *XWP* had a significant early impact, again in part because of the role of the internet, but also because Lawless acted as a gamechanger. In addition to posting that general thank you on the internet after she broke her pelvis, Lawless visited Meow Mix, the lesbian bar in New York City that hosted *XWP* nights, and communicated directly with dedicated fans whom she dubbed "hardcore nutballs" (Stafford 137). Unlike earlier generations of actors (with the exception of one or two such as Louise Brooks), Lawless seemed completely unconcerned about these activities being interpreted negatively as evidence of lesbianism. As Boese reports, Xenites "believe in the show's star, an unknown actor from New Zealand who bluntly says what she thinks and isn't afraid of lesbians" (Boese, "Ballard," 44). This endeared her to her lesbian fans but also seemed to signal a change in how other actors dealt with fans who sought confirmation that there was a lesbian subtext.

Chappell's decision to set up Open Book Productions to make a webseries directed at her Otalia fans is one good example of this increased level of openness and dialogue. The actors Joanne Kelly and Jaime Murray

provide another one. Kelly and Murray, who portrayed Myka Bering and
H.G. Wells respectively on *Warehouse 13*, spoke at fan conventions and in
interviews about their interpretations of their characters' relationship. As
the penultimate season was airing they gave an interview to Heather Hogan
for AfterEllen.com in which they talked about how they came to decide
that their characters were in love with each other. Murray explained that
the show typically wrote women to flirt with Myka's Warehouse partner
Pete (played by Eddie McClintock). However, Murray reports that she
remarked to Kelly that she believed her character would not be impressed
by Pete and would be more attracted to Myka.

She claimed that she and Kelly began making small interventions into
their characters' interactions, and although they expected these would be
overlooked on set and only picked up by fans, the writers began to script
their connection into the show and gave Murray a line about H.G. Wells
having had both men and women lovers in the past. The writers teamed
the two women up to give them multiple opportunities to exchange subtextual gazes. They also had major opportunities to sacrifice themselves for
the other and, in Myka's case, to prefer that the whole world be put in
jeopardy rather than lose H.G. Wells. When H.G. Wells betrayed Myka,
Myka's response was on the scale of a devastated and emotionally bruised
lover, not a disappointed friend. Small wonder, then, that fans followed
Kelly and Murray and began to ship "Bering and Wells." In common with
other actors whose characters "represented" the LGBT community, they
acknowledged the support of loyal fans and the importance of realizing
that any "queerness" they had managed to interject into their characters
was perceived as positive representation by fans who felt marginalized or
isolated in real life (Hogan, "Jamie").

A Lesbian Version of Facebook?

Chappell and Turrisi put their efforts into creating new content for
the Big Purple Dreams community and maintained some level of open
dialogue with them through social media, while Murray and Kelly shared
their commitment to the "Bering and Wells" ship. Recognizing the incred-
ible power of dedicated fans to generate interest in a series, some other
shows have tried to capitalize on their energy in different ways. Five years
after *XWP* ended the Xenaverse remained active. Its model of dedicated
community engagement, deep commitment to a show and respectful communication between the creative fans and the show's creators, and overall
loyalty to the ideals of "The Greater Good" still seemed extraordinary. It

was the sort of organic development of a buzz around a television show that marketers could only dream of. When the show that was *actually* about lesbians came to air some corporations tried to cash in on the idea that *The L Word* would generate the same level of excitement. This first dramatic series about lesbians generated a lot of interest. Lesbian bars (which at that time still existed) held viewing parties (as they had for *XWP* during the previous decade), scholars analyzed the characters, storylines, and limitations of the show and women compared Bette, Tina and the women around them to their own circles of friends.

One of the characters on *The L Word*, Alice Pieszecki, maintained "The Chart," an initially paper-based chart showing how everyone in her community was connected to her (and to everyone else) through their sexual encounters. The idea of "The Chart" is that any specific lesbian community in real life is tightly interconnected—that everyone is someone else's ex-lover. In 2007 TPTB tried to harness the potential of *The L Word*'s lesbian fan community by launching a virtual chart in the real world, "OurChart.com," to coincide with Alice migrating her paper version online in the show. It was pitched as a social networking site explicitly for lesbians that would have additional commissioned content beyond links to the show. Chaiken was the chief executive of OurChart.com which she co-founded with Hilary Rosen (a political lobbyist and former CEO of the Recording Industry Association of America).

While doing publicity for OurChart.com Rosen pointed out that "there hadn't been a specific social networking site for lesbians heretofore. Obviously, there are lesbians on MySpace and there are lesbians on Facebook. I hope to steal all their business" (qtd. in "Uncharted"). Using much the same set of ideas that had promoted lesbian chic a decade earlier, Rosen suggested that lesbians were potentially "superconsumers." She asserted that "lesbians have higher disposable income, are more college-educated, and are more into consumer products" than women as a whole (qtd. in "Uncharted"). For the duration of its short life OurChart.com was "a vibrant and highly successful blogging and social networking site" (Watson) but by the end of 2008 was basically dead: no longer updated with fresh content, it was then absorbed into the Showtime website (Showtime aired *The L Word*). OurChart.com's subscribers were frustrated with Chaiken for deciding to unceremoniously drop the site and erase the networks that had been built up through it without providing any explanation for her actions.

Later shows did not attempt quite so nakedly to capture fan excitement and sell it to advertisers, but some did try and generate buzz by using social media without, apparently, thinking through the potential for this tactic to backfire when the viewers they had courted used social media themselves to discuss the show and TPTB.

The Lexa Pledge

Bethonie Butler, writing in *The Washington Post*, argued that the fan revolt over Lexa's death was the result of "a show misunderstanding its audience and the politics of minority representation onscreen." Showrunners had used social media to interact with the fans, and when Lexa was shot the tools that TPTB used to draw in the LGBT audience were expertly used against them. Stunned audience members almost immediately set up an international Tumblr drive to try and persuade people to stop watching the show. They also circulated tweets containing the hashtags #BuryTropes NotUs, that trended nationally, as well as #LGBTfansdeservebetter which within hours had been tweeted more than 280,000 times.

Making the link between lives lived and lost both on screen and off, fans used the angry desire to do something with viewers' feelings of hurt betrayal in order to raise money for The Trevor Project, an LGBT youth suicide prevention charity. The social media campaigns were so extensive that they were featured on BBC Trending (a web page on the main BBC website which covers what is internationally popular). Commentary on the volume and nature of the online trends appeared as far afield as design and technology blogs including *Tech Insider* (Fussell) and io9.gizmodo.com (Cranz). What the fans did through their campaigns was not just find a community through which they could express their shock and grief, although this was an important component of the movement. But they also situated Lexa's death in a much wider context. Some commentators tried to undermine the legitimacy of fans' anger by spreading a narrative that positioned viewers as whining and overly entitled. After all, "to be perceived as too radical in the professional world of media producers is to be condemned, if not to invisibility then to the status of troublemaker" (Doyle 246). Fans responded with a counter-narrative: they argued that the lack of complex queer characters in general coupled with their frequently violent deaths is a social justice issue.

This anger was not only directed at *The 100*. Jacob Stolworthy of *The Independent* newspaper in the UK noted similar responses on Twitter by fans of *The Walking Dead* when its popular lesbian character, Denise, was violently sacrificed in a death that departed from the events depicted in the graphic novel on which the show was based. In *Vanity Fair* Joanna

Robinson raised concerns that Denise's violent end was not an isolated storyline but part of a "troubling TV trend" to deny women any chance of lasting relationships with each other. Both the U.S. and UK editions of the *Huffington Post* took up the discussion. Marisa Bruch read the online protests from the mostly young viewers of *The 100* as evidence that producers need to actually pay attention to the audiences they had been so busy trying to attract.

Presumably unaware of the long history of angry and hopeful attempts at intervention into the decisions taken by TPTB, Bruch expressed optimism that the community organizing around #LGBTfansdeservebetter might have the capacity to hold the industry accountable. Bella Roussanov argued in the *Harvard Political Review* that when 71 percent of television writers are white and 86 percent are men, then it is perhaps not surprising that they repeatedly demonstrated "confusion and misguided defensiveness" and a general unwillingness to carefully listen to and therefore understanding fan outrage. She compared the episode "Thirteen" in *The 100* and the "Seeing Red" episode in *Buffy the Vampire Slayer* fourteen years earlier in order to draw attention to the sense of betrayal when "the legitimate excitement in seeing characters like us on television" ends in their death or murder. Far from the specific death of Lexa being unprecedented and causing an outcry for that reason it was instead only too commonplace (Roussanov).

GLAAD responded to the outpouring of anger about the Dead Lesbian Trope by hosting a panel at the ATX Television Festival in Austin, Texas, on June 11, 2016. The "Bury Your Tropes" Panel included Javier Grillo-Marxuach (*The 100*), Krista Vernoff (*Grey's Anatomy*), Carter Covington (*Faking It*), Carina MacKenzie (*The Originals*) and Megan Townsend for GLAAD. The discussion focused on the death of Lexa and the freedom writers claim that they need in order to follow storylines of their own choosing without acknowledging that their supposedly individual choices follow a remarkably consistent pattern. As the comments on the LGBTFansDeserveBetter.com website pointed out afterwards, when lesbian and bisexual characters are only one per cent of all characters but ten per cent of all dead characters, there is a systemic problem. In a different context, Jennifer Mather Saul notes that when supposedly "individual choices" result in uniformity then they are clearly part of a cultural pattern, not an expression of individual freedom (143).

On June 12, 2016, the day after the GLAAD panel at the ATX Festival, 49 mostly Latino patrons were murdered and another 53 injured by a shooter at PULSE, a gay nightclub in Orlando, Florida. The massacre was deemed a hate crime and sent a shockwave around the world. It lent a terrible legitimacy to the concerns fans were raising about the relentless media diet of expendable characters and its impact on real people in their real lives.

Outrage over the Dead Lesbian Trope on television, the determination of TPTB to insist their hackneyed stories were unique, and dead and injured LGBT community members IRL fueled a number of people to set up a website to explain the reasons for their anger and to encourage viewers to hold those producing distorted representations to account. The LGBT-FansDeserveBetter.com website includes a fund raising initiative linked to The Trevor Project. To date over $135,000 has been raised: that the average donation is $33 indicates that this is a grassroots community response. A further response is the so-called "Lexa Pledge, A Pledge to the LGBTQ Fandom." Its preamble exhorts writing rooms everywhere to learn from and respond to fan frustration. It asks writers and producers to consider LGBTQ representation by committing to seven statements.

The Lexa Pledge

1. We will ensure that any significant or recurring LGBTQ characters we introduce, to a new or pre-existing series, will have significant storylines with meaningful arcs.

2. When creating arcs for the significant or recurring characters we consult with sources within the LGBTQ community, like queer writers or producers on staff, or members of queer advocacy groups like GLAAD, the Trevor Project, It Gets Better, Egale, The 519, etc.

3. We recognize that the LGBTQ community is underrepresented on television and, as such, that the deaths of queer characters have deep psychosocial ramifications.

4. We refuse to kill off a queer character solely to further the plot of a straight one.

5. We acknowledge that the Bury Your Gays trope is harmful to the greater LGBTQ community, especially to queer youth. As such, we will avoid making story choices that perpetuate that toxic trope.

6. We promise never to bait or mislead fans via social media or any other outlet.

7. We know there is a long road ahead of us to ensure that the queer community is properly and fairly represented on TV. We pledge to begin that journey today.

Source: http://lgbtfansdeservebetter.com/pledge/

The Pledge was created by Noelle Carbone and Sonia Hosko, writers and producers of the Canadian drama *Saving Hope*; producer, director and writer Michelle Mama; and Gina Tass creator of the Leskru Fundraiser in support of the Trevor Project. The mix of advocacy groups mentioned (Egale and The 519 are both Canadian, It Gets Better is international) indicate that the Pledge's creators see this as a very widespread problem.

While the pledge has been signed by a number of writers and producers, others have resisted on the grounds that the Pledge would hamper their creativity. Yet it is precisely more creativity that LGBT Fans Deserve Better is seeking, asking writers to avoid these lazy storylines for lesbian and bisexual female characters. One signatory to the Pledge, Sherry White, has added a statement to the site regarding her own series (*The Catch*) and the recent death of a bisexual character, an episode she now wishes had been handled differently.

Shadrach Kabango, then-host of the radio show *q* on the CBC, interviewed two of the founders of the Lexa Pledge, Noelle Carbone and Gina Tass in May 2016. They explained that the overarching goal of the Pledge was to improve lesbian and bisexual representation on television, to have showrunners seriously consider placing queer women at the center of their stories and to genuinely consider the impact of lesbian characters' violent deaths on the viewers who most identify with them. They also stressed that communication with the fan community via social media and repeated assurances that the audience would be pleased with the romantic story arcs were, in fact, only about ratings and constitute queerbaiting at best.

Queerbaiting

Point number six of the Lexa Pledge asks TPTB not to bait or mislead fans. "Queerbaiting" can be defined as:

> a strategy by which writers and networks attempt to gain the attention of queer viewers via hints, jokes, gestures, and symbolism suggesting a queer relationship between two characters, and then emphatically denying and laughing off the possibility. Denial and mockery reinstate a heteronormative narrative that poses no danger of offending mainstream viewers at the expense of queer eyes [Fathallah 491].

Although "queerbaiting" as a term only appears to have entered the lexicon recently, the practice—just like reading for subtext—was established by Hollywood. Andrea Weiss claims that even though, during the Hays Code era, no "inference" of "sex perversion" was permitted, "the public could be teased with the *possibility* of lesbianism, which provoked both curiosity and titillation. Hollywood marketed the suggestion of lesbianism, not because it intentionally sought to address lesbian audiences, but because it sought to address male voyeuristic interest in lesbianism" (Weiss, "Queer" 290). Rhona Berenstein also argues that Hollywood advertising campaigns deliberately hinted at same-sex desire, using intertextuality to achieve this aim without having to directly refer to lesbianism. Thus, she asserts, the promotion for the film *The Uninvited* explicitly referred to the earlier film

Rebecca in order to attract audiences to the idea of a new film which also dealt with "a strangely haunting love" (Berenstein 21).

Queerbaiting is a strange phenomenon. From the perspective of frustrated fans, it refers to a manipulative process by which showrunners "tease" the possibility of a same-sex relationship between major characters. This can be achieved through the storylines or blocking of shots, techniques which suggest that the producers and directors are aware of the lesbian subtext and are deliberately playing it up. Sometimes this can be interpreted by audience members as a sign that they intend to develop the relationship (perhaps in response to demands from a vocal subsection of the audience), although it often seems to lead to nothing more than an off-key heterosexual romance and fewer shared scenes between the two relevant women. The show *Rizzoli & Isles*, in which Jane and Maura spent all their free time together, exchanged banter like a romantic couple, and were even shown in bed together, yet both had unconvincing male love interests is a good example of this type of queerbaiting.

Another common queerbaiting technique is when showrunners give interviews in which they suggest the viewers who are dissatisfied with the lack of lesbian or bisexual representation on their show should keep watching, because something is coming that will please them. Such pronouncements might take place at conventions such as Comic Con, during press interviews, or while promoting an upcoming season. This was the approach taken by the creators of *The 100*. Perhaps not surprisingly, the fiasco around their show seems unlikely to persuade their colleagues that they might need to actually define "pleasing" the audience before they make such promises.

Once Upon a Time in ... Oz

An interesting example, which combines some queerbaiting with an attempt to respond respectfully to fan demands for hopeful stories, can be found in the fairytale fantasy show *Once Upon a Time*. Almost from its first episode, the relationship between two of the main characters, Emma Swan and Regina Mills, positively crackled with energy. In classic Harlequin romance novel style, they start by hating each other. They are opposites: one is fair and the other one dark, one is the Savior and the other one is the Evil Queen. They are sworn enemies. Yet they, like Olivia and Natalia, represent "my two mommies," in this case of Henry, a boy Emma gave up for adoption and Regina adopted and raised since infancy. They are also connected because Emma's mother, Mary Margaret, has a long history with

Regina who was her stepmother (when they were Snow White and the Evil Queen respectively in another realm). Locked together by their shared love of Henry and their combined magical powers, Emma and Regina have to learn first to work together and then to mature past their mutual mistrust until they come to love and support each other. As the seasons progress these two women become friends, confidants, and the only ones who believe in each other when various plot points mean that no one else does. Both are also willing to sacrifice themselves to save the other.

The series as a whole effortlessly passes the Bechdel Test and offers innovative and rich depictions of a many complex women who are motivated by a range of factors. Since shows which pass this test lend themselves to subtextual readings, and since Emma and Regina's relationship hits so many of the classic notes of an epic romance, it is not surprising that many fans jumped on board what they called the SwanQueen ship. Like other fan communities before them, these fans campaigned to make SwanQueen a reality, crafted videos they posted to YouTube and generally created fan art to share the way they saw these two characters. In a separate storyline, the show had also depicted two other women who seemed to have a very close and intense bond, Mulan and Aurora. *Once Upon a Time* has as its central premise the idea that each character has a true love (whose kiss is the only thing that can break a strong curse), and while fans acknowledged that it was highly unlikely that such a successful show would risk a romance between Emma and Regina, they could not help noticing that Mulan and Aurora were behaving like a couple. Was it possible that the show would give two women a fairytale ending, even if it was not SwanQueen?

In October 2013 Mulan almost told Aurora she was in love with her (one infers this of course: nothing was actually said, except in press junkets after the fact). What stopped her was Aurora's news—since she was already with *her* true love, Phillip, she was excited to tell Mulan that she was now pregnant. Mulan pretended to be happy for her but then walked away, crying. Other characters had lost their true loves in the show but only through death, not because their opposite number did not feel the same way about them. For a fantasy show, the lesbian in love with her straight best friend felt a little too close to reality and an appalling misstep by TPTB. The message they seemed to be sending was that every heterosexual person can have a happy ending but the only lesbian in sight is doomed to tearful loneliness. The fact that Mulan (played by Jamie Chung) was one of the only people of color on the show did not go unnoticed either.

It took two and a half years for the showrunners to try to correct the mistake, but they promised that season five would have a same-sex relationship. In April 2016 they brought together two different women, Ruby (or Little Red Riding Hood) and Dorothy (from the Land of Oz), whose ship was immediately and wittily dubbed "RubySlippers." These two only had one episode together, their plot necessarily interspersed with the others that were ongoing, so there was not much time for them to indicate that they were potentially soulmates or even exchange meaningful glances. Dorothy was then laid low by a sleeping curse and Ruby, frantic to work out who could give her the true love's kiss that would wake her, had to admit to herself (and to a very supportive Mary Margaret) that she loved her. The problem with true love's kiss, as formulated on the show, is that it only works if both parties are in love and so Ruby's anxiety was not alleviated by her admission. She might not have been watching the episode when Mulan realized Aurora was just not that into her, but she had no reason to suppose that it would be any different with Dorothy. However, Mary Margaret encouraged her to at least try and so she did. To the delight of Ruby, Mary Margaret, and the watching Munchkins in Oz, her kiss broke the spell and the women were able to kiss again—awake this time— and live happily ever after. Or so one infers, since their story takes place in the Land of Oz, a realm barely visited by the show and unlikely to be seen again before *Once Upon a Time* ends its run.

The lack of a fully developed RubySlippers storyline and the swift resolution of their particular crisis (other characters had taken up to half a season to save their true loves) caused some disappointment. Nevertheless, negotiating many different pressures, the show's creators, Edward Kitsis and Adam Horowitz, took the line that "love is love" and that the love RubySlippers shared should not be treated any differently from that of the other characters. The fact that these women had a conventionally happy ending, especially in the spring of 2016, was remarkable.

Conclusion

Reflecting on the strategies employed by GLAAD, Doyle remarks that "if engaging in media activism depends on competing for the organizational prestige, visibility, and standing that only media companies can grant, for example, then media companies will always maintain the upper hand, no matter what victories might be fought and won on this uneven terrain" (245). The fans have been pushing back against this inevitable inequality for decades. They have repeatedly shown TPTB the devastating impact of relentless symbolic annihilation and the many better alternatives available. They have demanded better representation, more nuanced characters, and fairytale endings. But these arguments have only had marginal success in shifting industry practices. For every Crystal Chappell or Noelle Carbone there is an Ilene Chaiken or Jason Rothenberg. However, that some of TPTB, such as Edward Kitsis and Adam Horowitz, are willing to recognize the crucial importance of giving same-sex couples a happy ending and use their institutional power to do so, indicates that change is possible.

The feeling of belonging to a community is perhaps more important than the outcomes of campaigns to keep *Guiding Light* on the air or to get industry professionals to sign the Lexa Pledge. Just as the Xenaverse provided the framework through which to see lesbian subtext and a space for online fan fiction, it was also the motive force for community organizing and the development of a network of sites, community "elders," and ideas about how to use social media to influence storylines and speak directly to "The Powers That Be." That legacy is activated each time that a new generation of viewers intervenes in an attempt to change an outcome or express their rage, and it also provides support to a wide range of people feeling collective grief when a character is killed and (sometimes short-lived) elation when two women finally get to kiss on screen.

7

REJECTING DEATH
NARRATIVES

When a character plunges into the sea of the lesbian dead the immediate reaction of fans tends towards shock, disbelief and grief. Many then turn to fan fiction sites such as Archive of Our Own (AO3) or Passion & Perfection to either read a "Fix-it" or write one themselves. For at least two decades femslash writers have been engaged in a low-level form of guerrilla warfare against symbolic annihilation. They abduct characters (and sometimes plots) from television shows and occasionally films. They give them dialogue they could never speak on screen, encourage them to have sex with one another, and send them on epic journeys. They place these characters in unfamiliar settings, bring the heroes of different shows together, and bend the rules of time and space in order to re-animate the dead. All of this creativity is a way to tell alternative stories and to flesh out the love between women that may be implied in a show but is never explored. It also resists the authority of "The Powers That Be" (TPTB) who try to insist on a final, correct interpretation of their copyrighted material.

Symbolic annihilation does not just kill characters. It also removes their power, destroys any sense of possibility they might bring and tells stories over and over again which emphasize the impossibility of long-term happiness between women. The reiteration of "types" similarly produces limited ideas about lesbian desire. Patricia White argues that lesbians' stories are almost always sidelined through a combination of intertextuality (the audience recognition of a particular actress in a supporting or character role), and the fact that supporting characters are "the same types [that] come back again; their very continuity across texts foregrounds cinema's repetition compulsion and the need constantly to reestablish heterosexual normalcy in the same old stories" (White 143). For fan fiction writers, rejecting the death narrative also means rejecting the dominant tales of lesbian loneliness and unhappiness. In a direct re-working of the saturation techniques used on screen, femslash writers attempt to ensure that the possibility of lesbian lives is affirmed by repeating particular tales over and over again—both within a specific fandom and across fandoms. The authors and readers who have been immersed in one fandom frequently transfer into fresh fandoms which emerge around new shows, promoting cross-pollination and intergenerational community. They maintain over the long haul the idea that women can live happily ever after.

Once Upon a Time in ... the Xenaverse

The fan fiction reviewer Lunacy explains the appeal of femslash: "unrestricted by time constraints, or censors or any of the other sensibilities imposed by film or TV, fan fiction allows for a fuller exploration of characters and themes and storylines" (Lunacy "History" para. 1). Since at least the 1960s when the bromance between Kirk and Spock on *Star Trek* struck some viewers as being a very special kind of friendship, fans have written slash fiction which pairs their favorite male characters. Once there were enough women on screen for them to start writing about women getting together femslash was born. This type of fiction was originally written for private consumption or sharing via fanzines among a small group of friends, but by the 1990s the internet began to provide a space in which complete strangers living in different parts of the world could "meet" each other and share their enthusiasms. Reflecting in 1998 on her experience as a *XWP* fan, Christine Boese noted that when she discovered the online Xenaverse during season two of the show she "unknowingly participate[d] in the greatest explosion of alternative fan fiction migrating on to the Web" (Boese, "Spinning," para. 05).

There are many sub-genres of fan fiction. There is "Adultfic" which includes sexual or very violent content; "Genfic" that has no sexual content; "Fluff" which is usually a humorous vignette; and the very short "Drabble" at about 100 words. "Challenges" appear when a writer writes a story in response to a specific "challenge," such as a suggested opening line or scenario, while "PWP" stands for Porn Without Plot or Plot? What Plot? A story marked "Hurt/Comfort" is one in which a character experiences some type of trauma (physical or emotional) and is then comforted by another character—in terms of the material we are discussing here, typically one with whom she is in a femslash relationship.

A specific subset of stories is of particular interest for understanding how fan fiction writers resist the death narratives they see on screen. They all come under the broad heading of "Alternate Universe" or "AU" fiction. When this term was originally coined it was known as "alt.fic." Lunacy categorized this type of work as being "ADULT stories that add a romantic element to the relationship between Xena and Gabrielle, depicting them as more than just friends. Be aware that most of the stories reviewed in the alt. section depict a sexual relationship between women" (qtd. in Wilder para. 8). The early alt.fic departed from the main narrative of *XWP* and took the characters in a new direction. This now describes AU fiction in general: it typically ignores something that happens on the show, such as a heterosexual relationship or a change in the relationship between the favorite characters. "Fix-its" are a specific type of AU because they restore a dead character to life and then develop her story. "Crossovers" bring characters from different shows together. Finally, "Uber" fiction creates completely new versions of the characters and places them in different times or places from those depicted in the original show.

The online fan fiction universe is now immense, but its initial migration from private mailing lists to the web was tightly linked to *XWP*. The Universal Studios website launched a *Xena: Warrior Princess* NetForum in October 1995, a month after the television show first aired. The following month an "alt.tv.xena" discussion group appeared, and Lunacy notes that fan fiction was first shared through these two online sites. By the spring of 1996 a couple of pieces of new fan fiction would be posted to the Net-Forum each week. Lunacy recalls the feelings of excitement as readers consumed this new material and anticipated what would come next. They started calling the writers "bards" in honor of Gabrielle, and these "bards" began to develop celebrity profiles themselves (Lunacy, "History" para. 4–5; Kerr).

Alt.fic or AU work was initially reserved for private mailing lists, but once both fans and the show had begun to mainstream the subtext AU was able to appear online without being viciously attacked, and Lunacy argues that it rapidly became a very popular type of fan fiction. Some writers embraced the opportunities to write about being lesbians. L.N. James explains that her stories about Xena and Gabrielle "tend to mirror the emotional bond between women. So, in part, yes, I think that in the privacy of our own homes, what I write about reflects what it's like to be lesbian. More or less" (Wilder para. 542). AU stories were not only written by lesbians, however: various fan fiction writers discuss the challenges of writing about same-sex love when they had no experience of this themselves. Baermer, for example, comments on the fact that as one of the heterosexual women writing alt.fic she felt that she took a huge risk the first time she wrote an explicit sex scene (Wilder para. 47). Another fan fiction writer, Rooks, reflects on why the love between Xena and Gabrielle appealed to men as well as women. He argues that "overwhelmingly, alternative fan fiction contains the theme of soul mates" and this type of deep connection is attractive to both women and men (Rooks para. 9–10). Tackling sex scenes is tricky, he acknowledges, but argues that for any writer this improves with practice and that by asking women beta readers (editors) to review the material he can feel reasonably confident that his work is not jarring to lesbians (Rooks para. 24).

The personally transformative experience of immersing oneself in the Xenaverse that we discussed in the last chapter extended into the desire to create more and more stories and not to merely passively consume other people's work. As Driscoll and Gregg point out "fanfic communities seem tailor-made for claims about un-tapped creativity that remains to be discovered outside the realms of existing corporate practices" (573), not least because the volume of fiction written in these communities is quite astonishing. Xenaverse fan fiction writers were "drawn in to the point that they have seized the means of production and created their own Xenaverse in cyberspace, a space where their agendas are the top priority and where TPTB have absolutely minimal control or influence" (Boese, "Spinning," para. 50). Other writers in more recent fandoms have followed in their footsteps.

Collecting Stories

Science fiction shows like *Stargate SG-1* and *Star Trek: Voyager* and fantasy series such as *XWP*, *Warehouse 13*, and *The 100* tend to present a diverse range of female characters in unfamiliar roles. As Nell Frizzell has noted in her assessment of the possible re-boot of *Xena: Warrior Princess*, "lesbian relationships in popular culture have often been disguised through the lens of science fiction [and fantasy] because that is the easiest way to sneak them into public consciousness." It is perhaps not surprising, then, that these are the types of shows which lend themselves to lesbian subtext and sometimes actual maintext and therefore inspire femslash in a way that other genres do not.

Femslash fan fiction provides a creative outlet primarily for women (the form is numerically dominated by women) who want to read and tell stories about women lovers who live to tell their tales. However, the early stories tended to disappear from spaces like NetForum quite quickly. As the overall number of stories dramatically increased it also became a challenge for readers to locate work they were interested in. Responding to the new demands generated by online fan fiction, various people began to preserve and organize the material. Tom's Xena Page (www.xenafan.com), set up by Tom Simpson, was the first example of this practice and a crucial entry point for many readers and writers who followed, including Mary D. Brooks who was inspired by Tom's Xena Page to set up AUSXIP.

For more than twenty years AUSXIP has been supplying news, updates and interviews with cast members to its global readership, but a major component of the site has always been its large fan fiction section. As AUSXIP grew rapidly in the 1990s, Mary D. Brooks organized the enormous amount of material into different sections to help her millions of visitors navigate their way around it. The Bard's Corner houses the fan fiction and Bards of the Xenaverse contains interviews with the authors. There is a multimedia section, pages specifically about Lucy Lawless and Renee O'Connor, and episode guides. Once *XWP* ended AUSXIP continued the series through Virtual Subtext Seasons which combined script-style writing with illustrative screengrabs. Lunacy's real life skill set as a librarian prompted her to start posting fan fiction recommendations and reviews to help readers find work they would be interested in, and in May 1997 Mary D. offered her some space on AUSXIP to post her reviews. In this way Lunacy was able to "try to encourage bards so that we get more stories, more variety, and better quality fiction" (Wilder para. 5).

Over the years, AUSXIP, Tom's Xena Page, and other sites such as the Royal Academy of Bards, Passion & Perfection, ShatterStorm Productions, Pink Rabbit Productions, the Atheneum and Archive of Our Own among others have provided around 25,000 links each week for readers of fan fiction. Other sites, such as Whoosh.org, do not contain fan fiction archives, but do have interviews with various popular fan fiction authors with links to their work. Many of these sites continue to publish Xena/Gabrielle stories more than twenty years after the show first appeared, in addition to fan fiction based on other shows that have come and gone since then. People interested in a particular fandom visit one of these sites and there encounter femslash that places new (lesbian) interpretations on their favorite characters (copyright holders and host sites permitting). Supportive communities form where members of a fandom share the work of writing, reading and critiquing each other's stories (Hellekson and Busse 7). This collective experience creates a space where women can explore different aspects of lesbian identity, share their fan fiction, and be affirmed in exploring their sexuality (both real and virtual).

The fan fiction archives are therefore crucial spaces through which the fan community developed. The sites provide a relatively supportive environment for writers who are inspired to try their hand at this genre, access to beta readers who provide invaluable editorial assistance, a place to go for readers who are hungry for more same-sex interaction than they are getting from their favorite show, and a sense of community. Unlike mainstream publishers, the people who run the sites, collect, archive and share fan fiction often come from the ranks of "journalists, professional communicators, educators and arts workers" and take the fans' writing seriously (Driscoll and Gregg 573).

Anonymity is an important component of the fan fiction universe. The explosion of fan fiction postings made possible by the evolution of web-based fan communities thrives, in part, because many producers of fan fiction can keep their on-line participation anonymous. L.N. James, for example, started posting her stories in February 1997 but at that time she writes that "I wasn't in a place (for privacy reasons) where I could put my email address on the stories I wrote" (Wilder para. 547). A serious challenge to this type of anonymity (#nymwars) occurred in 2011when Google insisted that people posting to Google-Plus social media could not use pseudonyms or memes. This seemed reasonable as a response to trolls who were increasingly posting threatening comments to women on social media (for example, the racist and misogynistic attacks against Leslie Jones who played Patty in the *Ghostbusters* movie). However, Francesca Coppa argues that some fans "accrue significant and traceable reputations" under their pseudonyms (Lothian 542). Insisting on digital surveillance was not only unwarranted, it would undermine this hard-earned capital.

Another serious challenge came in 2012 when the popular site Fan-Fiction.net removed about 8000 works they felt should have been rated "Fiction MA" for explicit sexuality and/or violence, and only suitable for mature adults. Stories with this rating were not permitted on the site, which only allowed material up to the rating "Fiction M" (covering adult themes but no explicit descriptions of sex or violence). The sudden loss of all of this work by unpaid authors, who borrow their characters and defy copyright rules, barely created a ripple because fan fiction is perceived "as lowbrow geek fodder undeserving of any real attention" (Ellison). In addition, fans who have devoted a lot of free labor and emotion to maintaining a particular fandom may feel pressure to conceal their level of involvement because of the stigma associated with this activity, thus making them less likely to protest (Stanfill 128–130).

Aware of the various threats to fan fiction work, including the tendency for sites to shut down when the person hosting it died, lost interest, or had to refocus on other life events, a group of fans set up a non-profit organization called the Organization for Transformative Works (OTW) in 2007. The term "transformative" is a nod to American copyright law that identifies the ways in which "fair use" can be defined. OTW aims to have fan-produced culture, including media, real person fiction, anime, comics, music, and vidding, "recognized as legal and transformative" and "accepted as a legitimate creative activity." The overall goal of the Organization is to "provide access to and preserve the history of fanworks and fan culture in its myriad forms." Arguing that "fanwork" is "historically rooted in a primarily female culture," they explain that they value their "identity as a predominantly female community with a rich history of creativity and commentary," as well as their roots in volunteer work and a gift economy (for example, by volunteering one's skills as a beta reader to support other writers' efforts) (www.transformative.org).

One project of the OTW was to set up Archive of Our Own as a place to post and archive fan fiction and to invite both comments and instant anonymous positive responses called "kudos," which are equivalent to the "Like" button on Facebook. Through the efforts of these and other women, particular fandoms created various awards for fan fiction. To acknowledge excellence in *XWP* fan fiction Brooks also set up Xippy Awards, while the International Day of Femslash, held annually since 2008, draws attention to audiences' frustration with the lack of compelling lesbian characters and celebrates femslash culture. Women such as geekgrrllurking organize various "ficathons," intensive writing periods around particular femslash characters. FemslashCon continues as an on-line forum to discuss new series of interest and the approaches various fan fiction writers are using to create their stories. Much of the interaction includes identifying femslash stories that participants have particularly enjoyed or been moved by. Challenges have included writing PWP sexually explicit stories as Advent Calendar treats for daily consumption to share during the Christmas holiday season.

The development of these large archives that are not specific to a particular fandom but host stories based on a wide range of popular cultural media has steadily reshaped the fan fiction landscape. Searchable archives permit readers to find stories by author, fandom, genre, character, slash category, and a number of other tags that can be selected by the author. Archive of Our Own, for example, has a tag that identifies stories as "Bechdel Test fix." Readers search for other works by an author whose stories they have enjoyed. By using tags and following specific writers, readers as well as writers move across to new or emerging fandoms.

Hellekson and Busse explain that in fandoms, "rather than inhabiting a space and then moving out when a new space comes open, the spaces are continuously inhabited, with fans moving in and out of the spaces as their inclination and technological limitations dictate" (16). Examples of this constant movement include the extensive work done by a number of fan fiction writers in several different fandoms. Gina L. Dartt has more than eighty stories on the *Star Trek: Voyager* characters Captain Katherine Janeway and cyborg Seven of Nine; readers will also find her fiction about *Bad Girls* and *Warehouse 13*. Readers who have followed Geonn Canon for *SG-1* Sam/Janet femslash (more than forty stories) will discover femslash based on the character Helen Magnus in *Sanctuary* (more than sixty stories) and the characters of Maura and Jane in *Rizzoli & Isles* (more than 30 stories) plus smaller numbers of works in other fandoms including *Once Upon a Time, Lost Girl, Warehouse 13* and *The Good Wife*. Geekgrrllurking contributes femslash to more than twenty different fandoms including science fiction and fantasy (*XWP; Stargate SG-1; Battlestar Galactica; Bionic Woman; Once Upon a Time*), criminal dramas (*CSI; CSI: Miami; CSI: NY; NCIS; Women's Murder Club*) and soap operas (*The Bold and the Beautiful; Guiding Light; Venice the Series*). Similarly, Ralst contributes to more than twenty different fandoms, in addition to organizing the large femslash archive and website *Passion & Perfection*.

These are just a few examples of more than twenty-five femslash authors who have written for more than three different fandoms, many of whom have also gone on to publish their fan fiction or original fiction in a more conventional manner. Thus new fans may move into the world of Xena/Gabrielle fan fiction from a Clexa space (where various Clarke and Lexa stories would be found). In doing this they are going "backwards," as it were, to read stories that might be more than fifteen years old, but experiencing the Xena/Gabrielle material as "new." Furthermore, by bringing their pre-existing knowledge to fresh fandoms, fan "elders" who write for multiple fandoms, as well as experienced readers who have seen all the comments and rebuttals before, can deepen and strengthen the community as a whole.

Resistance Is Not Futile

Vocal fans may encourage what seem to them to be logical storylines for women characters, perhaps in dialogue with the actors who have spotted a subtext or inserted one into the interactions between their characters. Yet it seems that once TPTB are aware that a lesbian subtext is threatening to drive the way a show can be interpreted they tend to promptly wheel in a heterosexual love interest, separate the characters, or kill one of them. Examples of shows where this has happened include *Warehouse 13, Stargate SG-1, Star Trek: Voyager,* and *Once Upon a Time.*

The fantasy show *Warehouse 13,* for example, has a number of strong women characters including Myka Bering, one of the main pair of agents who work for the Warehouse to retrieve magical artefacts that are causing mayhem in the world. Her work partner is Pete, who occupies the role of surrogate brother for the duration of the series. In season two Helena G. Wells arrives, initially functioning as nemesis to the Warehouse agents. Over the course of the following seasons she and Myka become very close, and as we discussed in the last chapter the actors who played them, Joanne Kelly and Jaime Murray, began to see their characters as being in love with each other.

The writers took this idea and played up the subtext without, however, ever making it into maintext. At the end of season two, having deeply bonded with each other, only Myka can persuade Helena not to destroy the whole world. Although that crisis is averted, Helena remains so dangerous that she offers to sacrifice herself to prevent her knowledge being used for evil in season three, and a devastated Myka tries to persuade her not to. In the end, she does sacrifice herself in the season finale to save Myka and the other Warehouse operatives when the Warehouse explodes. The final shots of the two women gazing at each other as they say goodbye leave little doubt about their feelings.

Because *Warehouse 13* is a fantasy show Helena is reanimated in season four, but the experience of her death was felt by fans. Unlike the characters of Artie and Steve, who also both die and are brought back to life, she never fully returns to the Warehouse. She leaves the Warehouse where she and Myka had worked together and is paired on-screen with a man and his daughter in a stifling domestic setting (which appeared to frustrate fans even more than the show's failure to let the two women become lovers). At the show's conclusion the audience is informed that (off-screen), Helena is in a new relationship with a woman. Myka, controversially and uncomfortably, ends the show in a relationship with her surrogate brother and work partner Pete. What TPTB did, then, was to first kill Helena and then—having reanimated her—placed both her and Myka into relationships with men.

The show *Stargate SG-1* performs a similar maneuver. The ten-season series depicts the activities of the "SG-1" team consisting of two U.S. Air Force personnel, a civilian, and an alien as they travel between worlds through a wormhole created at both ends by a "stargate." As we have argued elsewhere, in this show Samantha (Sam) Carter (a member of the SG-1 team) and Dr. Janet Fraiser (the Air Force base's Chief Medical Officer) were easily decoded by fans using a "negotiated" reading as being in a romantic relationship, constrained by the limits of the U.S. military's "Don't Ask, Don't Tell" policy which coincided with the run of the show (Millward and Dodd, "Mid-Course"). In addition to working closely with each other to solve innumerable scientific problems, Sam and Janet jointly bring up an alien daughter called Cassie, wear matching pink and blue cardigans, provide emotional support to each other, and are constantly in the frame together. As if the showrunners suddenly realized how this material could be decoded, Sam is given a serious boyfriend (another Pete) who proposes to her and Janet inexplicably shows romantic interest in a male documentary film maker just before she is killed off, although Sam is still the chief mourner at her funeral.

Both *Warehouse 13* and *Stargate SG-1* kill off one half of the subtextual pair *and* write in heterosexual romances, although the former show does at least bring its bisexual Helena back to life so that she can finally end the series in an unseen relationship with a woman. *Star Trek: Voyager* focuses purely on heterosexuality as the solution to its pressing subtextual problem. The show was part of the ever-popular Star Trek franchise and was the first to have a woman commander, Captain Janeway. At the end of season three the crew take on board a cyborg woman who had lived for many years as part of the Borg Collective. Known as Seven of Nine, she consistently challenges Janeway over her assumptions about the benefits of individualism over collectivism and her education in social conventions provides much of the comedy (and pathos) of the show. Although Janeway had previously engaged in a mentoring relationship with another woman on the ship, Kes, to a substantial number of viewers her dynamic with Seven of Nine seemed more electrifying and carried an erotic charge. In addition to their storylines, the pair shared intimate moments: Janeway frequently touched Seven (which she also did with Chakotay, her second in command and the ultimate heterosexual love interest for both women), gazed at her while she was dormant (recharging), sat beside her in firelight, and was willing to risk dying, messing with the otherwise sacrosanct timeline, or becoming part of the Borg herself in order to save Seven's life.

While many viewers saw their relationship as a mother-daughter bond, David Greven discusses the two-parter "Dark Frontier" in which Janeway rescues Seven from her former leader, the Borg Queen—a cyborg who interacts with Seven in ways that are more typically used by male villains to suggest sexual menace. Janeway's crew, meanwhile, becomes nonplussed and even disturbed by her cavalier actions as she attempts to rescue Seven. Greven argues that "Janeway's strangeness throughout this narrative is interpretable as code for the effect her emerging, newly revealed lesbian desires have on the crew; estranged from them yet determined all the same, Janeway fights for the right to express her desires, whatever effect they have on others" (Greven 177). The rescue is a pivotal point in the overall transformation of Janeway during what Greven defines as a "feminist version of an epic quest narrative," and he suggests that the show contains a "lesbian subtext that became an increasingly potent theme, at times almost threatening to be explicated in the text itself" (169). Both women did (in spite of some deaths along the way) make it to the end of the series alive, but their subtext did not. The showrunners behind *Star Trek: Voyager* chose a male love interest as their solution to the troubling suggestion that two women might fall in love with each other.

Because the women in science fiction and fantasy shows are independent, in positions of authority, and living in unfamiliar settings, it is easier to read lesbian potential into their lives than it is in other series set in the more mundane world of the here-and-now. The shows also have science fictional and fantasy elements that can be used by fan fiction writers to explore alternatives to everyday life, whether through AU fiction in general or Fix-its in particular. Through this type of fan fiction the writers suggest that it is possible to resist the banal heteronormative futures (or deaths) that TPTB prefer for these women characters.

Almost as soon as H.G. Wells arrived fan fiction writers started writing her into a relationship with Myka. In common with other *Warehouse 13* fan fiction, most stories revolved around the two women using various artefacts from the Warehouse to have sex or adventures. Once season two ended with Myka's realization that Helena had betrayed her and then given up her plan to destroy the world in order to save her, AU fiction and "Fixits" sprang up. Femslash exploring Sam and Janet's relationship began to appear on the internet by the end of the first season of *Stargate SG-1*. Both the show and much of the Sam and Janet femslash include realistic representations of the issues facing lesbians in the military at that time, including the need to provide evidence of heterosexuality and the impact of secrecy and social isolation on their personal lives (Millward and Dodd 48–52). In *Star Trek: Voyager* the whole point of the Janeway-Seven relationship on the show is that Janeway is socializing Seven but that Seven has no preconceived framework about how to behave, including no heteronormative perspective. She just views humanity as inefficient and that the sacrifice of one Borg drone (such as herself) or personal relationships should be irrelevant to the well-being of the whole collective. Her questions about humanity constantly challenge Janeway to reconsider some of her own assumptions. Femslash writers pounced on this material to explore how both women could learn from the other about their sexual and romantic desires.

These brief examples from just a few shows provide a general sense of the ways in which femslash writers have taken elements of what is shown in these series and adapted it to tell the stories from a completely different point of view. They may not be able to change what appears on the screen, but they can and do suggest that there is another story entirely taking place off screen.

Fix-Its

In the final episodes of *XWP*, entitled *A Friend in Need, Parts 1 and 2* and shortened by fans to FIN, Xena lets herself be killed in battle and her body is beheaded. Her death is a trade-off for the souls of 40,000 individuals who have been trapped in a limbo due to her actions in the distant past alongside a woman (or former lover) named Akemi. Xena could be restored to life, but asks Gabrielle to respect her decision to stay dead so that she can redeem herself for the sins of the past. As the sun sets the warrior bard is left to contemplate a future without her soulmate. In season seven of *Stargate SG-1* during the episodes entitled *Heroes 1 and 2* Janet is killed by a weapons blast in an off-world battle with alien enemies, where she had gone with the rest of the team in order to work as a field medic. At her memorial in front of all their military family, Sam eulogizes Janet who had saved so many of their lives in the past.

The season three premiere of *Chicago Fire* reveals that the paramedic Lesley Shay has died in the explosion that provided the cliff hanger at the end of the previous season. In the season six episode of *Buffy the Vampire Slayer* entitled "Seeing Red," after reconciling and making love with Willow, Tara is hit by a bullet meant for Buffy. Tara dies in Willow's blood-stained arms. And of course the same tragedy takes Lexa from Clarke in *The 100*.

The trappings of heroism and self-sacrifice were used to make most of these deaths (as well as many of the others that wiped out the lesbian or bisexual contingent of various shows) permanent and therefore beyond the reach of the types of magical or other-worldly solutions that had brought other characters on these shows back to life. For fans of *XWP*, Xena and Gabrielle had looked death in the eye many times and always returned to life to reunite with each other. Why was this sacrifice so final? Another member of the SG-1 team, Daniel, had died a very human and horrible death of radiation poisoning on *Stargate SG-1* and ascended to a higher plane of existence where he joined the Ancients. But he managed to make it back into his mortal body after just one season. On *Buffy the Vampire Slayer* magic had (rather disastrously) brought Buffy back to life. Why could it not do the same for Tara? Fans' sense of betrayal, both on behalf of the characters and for themselves, grew. Each of these deaths distressed their respective fan communities and generated an outpouring of fan fiction responses. Fans felt a compulsion to "fix" these stories and re-open the horizon of possibility for the same-sex relationships that they had been following with such loyalty.

As its name suggests, "Fix-it" is a fan fiction story that repairs the damage done (typically to a subtext) by a storyline that has occurred on the relevant show. In order to effectively integrate Fix-its into the world created by the show, writers will draw on elements already present in that show. For example, *XWP* includes the ideas that Xena and Gabrielle are soulmates, destined to be together for eternity. They will be reincarnated and they can be cloned. The science fictional elements of *Stargate SG-1* include sarcophagi that can reanimate the apparently dead, healing devices that can cure the nearly dead, cloning technology that can reproduce the dead, parallel universes where all alternate possibilities are being lived simultaneously, and ascension to a higher plane. Magic is real in *Buffy the Vampire Slayer* and is used to raise the dead: most noticeably Buffy herself in season six. In *Warehouse 13* the magical properties of the various artefacts that the team protects in the Warehouse can reanimate the dead and undo the timeline.

Once *XWP* fans were able to pick themselves up after the dreadful events of FIN they responded with their own versions of the episode. In a finale rewrite entitled "The Lie" by My OSage, the Greek goddess Aphrodite seeks Apollo's help in delaying the sunset, forces Akemi to confess her lie to trap Xena with her in the afterlife, and restores Xena to life and her true soulmate, Gabrielle. Other stories reflect efforts by both parties to restore their union, as Gabrielle works on earth to get Xena back and Xena tries to connect with her from the afterlife. In "Watching and Waiting" by CN Winters the ghost of Xena tries to decide what to do, reflecting that haunting Gabrielle was starting to have a worrying effect on Gabrielle who could not move on with her life.

Many of these stories start in the kinds of dark places that are dictated by the series finale. For example, in "The Black Dragon" by Aiglon,

Gabrielle sits watching a sunset and ponders what it now means to be a single warrior bard. However, these stories move through adversity to a much better outcome. Not only do the femslash writers restore the lives of the lesbian characters, they do so within the tenets of the show by using its own mythologies or tools. The often-repeated trope of "soulmates forever," who will find each other no matter what, is essential to much of this femslash. In "Bonding Souls" by CN Winter, Gabrielle muses "We can never die because in a way—we are never born." In Marion Tuttle's "Strange Alliance" and in Aiglon's "The Black Dragon" Gabrielle turns to the Olympian gods Ares and Aphrodite to help find Xena and plot her rescue. Verrath's "The Sad One" shows Gabrielle tracking down the Fates, the three sisters who control the length of one's life and who had appeared several times in the show. She insists that they restore the threads of Xena's life and change its outcome in a storyline which partially echoes the season six episode "When Fates Collide."

Fans of *Stargate SG-1* were similarly outraged by the loss of Janet Fraiser and the apparent determination of TPTB for her to remain dead. This was notable because every other major character in *Stargate SG-1* had been brought back from the dead, some more than once, some by the use of alien technologies, and often by Janet's innovative scientific and medical skills. Prolific *Stargate SG-1* femslash writers Celievamp and Elizabeth Carter had a discussion on their *Dark Matter* website which captured the sense of loss that fans felt at the death of Janet. There was an outpouring of femslash rewrites that "fixed" the event or simply ignored it. Celievamp's own story entitled "Fight or Flight" starts with the author's note: "Oh, and Dr. Fraiser, she's alive and well and living in Colorado Springs."

Other authors use the tools afforded by the science fictional elements of the show to tackle the restoration of this subtextual pair. In "Back from the Abyss" by Romansilence, Janet has ascended (like Daniel did) to a higher plane of existence with the Ancients, but in her grief Sam has started drinking and taking unnecessary risks. The Ancients know that the safety of Earth is dependent on Sam being in top form so they restore Janet to her old life. In "The Unexpected" by Dhamphir Sam turns to SG-1's alien allies, the Asgard, who have invented advanced cloning technologies, for help in restoring Janet. In Geonn's clever rewrite "Steam-Modern Prometheus," Janet is wounded but not dead and Sam rebuilds her from parts (with a nod to Mary Shelley's classic novel *Frankenstein*). *Stargate SG-1* femslash authors also exploit time travel to fix the past or to offer other parallel realities. The story "When you feel longing" by Romansilence shows Sam using Asgard technology to travel back in time so that she can ensure that Janet never enters the battle zone. Professions of love that could not or did not happen in one reality can be made in another. In "The Doctor's Patience" by Geonn, for example, Janet returns from another reality via a quantum mirror: when this happens in the series itself Sam and this other Janet from another world hardly interact, but Geonn's version corrects that. In an episode rewrite entitled "A New Affinity" by Elizabeth Carter, it is Janet who proposes marriage to Sam, not her boyfriend Pete.

Fans of *Buffy the Vampire Slayer* were concerned by the apparent equating of lesbian sexuality with both death and villainy. Judith Tabron observed that Tara's violent death and Willow's use of black magic distort and undermine the otherwise progressive representation of their relationship. Other fans have responded by using the mythology of witchcraft from the show to allow Willow and Tara to reconnect. In "United" by Wereleopard58, Willow can communicate with Tara after her death but only on the Day of the Dead. In "Everything Slows Down" by Alishsathewallflower, Tara and Willow first meet at a Wicca meeting and become consciously aware of their future together. The story follows their attempts to fix the outcome and avoid the torment ahead.

For fans of *Chicago Fire*, with no science fiction or fantasy elements to draw on, Fix-its depend on simply changing the outcome of the season two finale. Rewrites have included the aptly titled "Episode Rewrite: 2X14" by Lost-at-Sea. In it Leslie Shay survives the explosion that ended season two (that is, episode 2x14). Her co-worker Allison Rafferty refuses to leave her side as she recovers, eventually professing her love. Leslie survives and Allison struggles to deal with her growing attraction to her, feeling jealousy about Leslie's previous lovers and anxiety about taking on a lesbian identity, in "Homing Beacon" by P Kristen. In the story "Three Simple Words" by Msweener19, Leslie is in a near-fatal crash but becomes delightfully unguarded in her comments when drugged with pain killers. A text message from Allison Rafferty professing love starts the tale and a passionate kiss ends it.

There are more than 17,000 fan fiction posts on Archive of Our Own for *The 100*. The responses to Lexa's death include stories that deny it, such as "I Will See You Again" by Sgafirenity and "Commanders of Peace" by Lynniedthebeegirl. In this story the conflict has ended, Clarke and Lexa have a household together, and are wishing for a child. The author's notes for "The White Owl's Egg" by Coldwise use the phrase "canon divergence from the end of 3x07 and onward" in order to claim the space to undo Lexa's death (which took place in episode 7 of season 3) and explore other possible futures. In "How Deep Is Your Love" by Romi364, the author uses a crossover format with *Fear the Walking Dead* to give Clexa another chance in a zombie universe (Alycia Debnam-Carey, who played Lexa, stars as Alicia Clarke in *Fear the Walking Dead*). The author's notes include the statement that "Clarke and Lexa are meant for each other. Because I love zombies and I need happiness for Clexa. PS: fck jroth…"

"Fish, Swords, and Love" by DanieXJ is a *XWP—Stargate SG-1* crossover fan fiction in which both *Heroes* and *A Friend in Need* are "fixed": Xena, Gabrielle, Sam and Janet all end up in a hot tub. An intertextual example, "My Brunette with the Golden Eyes" by Babydykecate, points readers to a wealth of existing lesbian literature. In an alcove at the college library, Willow reads Tara some of the great lesbian love poems by Audre Lorde, Renee Viven and Angelina Grimke.

A particularly clever femslash Fix-it of a substantial portion of the Dead Lesbian Ur-text is "The Travellers" by Fleimgona, posted on Archive of Our Own. This uses the crossover format to "Fix" both the lesbian deaths and frustrating storylines on *The 100, American Horror Story, Lost Girl, Glee, Chicago Fire, Xena: Warrior Princess* and the movie *Carol.* The author's notes explain that the premise of this incomplete piece of fan fiction is that "The dead lesbian squad must find a way back to their worlds so they can return to their soulmates."

The opening scene of "The Travellers" is set in a bar in Valhalla where four heroic dead lesbians, Tasmin (from *Lost Girl*) Lexa, Xena and Leslie Shay, have gathered to plot their escape. Tasmin explains that "there is a realm above our own that belongs to the creators, they write our reality, every person you ever met, every friend you ever lost, it was written. I don't know why or how, but they've been killing all of us and it's sending ripples across all the worlds" (Fleimgona). The women travel through time and space to New York City in 1950 where they are joined by Carol and Therese from the film *Carol* who are convinced their so-called happy ending cannot last. Knowing that many of the writers are in California, they head to Los Angeles to find them and correct their story lines.

In spite of some scholarly dismissal of the form, much fan fiction is extremely well written and indicates that its authors are thoroughly versed not just in their favorite shows but in the wider constraints of the entertainment industry. Fleimgona's characters are fully "in character" in their interactions with each other, even though they engage with characters from other shows. This level of consistent characterization is rarely achieved by the products of the writers' rooms on the actual shows themselves. Allusions are also made to the requisite ratio of blonde to brunette lesbians in pop cultural products. Though not yet complete, this solidly tongue-in-cheek piece of fan fiction clearly identifies the source of the problem as a long-standing and profound failure of imagination by TPTB. It also identifies lesbian community organizing, including in this case among fictional lesbians, as not only necessary for political action, but viable and enjoyable.

Post-death

The tag of "Post-3x07" is used by some 262 stories and counting in Clexa fan fiction. The term "Post" hyphenated to the name or number of a specific episode is a way for authors and readers to identify AU fan fiction that writes futures for the characters who died in the named episode. In other words, it ignores or "fixes" the death and then carries on, writing fiction in which the femslash couple remains together. It was used by femslash authors in both the Xenaverse (Post-FIN) and *Stargate: SG-1*communities (Post-HEROES). Not only do writers and fans move from fan community to community but they maintain these types of paratextual conventions (such as tags) to identify their disappointment with specific episodes and their own efforts to make the endings better for the characters. Seasoned femslash readers (after all, from post–FIN in 2001 to Post-3x07 in 2016 means this tag has been around for a long time) can relax and confidently enjoy new stories by recognizing the nature of the tag as a refusal of the death trope. New readers can also see a pattern through the "Post" tag of stories across fandoms collectively refusing the (literal) master narrative.

Taking the time to tell femslash stories at all is a major achievement, and this tag matters because it directly negates symbolic annihilation. One of the disturbing elements of the Dead Lesbian Trope is how persistent it is. Very few viewers who are aware of it can sit down in front of their television set or laptop or watch their mobile device screen and comfortably relax into a show featuring a same-sex couple. The "Post" tag, on the other hand, is better than the Vito Russo Test or the Lexa Pledge, because it does not promise something that it is unlikely to deliver given media industry limitations. Instead, this tag reassures the reader that rather than disposing of the lesbian, her death itself has already been disposed of and she lives on.

Secretly Mining the Subtext

Archive of Our Own contains millions of stories and hundreds of thousands of them are related to television series. However, it seems that series which have identifiable lesbian or bisexual women as continuing characters have relatively fewer fan fiction posts than series which lend themselves to a subtextual reading. In August 2016, examples with continuing lesbian story arcs include *Bomb Girls* (142 entries), *Call the Midwife* (318 entries), *Chicago Fire* (229 entries), *Empire* (57 entries), *The L Word* (74 entries), *Lost Girl* (1062 entries), *Orange Is the New Black* (547 entries), *Pretty Little Liars* (926 entries), and *The Good Wife* (812 entries). Two shows with central same-sex relationships buck this trend: *The 100* has 17,377 entries and *The Walking Dead* 11,183 entries, although the compulsion to write Fix-its may account for some of them. In contrast, recent shows in which central female characters could be read through subtext have much higher number of posts including *Once Upon a Time* (28,108 entries) and *MARVEL: Agents of S.H.I.E.L.D.* (17,370 entries). The exception appears to be *Rizzoli & Isles* with only 1153 fan fiction entries on Archive of Our Own, but it is a significant part of many other femslash sites including Passion & Perfection. An extensive portion of AUSXIP is devoted to the show and its actors but the site sends those who are seeking fan fiction to FanFiction.net which includes about 5200 posts on *Rizzoli & Isles*, of which 4900 are Jane/Maura femslash.

As the fan community that developed around *Xena: Warrior Princess* and later shows such as *Guiding Light* suggests, many women come to same-sex love stories with no particular sense of themselves *as lesbians*, or even as attracted to women at all. Viewers tend to identify with characters from their own identity group. This means that women who do not think of themselves as lesbians might be less invested in an overt lesbian storyline than in storylines about ostensibly heterosexual characters. In *Lesbian Epiphanies: Women Coming Out in Later Life* Karol Jensen suggests that "if women were allowed to understand their sexual feelings, to be unashamed of them, they might recognize that they want to seek out other women as more than friends, as potential life partners," but because, historically, women have not been encouraged to do so, then "when, or if, she does experience her feelings of attraction for a female, she is likely to deny it, push it down and away, or she may miss the meaning or significance of it altogether" (Jensen 40). Women who can be described in this way are likely to find the subtext attractive. In addition, subtext is rich with possibility compared to maintext dealing with named lesbian characters, because subtextual stories are generated in the viewers' imaginations.

Uber Fiction

Although Uber fiction would probably have developed quite rapidly anyway, it started as an outcome of a particular episode of *XWP*. In season two a clip show, "The Xena Scrolls," introduced two new characters, Janice Covington (Renee O'Connor) and Melinda Pappas (Lucy Lawless). The action of the episode takes place in Macedonia in the 1940s, where the two women are working at an archaeological dig and uncover the Xena Scrolls, written by Gabrielle millennia earlier. Janice and Mel are revealed to be the descendants of Gabrielle and Xena and they ride off into the sunset together. This conceit, that the original (ancient) characters could live on in some form as descendants, reincarnations, or clones reappeared in several other episodes but this first incarnation gave rise to a new subset of fan fiction which Kym Taborn named "UberXena" fiction. Boese notes that initially all Uber-Xena fiction was "Janice and Mel" fiction, but "before long, writers began branching out, placing new descendants of Xena and Gabrielle all over the timeline, often with complex, novel-length offerings" (Boese, "Spinning," para. 84–85). Taborn herself gives a slightly different explanation of the meaning of the term "Uber." Taborn argues that "The Xena Scrolls" was actually the third of three episodes that made it possible for fan fiction writers to see that:

> The characters of Xena and Gabrielle were in fact archetypes that could be explored in different times and diverse cultural backgrounds. This phenomena could also be seen as an attempt at rewriting women's mythology of the past—creating new versions of past, present, and future, and using Xena and Gabrielle as the archetypal hero and companion exploring these new views of the old stories and stereotypes previously dominated by male characters ["What"].

For Taborn's definition the two other relevant episodes were "Dreamworker" from season one, which indicated that Xena and Gabrielle shared a mystical link that made them soulmates, and "Remember Nothing" from season two in which the story suggested that their lives were destined to be intertwined.

Taborn dates the very first example of Uber fiction to an incomplete short story called "Get Your Kicks on Route 66" by Miss and Aisa which circulated on a private mailing list in June 1997. This was followed by a completed story, "Toward the Sunset" by Della Street, which circulated on a private mailing list as well. It was not until July 22, 1997, when Bongo Bear posted "The Hitch Hiker" to the web that "the world was first exposed to UberXena" and by that act initiated "one of the most exciting and creative movements within all of fan fiction culture" ("What"). By the end of that summer of 1997 the Uber genre had exploded. Boese argues that "this fan fiction universe is the height of rebellion away from TPTB because it in essence says, 'We don't need the television show to sustain this space'" (Boese, "Spinning," para. 51). Although Uber characters were clearly based on Xena and Gabrielle, they were not the property of the studio and this branch of fan fiction was therefore able to make the leap off the computer screen and into published book form. Three women in particular made this transition: Melissa Good, Mary D. Brooks, and Len Barot.

One of the best-known Xenaverse bards is Melissa Good. She posted her first piece of Xena and Gabrielle fan fiction to the web in April 1997 after watching the episode "The Quest." Like Brooks and others, it only took one episode of the show, watched reluctantly (she has more than once recounted the story that when she first saw *XWP* Good was painting some wrought iron with the television on and was unable to change the channel) to unleash Good's creativity. She followed her first foray into writing with many lengthy stories, into one of which she introduced a wolf pup called Ares. Given that Good's username was "Merwolf," her fans started to call themselves "Merpups" (Lunacy "Very" para. 12). Good's productivity was extraordinary. She became a very prolific fan fiction writer and was invited to write the scripts for the season six opener "Coming Home," as well as "Legacy," an experience she describes as a writer's dream come true (Stafford 155). In addition to multiple novel-length stories posted online, including her "Journey of Soulmates" series, Good wrote "Uber" fiction, and the enormous interest in her work from the Merpups as well as from more casual readers encouraged her to publish some of her "Dar and Kerry" Uber fiction in book form. There is no mistaking who they are—Dar is the comtech executive with many skills and killer instincts sent to swallow up smaller enterprises, while Kerry is the people-savvy junior partner who always uses words first in any conflict. They face contemporary issues such as coming out to family, work/life balance, sexual harassment and homophobia in the workplace and emerging lesbian identity. Six of the Dar and Kerry novels have been published by Yellow Rose Books.

In addition to initially working as an editor for Tom's Xena Page and running AUSXIP, Brooks also writes her own Uber fiction. To date she has published six books in her "Intertwined Souls" series, following the lives of Eva Muller and Zoe Lambros (Uber versions of Xena and Gabrielle, respectively), relocated to Second World War Greece and postwar Australia. She has also written a lesbian romance novel as a spin-off from the main series. In 2015 she launched her own publishing company, Ausxip Publishing.

Len Barot, who writes under the names Radclyffe and L.L. Raand, was another Xenaverse fan fiction writer who has ended up with her own publishing company. In addition to Xena fan fiction she also wrote stories based on *The X-Files* in which Scully was a lesbian. Writing as Radclyffe she took advantage of the demand for Uber fiction in order to develop several series of novel-length works which became extremely popular. In keeping with the intertextual world of lesbian storytelling, Barot explains that she chose the name "Radclyffe" to make reference to Radclyffe Hall, the author of *The Well of Loneliness*. Once she started publishing original fiction in book form she kept this fan fiction author name so that potential readers would recognize her work. In 2004 Barot founded Bold Strokes Books to publish mostly lesbian genre fiction and this company now dominates the marketplace for that type of work.

One Thing Leads to Another

Lesbian fiction first received a massive fillip in the 1970s when several publishers established themselves to meet the demand generated by second-wave feminists and other women seeking lesbian content. These women were no longer willing to put the effort in to try and imagine alternative happy endings for lovers in the doom-laden tales available in pulp fiction. They wanted new stories that spoke to their experiences interacting with lesbians in women's groups, women's studies courses, and women's cooperatives. Naiad Press, for example, was founded in 1973. It published genre fiction and became the largest publisher of lesbian books in the world. When it shut up shop forty years later it transferred its titles to Bella Books, another lesbian genre fiction publisher established in 2001. To publish yet more genre fiction, Barot set up Bold Strokes Books, recognizing that the demand for her own Uber fiction and that of her fellow bards—demonstrated through the fan fiction sites—meant that there was now an even larger market for lesbian stories. The Xenaverse was therefore largely responsible for this reinvigoration and ongoing health of lesbian romance fiction, both in terms of the market for it and in terms of content.

In her study entitled *Lesbian Romance Novels*, Phyllis Betz discusses the impact of *XWP* on the proliferation of a specific sub-genre of romance. She points out that when the series started Xena and Gabrielle "dramatically altered the physical look, behavior, and emotional development of the romantic couple in the novel. Where previously the women would reflect a more varied range of physical types, the impact of these new models set up, surprisingly, some descriptive limitations" (Betz 106–107). As Betz explains:

> The requirements for keeping a mainstream audience prevented that relationship [between Xena and Gabrielle] from crossing the boundary from play to actual romantic connection. Yet, it is this consummation that recent lesbian romance novels play out

again and again. Having the two women not only openly declare their love, but initiate a physically intimate relationship can be seen as just the wish fulfillment of avid lesbian Xena fans. What is striking in the majority of recent lesbian romances, however, is the authors' insistence on incorporating what can now be seen as iconic images and characterizations, especially since the show went off the air [Betz 107].

Betz suggests that by drawing on *XWP*, lesbian romances now cover territory that focuses on how to survive and negotiate a relationship, rather than on coming out or dealing with homophobia. "The lesbian romance that replicates the series' character and plot configurations gives the majority of the narrative to tracing a similar movement; questions of trust, depth of feeling, willingness to adapt, and other aspects needed for building a complete relationship become the central concern of the story" (Betz 109). In this way *XWP* and Xenaverse fan fiction provided a blueprint for thinking through same-sex relationship dynamics, and lesbian romance writers explore these in detail in their novels. These books and others by femslash authors indicate the strong desire and dogged persistence of both writers and readers to continue the stories of lesbian characters long after the television shows that gave birth to them have attempted to create a final version of the characters' lives.

Conclusion

Fan fiction writers spend many unpaid hours crafting their stories. Beta readers offer editorial advice for free. The women and men who set up and maintain fan fiction archives preserve these stories and help others to find them, enjoy them, provide feedback, and, often, start writing their own stories in turn. The level of energy dedicated to this volunteer-run community, managed on a shoestring and relying on donations, is impressive by any measure. Most significant here, however, is that it offers a damning corrective to TPTB whose own stories lack luster and originality. Readers are drawn to the world of fan fiction because it provides them with richer, deeper, and more complex stories about women than those they can find in the material offered up by the entertainment industry. Driscoll and Gregg call this "the situated context for producing fan texts—whether zines prior to the Internet or online fanfic after—and the wider structural questions such practices respond to if not fully answer" (572). Fan fiction writers and the hosts of fan archives, who are heterosexual men and women as well as lesbians and bisexual women, collectively respond to homophobia and lesbian invisibility.

Clearly stories about women loving women still matter to many viewers, decades after the first versions of them appeared online. Fan fiction communities overall are places to affirm lesbian desire and to act as sites of resistance. Exposure to the kind of insight into characters and refusal of the master narrative that comes through reading femslash can help engaged viewers to learn to read against the grain for themselves and bring that skill to all of their media consumption and, potentially, production. Fan fiction can also tell a story that offers a respite from reality. L.N. James says of her own work that "I get enough of [homophobia] in real life, I don't want Xena and Gabrielle in their own little world to have to deal with that bullshit" (Wilder para. 544). Online and now in the published books that have come out of fandoms, lesbians do not only survive, they thrive.

CONCLUSION

In her review of the ways in which lesbians have been erased from history Adrienne Rich points out that symbolic annihilation is one component in the "rendering invisible of the lesbian possibility, an engulfed continent which rises fragmentedly to view from time to time only to become submerged again" (Rich 647). Is it possible that the present time is one in which an emergent sense of lesbian possibility is in the process of being deliberately forced back beneath the waves? And, if so, why now?

One argument is that lesbianism (not just sex acts between women) threatens patriarchal power structures which rely on heteronormativity and women's subordination to prop them up. This might seem like a dated argument but contemporary audiences find it relevant. Heterosexual and lesbian women alike, in Alison Hopkins's study for example, argued that the patriarchy still dictates how lesbians appear on the screen. Her focus group participants said that the reason why there are no (or very few) realistic or diverse lesbian characters is because, from a patriarchal perspective, lesbians "must be subjugated, marginalised and put down by attributing qualities opposite to those the patriarchy finds attractive" (Hopkins 95). Those characters which are labeled "lesbian" on television are therefore "appealing to men" and the "girly lesbian is a construct of straight-male fantasy which they find erotic" (Hopkins 97). And as Terry Castle argues, it can be difficult to see the lesbian "in part because she has been 'ghosted'—or made to seem invisible—by the culture itself. It would be putting it mildly to say that the lesbian represents a threat to patriarchal protocol: Western civilization has for centuries been haunted by a fear of 'women without men'—of women indifferent or resistant to male desire" (Castle 4–5). This argument helps to explain why the "on-screen lesbian landscape [is] distinguished more by continuity than change" (Eaklor, "Kids" 165).

The entertainment industry does not merely provide diversion. It is a major global industry and its ability to set the parameters on what stories are told should be taken very seriously since, as Angela McRobbie asserts, "relations of power are indeed made and remade within texts of enjoyment and rituals of relaxation and abandonment" (38). Adolescents in particular now find out about sexuality primarily through media (television, film, magazines, and social media) rather than older institutions such as the family, religion or education (Cover, *Queer* 18). Rob Cover's study of queer youth suicide reassures that simply consuming media texts which suggest suicide is a "logical solution to a seemingly unliveable life" does not drive anyone to actually attempt suicide, but he nevertheless cautions that entertainment media can (and does) reinforce "existing cultural knowledge that *associates* non-normative sexuality with self-harm and suicide" (Cover, *Queer* 20, emphasis in original). While almost none of the current crop of dead lesbians killed themselves, his point remains relevant here: globally, the entertainment media is still peddling a powerful and relentlessly reinforced message that women cannot live full and happy lives together.

Thus, even when actors, writers, directors and fans attempt to argue for an alternative storyline, one which, to them, seems more honest and true to the characters or to the complexity of real life, their voices are in competition with a large number of other ones. The mix of groups vying to control which lesbian (and other GBTQ) stories made it to the screen is a true mélange. Doyle lists the stakeholders as including:

> LGBT movement activists, entertainment industry producers, mainstream journalists, LGBT journalists, other national movement organizations, media executives, marketing professionals, media scholars, corporate donors, GLAAD's membership, the LGBT community writ large, LGBT artists and independent media producers, and anti-gay conservative groups, among others [Doyle 22].

While lesbian, bisexual and queer women—all of those women who fall so nicely into Jeanette Foster's category of "sex variant"—are perfectly capable of telling their own stories, it is a fact of homophobia and patriarchy combined that they are not always well positioned to do so. These women are everywhere and are very talented, but other ("straight") networks are more extensive and have more money. Thus the most widespread images of women-loving women are mainstream ones, and Elaine Marks argues that "images of the lesbian are related in any given time and place to prevalent images of women. They are influenced by the same fear, loathing, or ignorance of female sexuality" (360). If women who love women are being wiped off the screen, what is happening to heterosexual women?

Joanne Clarke Dillman reminds us that although women are not telling their own stories in popular media, dead women do fill our big and small screens each and every day. She argues that the symbolic annihilation of women as a group is the price exacted for the successes of feminism: the dead women are meant to discipline living women viewers who might challenge patriarchal restrictions on their lives. She also argues that dead women (both fictional and real) achieve visibility *because* they are dead, often acting as a plot device or placeholder in someone else's story. Examining films from the first decade of the twenty-first century including *Minority Report* (Steven Spielberg, USA, 2002), *Déjà Vu* (Tony Scott, USA, 2006), *The Lovely Bones* (Peter Jackson, USA, 2009), *Disturbia* (D. J. Caruso, USA, 2007) and even the animated film *The Corpse Bride* (Mike Johnson and Tim Burton, USA, 2005), she draws attention to the linkage of sex/y with death, and especially with graphic acts of gender-based violence. Similar scenarios play out in almost all television crime dramas with entire series devoted to sexual violence cases or serial killers, in *Law & Order: Special Victims Unit* and *Criminal Minds*, for example.

All of this marks a dramatic shift from the strong women taking charge in the 1980s and 1990s when advertisers sought to hook urban, white, affluent women viewers whom they assumed were interested in feminism. By the twenty-first century those strong women had become a nightly staple—even, finally, including black women—but the risk that they could signal women's empowerment at the expense of patriarchy had to be tempered. Antifeminism, as a hostile reaction by tiny fringe groups to even the most basic feminist claims, is easy to dismiss as extremist and outmoded when it makes its presence felt—the orchestrated campaign against the all-women remake of *Ghostbusters* is a good example of this approach. Although social media gives its more virulent strains of death and rape threats new vectors of transmission and it therefore feels very threatening to the women and men who are targeted by the antifeminists, its misogyny is crude and transparent and not to be taken seriously.

Postfeminism, by contrast, is firmly rooted in neo-liberal ideology and is therefore much more insidious. Each choice to remove lesbianism from the symbolic landscape is taken for supposedly rational reasons. The decision to mothball the AfterEllen website in September 2016—after fourteen years of sharing news and information about lesbians and bisexual women in the entertainment industry—because the site was not generating enough income, is only the most recent example of this process (Bendix, "Eulogy"). Lesbians are not "superconsumers" after all, it seems. Postfeminism insists to each viewer that she does not belong to any social group, that her struggles are the outcome of her individual failings and are hers to bear alone, and that each beloved character who vanishes into oblivion is certainly not the latest casualty in a war that she is foolish to believe is being waged at all.

Battle On!

In the "Puppy" episode of the *Ellen* sitcom Ellen Morgan accuses Susan, the lesbian to whom she is attracted, of trying to recruit her. Without missing a beat, Susan retorts that she will have to contact the lesbian "national headquarters" and confess her failure: if she had succeeded in turning Ellen into a lesbian they would have sent her a toaster oven. The implication is that by collecting enough lesbians (rather like loyalty points) Susan would have earned a reward. At the end of the episode, after Ellen has come out, Susan takes her to meet Melissa Etheridge, the lesbian musician and at the time one of only a handful of out lesbian celebrities. Etheridge asks Ellen to verify that she is gay, gets her to sign and initial a number of forms and then presents an excited Susan with her toaster oven. This is a fascinating moment, because while Susan's initial remark was read as mocking the closeted Ellen's homophobic assumption that lesbians are predatory and so women must be shielded from them, the end of the episode gleefully confirms the worst fear of patriarchal parents everywhere: that lesbians do recruit.

The attractive possibilities of lesbianism for women are why, arguably, symbolic annihilation still matters after all these years. When a woman encounters a lesbian she does not just meet someone new—she encounters lesbian possibility for herself. For many women, this encounter first occurs in the fictional realm (whether literary, on television, in film, or online). A number of television series and even the occasional mainstream film show the process by which a woman comes to realize that she is attracted to other women: how exposure to lesbian possibility becomes lesbian (or bisexual) reality for some characters. Thus on *Grey's Anatomy* Callie Torres and her colleague and friend Erica Hahn kiss each other as a joke in front of Callie's friend and former lover Mark Sloan. The kiss precipitates romantic and sexual feelings in both previously heterosexual women. They realize that they are genuinely attracted to each other and start a relationship. Although they break up, Callie subsequently begins a new relationship with another woman, Arizona Robbins.

In the British soap opera *Holby City* the newly out Bernie Wolfe comes to work at Holby City Hospital. Her colleague Serena Campbell is a dyed-in-the-wool heterosexual who had clearly never thought about women as potential romantic partners before meeting Bernie. She and Bernie become close and supportive friends, their relationship crackling with what Bernie calls their "undeniable sexual chemistry." After they share a kiss Serena tries out the word "lesbian" on herself. In the Venezuelan film *Liz in September* Eva encounters Liz and her group of lesbian friends and ex-lovers and falls in love not just with Liz but with the feeling of belonging to the group which embraces her. The British romantic comedy *Imagine Me and You* (Ol Parker, UK, 2005) shows the just-married (to a man) Rachel feeling intensely drawn to Luce, the florist who provided the flowers at her wedding. Before she knows that Luce is a lesbian Rachel believes that she simply wants to be Luce's best friend, but once she does find out she realizes that her feelings are romantic and (after surmounting appropriate barriers) the two women end up together.

The daytime soap opera *Guiding Light* provides a particularly good example of this whole process. Neither Olivia nor Natalia are lesbians, so their encounter with lesbian possibility comes from the outside. Olivia's daughter Emma gives a presentation on "My Two Mommies" at her school and a well-meaning teacher therefore assumes that Olivia and Natalia are a couple. Once Olivia sees their relationship through the teacher's eyes she realizes that that is, in fact, the relationship she wants with Natalia. Since Natalia is a devout Catholic passively receiving the attentions of a male love interest it takes her a lot longer to come around to the same position as Olivia, although she eventually does and the two women become romantic partners.

As this last example shows, women do not even have to encounter an actual lesbian to discover they are attracted to women: they just have to have that potential seem possible in their own lives. For characters this visibility is achieved through various means, but not usually because they were watching two women fall in love on television. For many viewers, however, the characters themselves, either in their on-screen romances or through their subtextual connections, make same-sex desire suddenly seem captivating. What kinds of characters exist, how they comport themselves and which ones survive is therefore immensely significant: a television season strewn with the bodies of dead lesbian characters is sending a clear message to all viewers and just because these deaths are fictional does not mean they have no bearing on reality.

Wondering how it is that older women decide to come out as lesbians, Karol Jensen conducted a series of interviews with a number of them. She wanted to know how it is that having built a heterosexual identity for themselves, they could:

live through a series of life events and transitions that develop into a critical level of information and awareness, a critical cascade, that leads to a *deconstruction* of their identities as heterosexual (predisposing factors, marriage as social fantasy, invalidation of that first relationship, pressures to leave, pressures to stay, responses of family and community, etc.), and come to reconstruct new identities as lesbian or bisexual women (enabling factors, role models, defining moments, finding a community, social support, etc.) [Jensen 11].

Women who love women on screen, as well as the supportive fan community that develops around them, are crucial—sometimes pivotal—sources of knowledge that can shift the entire direction of a woman's life at any age.

Whether through online fan fiction or in published novels, readers and authors insist on happy endings. The immense and sustained outpouring of activism and creativity around changing the stories that get told (given that one cannot simply change the channel in order to see something different) signals just how much on-screen lives (and deaths) continue to matter, not only to the women (and men) who have seen it all before, but to each new generation of viewers. The energy put into communities of women who love women and resistance to symbolic annihilation continues the work done by earlier generations of women who withstood a world which tried so hard to deny their humanity and refused to tell their stories.

BIBLIOGRAPHY

Aaron, Michele. *Death and the Moving Image: Ideology, Iconography and I.* Edinburgh: Edinburgh Press, 2014. Print.

Abrams, Natalie. *"Xena: Warrior Princess.* An Oral Herstory." *Entertainment Weekly* June 17, 2016. Web.

"The Act for Change Project." *act-for-change.com.* Web.

Adichie, Chimamanda. "The Danger of A Single Story." *TED Talks.* TED Global 2009. July 2009. Web.

Ahmed, Sara. *Queer Phenomenology: Orientations, Objects, Others.* Durham, NC: Duke University Press, 2006. Print.

Aiglon. "The Black Dragon." *ausxip.com.* Web. http://www.ausxip.com/fanfiction/aiglon/blackdragon.htm.

Ailaikannu. "Broken Heart." *archiveofourown.org.* Web. http://archiveofourown.org/works/6684094/chapters/15286351.

Anderson, Hanah, and Matt Daniels. "Film Dialogue from 2,000 Screenplays Broken Down by Gender and Age." Polygraph.cool/films. April 16, 2016. Web.

Anderson, Kate. "From A to Xena." *Xposé Special* #11. Spring 2000: 6–15. Print.

Anderson, Tre'vell. "#OscarsSoWhite Creator on Oscar Noms: 'Don't Tell Me That People of Color, Women Cannot Fill Seats.'" *Los Angeles Times* January 14, 2016. Web.

Anderson-Minshall, Diane. "I Kissed a Girl … The Evolution of The Prime-Time Lesbian Kiss." *Bitch Magazine* 23 (Winter 2004): 27–30; 87.

Aston, James, Basil Glynn and Beth Johnson. *Television, Sex and Society Analyzing Contemporary Representations.* New York: Continuum, 2012. Print.

Atwell, Elaine. "'Last Tango in Halifax' Writer Sally Wainwright 'Explains' Kate's Death." *AfterEllen.com.* January 19, 2015. Web.

Aurora Novarum. Comment on "Topic: 7.18—Heroes (Part 2)." Stargate SG-1 & Atlantis Solutions Forum. November 7, 2006, 01:37:48 PM., http://www.stargate-sg1-solutions.com/forum/index.php?topic=164.0.

BBC. *Portrayal of Lesbian, Gay and Bisexual People on the BBC: Executive Summaries and Recommendations.* September 2010. www.bbc.co.uk/diversity/audiences/lgb-consultation.html. Web.

_____. *Portrayal of Lesbian, Gay and Bisexual People on the BBC: Research Report.* September 2011. www.bbc.co.uk/diversity/audiences/lgb-consultation.html. Web.

_____. *Portrayal of Lesbian, Gay and Bisexual People on the BBC: Research Update.* November 2012. www.bbc.co.uk/diversity/audiences/lgb-consultation.html. Web.

Babydykecate. "My Brunette With Golden Eyes." *fanfiction.net*. Web. https://www. fanfiction.net/s/5139287/1/My-Brunette-with-Golden-Eyes.

"Back for Good." *Xena Magazine*, Issue 11. October 2000: 5. Print.

Badgett, M.V. Lee, and Jody L. Herman. *Sexual Orientation & Gender Diversity in Entertainment: Experiences & Perspectives of SAG-AFTRA Members*. Los Angeles: SAG-AFTRA/Williams Institute, 2013.

Barker, Kate. "Blond Ambition." *Xena Magazine*. Issue 10 September 2000: 20–26. Print.

Bassom, David. "Paris Match." *Xena Magazine* Issue 12, December 2000: 42–44. Print.

Booth, Stephen. *The Death of Tara, the Fall of Willow and The Dead/Evil Lesbian Cliché FAQ*. Stephen and Kaths Place, n.d. Web. www.stephenbooth.org.

Becker, Edith, Michelle Citron, Julia Lesage, and B. Ruby Rich. "Lesbians and Film." *Out in Culture: Gay, Lesbian and Queer Essays on Popular Culture*. Eds. Corey K. Creekmur and Alexander Doty. Durham: Duke University Press, 1995. 24–44. Print.

Beirne, Rebecca. "Screening the Dykes of Oz: Lesbian Representation on Australian Television." *Journal of Lesbian Studies* 13 (2009): 25–34. Print.

_____. "Teen Lesbian Desires and Identities in International Cinema: 1931–2007." *Journal of Lesbian Studies* 16 (2012): 258–273. Print.

_____, ed. *Televising Queer Women: A Reader*. New York: Palgrave, 2012. Print.

Bélot, Sophie. "Female Friendships in Contemporary Popular Films by French Women Directors." *Lesbian Inscriptions in Francophone Society and Culture*. Eds. Renate Günther and Wendy Michallat. Manchester: Manchester University Press, 2011. 63–79. Print.

Bendix, Trish. "Eulogy for the Living." http://trish-bendix.tumblr.com/post/150695653 921/eulogy-for-the-living. September 20, 2016. Web.

_____. "How to Grieve The Loss of Your Favorite Lesbian/Bi TV Characters." *AfterEllen.com* June 1, 2016. Web.

_____. "How the Trope of Queer Women Dying on Television Can (And Must) Be Stopped." *AfterEllen.com* March 21, 2016. Web.

_____. "Please Stop Killing Us! The State of Lesbians And Bi Women on TV." *AfterEllen.com* October 1, 2014. Web.

Berenstein, Rhona J. "Adaptation, Censorship, and Audiences of Questionable Type: Lesbian Sightings in *Rebecca* (1940) and *The Uninvited* (1944)." *Cinema Journal* 37.3 (1998): 16–37. Print.

Betz, Phyllis M. *Lesbian Romance Novels: A History and Critical Analysis*. Jefferson: McFarland, 2009. Print.

Biersdorfer, J.D. "In the Service of a Warrior Princess." *The New York Times*. March 5, 1998. Print.

"Body Language & the Male Gaze—Tropes vs Women in Video Games." *Youtube*, uploaded by feministfrequency (Anita Sarkeesian), March 31, 2016. https://www. youtube.com/watch?v=QPOla9SEdXQ.

Boese, Christine "The Ballad of the Internet Nutball: Chaining Rhetorical Visions from the Margins of the Margins to the Mainstream in the Xenaverse." PhD dissertation, Rensselaer Polytechnic Institute, 1998.

_____. "Spinning Off from the Source: Alternative Fan Fiction Changes with the Seasons." *Whoosh!* Issue 25, October 1998. Web.

Bremer, Carolyn, and Christine Boese. "The Convention as Authentic *Xena* Experience." *Whoosh!* Issue 57, June 2001. Web.

Bruch, Marisa. "Can Television Fandoms Change the Fates and Futures of Gay Characters?" *Huffington Post US Edition*. Huffington Post, April 2, 2016. Web.

Bury Your Tropes Panel Presented by GLAAD. ATX Television Festival, June 11, 2016.

Butler, Bethonie. "TV Keeps Killing off Lesbian Characters. The Fans of One Show Have Revolted." *The Washington Post*. April 4, 2016. Web.

Buzzfeed PSA: https://www.buzzfeed.com/skarlan/psa-stop-killing-queer-women-on-television?utm_term=.wgNXBv3Z9#.fjL0d2Wl6

Cairns, Lucille. "Lesbian Desire in Recent French and Francophone Cinema." *Lesbian Inscriptions in Francophone Society and Culture*, eds. Renate Günther and Wendy Michallat. Manchester: Manchester University Press, 2011. 45–61. Print.

Carter, Elizabeth. "A New Affinity." *slayerstime.net*. Web. http://slayerstime.net/stargate/elizabeth-carter-a-new-affinity-sam-janet-pg-15-sam-contemplates-a-proposal.html.

Cartier, Nina. "Black Women On-Screen as Future Texts: A New Look at Black Pop Culture Representations." *Cinema Journal* 53.4 (2014): 150–157. Print.

Castle, Terry. *The Apparitional Lesbian: Female Homosexuality and Modern Culture*. New York: Columbia University Press, 1993.

Caudill, Helen. "Tall, Dark, And Dangerous: Xena, The Quest, And The Wielding of Sexual Violence in *Xena* On-Line Fan Fiction." *Athena's Daughters: Television's New Women Warriors*. Eds. Frances Early and Kathleen Kennedy. Syracuse: Syracuse University Press, 2003. 27–39. Print.

Chiang, Jo. "Women Who Love Women Aren't Tragic." *The New York Times*. August 15, 2016. Web.

Child, Ben. "Ellen Page on Hollywood: 'Now I'm Gay, I Can't Play A Straight Person?'" *The Guardian*. January 27, 2016. Web.

Ciasullo, Ann M. "Making Her (In)Visible: Cultural Representations of Lesbianism and the Lesbian Body in the 1990s." *Feminist Studies* 27.3 (2001): 577–608. Print.

Clark, Danae. "Commodity Lesbianism." *The Lesbian and Gay Studies Reader*. Eds. Henry Abelove, Michèle Aina Barale, and David M. Halperin. London: Routledge, 1993. 186–201. Print.

Coldwise. "The White Owl's Egg." *archiveofourown.org*. Web. http://archiveofourown.org/works/6712990/chapters/15351781.

Collier, Noelle R., Christine A. Lamadue & H. Ray Wooten. "Buffy the Vampire Slayer and Xena: Warrior Princess: Reception of the Texts by a Sample of Lesbian Fans and Web Site Users." *Journal of Homosexuality* 56 (2009): 575–609. Print.

Conlan, Tara. "EastEnders and Other TV Shows to be Monitored for Diversity in New Scheme." *The Guardian*. August 24, 2016. Web.

Cover, Rob. "Mediating Suicide: Print Journalism and the Categorization of Queer Youth Suicide Discourses." *Archives of Sexual Behavior* 41.5 (2012): 1173–1183. Print.

_____. *Queer Youth Suicide, Culture and Identity: Unliveable Lives?* Burlington: Ashgate, 2012. Print.

Cox, Greg. *Battle On! An Unauthorized, Irreverent Look at Xena: Warrior Princess*. New York: RoC/Penguin Putnam, 1998. Print.

Cragin, Becca. "Lesbians and Serial TV: *Ellen* Finds Her Inner Adult." *The New Queer Aesthetic on Television*. Eds. James R .Keller and Leslie Stratyner. Jefferson: McFarland, 2006. 193–208. Print.

Craig, Shelley L., Lauren McInroy, Lance T. McCready, and Ramona Alaggia. "Media: A Catalyst for Resilience in Lesbian, Gay, Bisexual, Transgender, and Queer Youth." *Journal of LGBT Youth*, 12:3 (2015): 254–275. Print.

Cranz, Alex. "The History of Femslash: The Tiny Fandom That's Taking Over the Universe." *io9.gizmodo*. April 8, 2016. Web.

Crenshaw, Nadine. *Xena X-Posed: The Unauthorized Biography of Lucy Lawless and Her On-Screen Character*. Rocklin, CA: Prima, 1997. Print.

Crimp, Douglas. "Art Acts Up: A Graphic Response to AIDS." *Out/Look* 3.1 (Summer 1990): 22–30. Print.

Crosby, Sara. "The Cruelest Season: Female Heroes Snapped into Sacrificial Heroines." *Action Chicks: New Images of Tough Women in Popular Culture*. Ed. Sherrie A. Inness. New York: Palgrave, 2004. 153–178. Print.

DanieXJ. "Fish, Swords, and Love." *archiveofourown.org*. Web. http://archiveofourown. org/works/589265/chapters/1059727.

Dartt, Gina L. "Various Stories." *users.eastlink.ca*. Web. http://users.eastlink. ca/~ginadartt/OtherFanFicIndex.html.

Davidson Gluyas, Sophia. "Missing the Lesbian and the Missing Lesbian: A Study of the Forgotten Lesbian in 1970s Australian Cinema." *Gay and Lesbian Perspectives: Intimacy, Violence and Activism: Gay and Lesbian Perspectives on Australasian History and Society*. Eds. Graham Willett and Yorick Small. Clayton: Monash University Publishing, 2013. 90–104. Print.

Debbie. "Convergences in Time." ralstwww. Web. http://www.ralst.com/Convergencies Time.HTM.

D'Emidio, Tiffany. "A Conversation with The Girls from Big Purple Dreams." eclipse magazinewww. April 1, 2009. Web.

_____. "Fans Fight to Save Guiding Light." eclipsemagazine.com. April 6, 2009. Web.

_____. "Guiding Light/Otalia International Following Speak Out." eclipsemagazine. com. May 11, 2009. Web.

Dhaenens, Frederik. "Queer Cuttings on Youtube: Re-Editing Soap Operas as a Form of Fan-Produced Queer Resistance." *European Journal of Cultural Studies* 15.4 (2012): 442–456. Print.

Diamond, Lisa M. "Female Bisexuality from Adolescence to Adulthood: Results from a 10-Year Longitudinal Study." *Developmental Psychology* 44.1 (2008): 5–14. Print.

Diawara, Manthia. *In Search of Africa*. Cambridge: Harvard University Press, 1998. Print.

Dillman, Joanne Clarke. *Women and Death in Film, Television, and News: Dead but Not Gone*. New York: Palgrave Macmillan, 2014. Print.

Dionne, Stephens, and April Few. "Hip Hop Honey or Video Ho: African American Preadolescents' Understanding of Female Sexual Scripts in Hip Hop Culture." *Sexuality & Culture*. 11.4 (2007): 48–69. Web. 23 Jul. 2014.

Doyle, Vincent. *Making Out in the Mainstream: GLAAD and the Politics of Respectability*. Montreal & Kingston: McGill-Queen's University Press, 2016. Print.

Driscoll, Catherine, and Melissa Gregg. "Convergence Culture and the Legacy of Feminist Cultural Studies." *Cultural Studies* 25.4–5 (2011): 566–584. Print.

Duggan, Lisa. *Sapphic Slashers: Sex, Violence, and American Modernity*. Durham: Duke University Press, 2000. Print.

Eaklor, Vicki L. "The Kids Are All Right But the Lesbians Aren't: The Illusion of Progress in Popular Film." *Historical Reflections* 38.3 (2012): 153–170. Print.

_____. "'Seeing' Lesbians in Film and History." *Historical Reflections* 20.2 (1994): 321–333. Print.

Early, Frances and Kathleen Kennedy. "Introduction." *Athena's Daughters: Television's New Women Warriors*. Eds. Frances Early and Kathleen Kennedy. Syracuse: Syracuse University Press, 2003. 1–10.

Ellison, Hannah. "The Book Burning That Wasn't: Thousands of Works of Fiction Destroyed and No One Pays Attention." *The Huffington Post (UK Edition)*. June 13, 2012. Web.

Ellis-Petersen, Hannah. "BBC to stream 1974 Show with First Lesbian Kiss on UK Television." *The Guardian.* June 16, 2016. Web.

European Commission. *Gendered Innovations: How Gender Analysis Contributes to Research.* Luxembourg: Publications Office of the European Union, 2013. Print.

Faderman, Lillian. *Odd Girls and Twilight Lovers: A History of Lesbian Life in Twentieth-Century America.* New York: Penguin, 1991. Print.

_____. *Scotch Verdict: Miss Pirie and Miss Woods v. Dame Cumming Gordon.* New York: Columbia University Press, 1993. Print.

Fahs, Breanne. "Compulsory Bisexuality?: The Challenges of Modern Sexual Fluidity." *Journal of Bisexuality* 9 (2009): 431–449.

Fairman, Michael. "The Crystal Chappell & Kim Turrisi Interview—Venice." *Michael Fairman On Air On Soaps* April 9, 2009. Michaelfairmansoaps.com.

Fanatical Queer Geek. "Dead Lesbian Syndrome. Bury Your Gays...." *Killing Off The Queers.* October 9, 2014. http://fanaticalqueergeek.tumblr.com/post/99583146130/killing-off-the-queers-dead-lesbian-syndrome-bury.

Farr, Daniel. "Introduction: Special Issue on Global Lesbian Cinema." *Journal of Lesbian Studies* 16 (2012): 255–257.

Farwell, Marilyn R. "Heterosexual Plots and Lesbian Subtexts: Toward a Theory of Lesbian Narrative Space." *Lesbian Texts and Contexts: Radical Revisions.* Eds. Karla Jay and Joanne Glasgow. London: Onlywomen, 1992. 91–103. Print.

Fathallah, Judith. "Moriarty's Ghost: Or the Queer Disruption of the BBC's *Sherlock.*" *Television & New Media.* 16.5 (2015): 490–500. Print.

Fernandez, Maria Elena. "Orange Is the New Black's Samira Wiley on Poussey's Devastating Scene, Black Lives Matter, and Looking Straight Into the Camera." *Vulture.* June 17, 2016. Web.

Finch, Amanda. "The Most Intriguing Women in Science Fiction." *Sci-Fi Universe* 3.9 (1997): 24–34. Print.

Findlay, Heather. "8 Reasons to Canonize *Xena: Warrior Princess.*" *Girlfriends* (May 2001): 28–30. Print.

Fleimgona. "The Travellers." *archiveofourown.org.* http://archiveofourown.org/works/6907150/chapters/15755794.

Foolingducks (MochofHeda). "Did You Know You Wrote A Lifesaver?" *archiveofourown.org.* Web. http://archiveofourown.org/works/7653610/chapters/17426704.

Foster, David William. *Queer Issues in Contemporary Latin American Cinema.* Austin: University of Texas Press, 2003. Print.

Foster, Jeannette H. *Sex Variant Women in Literature.* Tallahassee: Naiad Press, 1985.

Foucault, Michel. "The Subject and Power." *Critical Inquiry* 8.4 (1982): 777–795. Print.

Framke, Caroline. "Queer Women Have Been Killed On Television For Decades. Now *The 100*'s Fans Are Fighting Back." www.vox.com March 25, 2016.

———, Javier Zarracina and Sarah Frostenson. "All The TV Character Deaths of 2015-'16, in One Chart." www.vox.com June 1, 2016.

French, Lisa. "Gender Then, Gender Now: Surveying Women's Participation In Australian Film And Television Industries." *Continuum: Journal of Media & Cultural Studies* 28.2 (2014): 188–200. Print.

Fried, Stephen. "Thing of Beauty." *Philly Mag.* February 2008. Web.

Friedman, Lyle, Matt Daniels and Ilia Blinderman. "Hollywood's Gender Divide and its Effect on Films." Polygraph.cool/bechdel. May 2016. Web.

Frizzell, Nell. "Xena: Lesbian Warrior Princess—Have The Rules of TV Just Been Rewritten?" *The Guardian.* March 15, 2016. Web.

Fussell, Sidney. "Fans Had a Big Problem With Part of Sunday's 'The Walking Dead.'" *Tech Insider.* March 21, 2016. Web.

Futrell, Alison. "The Baby, the Mother, and the Empire: Xena as Ancient Hero." *Athena's Daughters: Television's New Women Warriors.* Eds. Frances Early & Kathleen Kennedy. Syracuse: Syracuse University Press 2003. 13–26. Print.

Gardiner, Jill. *From the Closet to the Screen: Women at the Gateways Club, 1945–85.* London: Pandora, 2003. Print.

Geekgrrllurking. Master List. geekgrrllurking.livejournalwww. Web. http://geekgrrllurking.livejournal.com.

Geonn. "Badge of Honor." http://archiveofourown.org/works/7653610/chapters/17426704. Web. http://archiveofourown.org/works/528909.

_____. "The Doctor's Patience." *archiveofourown.org.* Web. http://archiveofourown.org/works/473409?view_adult=true.

_____. "The Steam-Modern Prometheus." *archiveofourown.org.* Web. http://archiveofourown.org/works/349533.

_____. "Various Works." *archiveofourown.org.* Web. http://archiveofourown.org/users/Geonn/pseuds/Geonn.

Gerbner, George, and Larry Gross. "Living with Television: The Violence Profile." *Journal of Communication* (1976): 173–199. Print.

Gever, Martha. *Entertaining Lesbians: Celebrity, Sexuality, and Self-Invention.* New York: Routledge, 2003. Print.

"Girls on Top." *Xena Magazine,* Issue 8. August 9, 2000. Print.

GLAAD. *Studio Responsibility Index: 2016.* glaad.org

GLAAD. *Where we are on TV: 2015–16.* glaad.org

Gomillion, Sarah C. and Traci A. Giuliano. "The Influence of Media Role Models on Gay, Lesbian and Bisexual Identity." *Journal of Homosexuality* 58:3 (2011): 330–354. Print.

Goodman, Kate. "Love and Death: An Examination of Death Scenes and Subtext in *Xena: Warrior Princess* Episodes." *Whoosh!* Issue 37, October 1999. Web.

Gray, Tim "Academy President Cheryl Boone Isaacs: New Members Represent a 'Major Step' in Oscar Diversity." *Variety.* June 29, 2016. Web.

Green-Simms, Lindsey, and Unoma Azuah. "The Video Closet." *Transition* 1 (2012): 32–49. Print.

Greven, David. *Gender and Sexuality in Star Trek: Allegories of Desire in the Television Series and Films.* Jefferson: McFarland, 2009. Print.

Gwenllian Jones, Sara. "Histories, Fictions, and Xena: Warrior Princess." *Television & New Media* 1:4 (2000): 403–418. Print.

Halberstam, Judith. "An Introduction to Female Masculinity." *Female Masculinity.* Durham: Duke University Press, 1998. 1–43. Print.

Hall, Stuart. "Encoding/decoding." *Culture, Media, Language: Working Papers in Cultural Studies.* Eds. Stuart Hall, Dorothy Hobson, Andrew Lowe and Paul Willis. London: Routledge, 1980. 117–127. Print.

Hamming, Jeanne E. "Whatever Turns You On: Becoming-Lesbian and the Production of Desire in the Xenaverse." *Genders* 34 (2001). Web.

Hammonds, Evelynn. "Black (W)holes and the Geometry of Black Female Sexuality." *Feminism Meets Queer Theory.* Eds. Elizabeth Weed & Naomi Schor. Bloomington: Indiana University Press, 1997. 136–156. Print.

Hanmer, Rosalind. "Internet Fandom, Queer Discourse, and Identities." *LGBT Identity and Online New Media.* Eds. Christopher Pullen and Margaret Cooper. New York: Routledge, 2010. 147–158. Print.

_____. "Lesbian Subtext Talk: Experiences of the Internet Chat." *International Journal of Sociology and Social Policy* 23.1–2 (2003): 80–106. Print.

_____. "Xenasubtexttalk: The Impact on The Lesbian Fan Community Through Its Online Reading and Writing of Lesbian Fan Fiction in Relation to The Television Series *Xena: Warrior Princess.*" *Feminist Media Studies* 14.4 (2014): 608–622. Print.

Harris, Angelique. "'I'm a Militant Queen': Queering Blaxploitation Films." *Contemporary Black American Cinema.* Ed. Mia Mask. Florence: Taylor and Francis, 2012. 217–231. Print.

Hart, Lynda. *Fatal Women: Lesbian Sexuality and the Mark of Aggression.* London: Routledge, 1994. Print.

Hayes, K. Stoddard. *Xena: Warrior Princess: The Complete Illustrated Companion.* London: Titan, 2003. Print.

_____. "Jacquelin [*sic*] of all Trades." *Xena Magazine* Issue 10, September 2000: 44–45. Print.

_____. "Who Would I be Without You?" *Xena Magazine* Issue 8, August 2000: 40–46. Print.

Heawood, Sophie. "Ellen Page: 'Being Out Became More Important Than Any Movie.'" *The Guardian.* January 30, 2016. Web.

Hedley, Mark. "The Geometry of Gendered Conflict in Popular Film: 1986–2000." *Sex Roles,* 47.5/6 (2002): 201–217. Print.

Heffernan, Virginia. "Critic's Notebook; It's February. Pucker Up, TV Actresses." *The New York Times.* February 10, 2005. Web.

Hellekson, Karin, and Kristina Busse, eds. *Fan Fiction and Fan Communities in the Age of the Internet: new essays.* Jefferson: McFarland, 2006. Print.

Heller, Dana. "Visibility and its discontents: Queer television studies. *GLQ: A Journal of Lesbian and Gay Studies.* 17 (2011): 665–676. Print.

Hogan, Heather. "Autostraddle's Ultimate Infographic Guide to Dead Lesbian Characters on TV." *Autostraddle.com* March 25, 2016. Web.

_____. "Jaime Murray and Joanne Kelly talk "Warehouse 13," Bering and Wells, and Nerdsbians." *AfterEllen.com.* April 23, 2013. Web.

_____. "Lesbiland: A TV Writer's Guide to Creating Lesbian Characters." *AfterEllen.com* October 3, 2012. Web.

Holmlund, Chris. "Cruisin' for a Bruisin': Hollywood's Deadly (Lesbian) Dolls." *Cinema Journal* 34.1 (1994): 31–51. Print.

hooks, bell. *Reel to Real: Race, Sex and Class at The Movies.* New York: Routledge, 1996. Print.

Hopkins, Alison Julie. "Convenient Fictions: The Script of Lesbian Desire in the Post-Ellen Era. A New Zealand Perspective." PhD dissertation. Victoria University of Wellington, 2009. Print.

Horn, John, et al. "Unmasking Oscar: Academy Voters are Overwhelmingly White and Male." *Los Angeles Times.* February 19, 2012. Web.

Hunter, Carson. "Life After Xena." *Girlfriends* August 2004. 44–47. Print.

Inness, Sherrie A. *The Lesbian Menace: Ideology, Identity, and the Representation of Lesbian Life.* Amherst: University of Massachusetts Press, 1997. Print.

_____. *Tough Girls: Women Warriors and Wonder Women in Popular Culture.* Philadelphia: University of Pennsylvania Press, 1999. Print.

Isaacs, Cheryl Boone. "Statement from Academy President Cheryl Boone Isaacs." January 18, 2016. www.oscars.org Web.

Jackson, Cassandra. *Violence, Visual Culture and the Black Male Body.* New York: Routledge, 2010. Print.

Jackson, Sue. "(Un)recognizable Lesbians: Young People Reading 'Hot Lesbians' through a Reality Lens." *Televising Queer Women: A Reader.* Ed. Rebecca Beirne. New York: Palgrave, 2012. 151–165. Print.

Janoff, Douglas. *Pink Blood: Homophobic Violence in Canada.* Toronto: University of Toronto Press, 2005. Print.

Jensen, Elizabeth. "*The L Word* Spins Off Its Chart." *The New York Times.* December 18, 2006. C5.

Jensen, Karol L. *Lesbian Epiphanies: Women Coming Out in Later Life.* New York: Harrington Park Press, 1999. Print.

Kabir, Shameen. *Daughters of Desire: Lesbian Representations in Film.* London: Cassell, 1998. Print.

Kann, Laura, Emily O'Malley Olsen, Tim McManus, et al. "Sexual Identity, Sex of Sexual Contacts, and Health-Related Behaviors Among Students in Grades 9–12—United States and Selected Sites, 2015." *MMWR Surveillance Summaries* 65.9 (2016): 1–202. Print.

Kaplan, Deborah. "Construction of Fan Fiction Character Through Narrative." *Fan Fiction and Fan Communities in the Age of the Internet: New Essays.* Eds. Karen Hellekson and Kristina Busse. Jefferson: McFarland, 2006. 134–152. Print.

Keeling, Kara. "'Ghetto Heaven': *Set It Off* and the Valorization of Black Lesbian Butch-Femme Sociality." *The Black Scholar* 33.1 (2003): 33–46.

Keller, James R., and Leslie Stratyner, eds. *The New Queer Aesthetic on Television.* Jefferson: McFarland, 2006. Print.

Keller, Yvonne. "'Was It Right to Love Her Brother's Wife So Passionately?' Lesbian Pulp Novels and U.S. Lesbian Identity, 1950–1965." *American Quarterly* 57.2 (2005): 385–410. Print.

Kennedy, Kathleen. "Love is the Battlefield: The Making and Unmaking of the Just Warrior in Xena, Warrior Princess." *Athena's Daughters: Television's New Women Warriors.* Eds. Frances Early and Kathleen Kennedy. Syracuse: Syracuse University Press, 2003. 40–52. Print.

_____. "Xena on the Cross." *Feminist Media Studies* 7.3 (2007): 313–332. Print.

Kerowyn. "These Exiled Years." *xenafiction.net.* Web.

Kerr, Sheryl-Lee. "The Good Life: Interview with Melissa Good." www.ausxip.com. n.d. Web.

Kesler, Jennifer. "The Hathor Legacy: The Search for Good Women Characters." thehathorlegacy.com. Original post July 6, 2006. Web.

Kessler, Kelly. "They Should Suffer Like the Rest of Us: Queer Equality in Narrative Mediocrity." *Cinema Journal* 50.2 (2011): 139–144. Print.

Kirby-Diaz, Mary, ed. *Buffy and Angel Conquer the Internet: Essays on Online Fandom.* Jefferson: McFarland, 2009. Print.

Krainitzki, Eva. "Ghosted Images: Old Lesbians on Screen." *Journal of Lesbian Studies* 19 (2015): 13–26. Print.

Kristen, P. "Homing Beacon." *fanfiction.net.* Web. https://www.fanfiction.net/s/10360827/1/Homing-Beacon.

Laćan, Sanja. "Concealing, Revealing, and Coming Out: Lesbian Visibility in Dalibor Matanić's *Fine Dead Girls* and Dana Budisavljević's *Family Meals.*" *Studies in European Cinema* 12.3 (2015): 229–245. Print.

Lady_Katana4544. "Untitled." *archiveofourown.org.* Web. http://archiveofourown.org/works/2457800.

Lauzen, Marth M. "Boxed In: Portrayals of Female Characters and Employment of Behind-the-Scenes Women in 2014–15 Prime-time Television." Center for the Study of Women in Television and Film. San Diego State University, 2015. Web.

_____. "The Celluloid Ceiling: Behind-the-Scenes Employment of Women on the Top 100, 250, and 500 films of 2015." Center for the Study of Women in Television and Film. San Diego State University, 2015. Web.

_____. "It's a Man's (Celluloid) Work: Portrayals of Female Characters in the Top 100 films of 2015." Center for the Study of Women in Television and Film. San Diego State University, 2016. Web.

_____, David M. Dozier and Nora Horan. "Constructing Gender Stereotypes Through Social Roles in Prime-Time Television." *Journal of Broadcasting & Electronic Media* 52.2 (2008): 200–214. Print.

Lawrence, Jacquie. "Where Have All the Lesbians Gone in TV And Film?" *The Guardian*. March 25, 2015. Web.

Lee, Benjamin. "From Ghostbusters to Star Trek Beyond: Gay Characters are there, but Only Just." *The Guardian*. August 4, 2016. Web.

Lee, Pei-Wen and Michaela D.E. Meyer. "'We All Have Feelings for Our Girlfriends': Progressive (?) Representations of Lesbian Lives on *The L Word*." *Sexuality & Culture* 14 (2010): 234–250. Print.

Leonard, Andrew. "Who Owns Xena?" Salonwww. August 3, 1997. Web.

Lewis, Rachel. "Towards a Transnational Lesbian Cinema." *Journal of Lesbian Studies* 16 (2012): 273–290. Print.

Linster, The. "The London Olympics Opening Ceremony Includes a Lesbian Kiss Seen around the World." *After Ellen.com* July 28, 2012. Web.

Lippman, Julia R. "I Did It Because I Never Stopped Loving You: The Effects of Media Portrayals of Persistent Pursuit on Beliefs About Stalking." *Communication Research* (2015): DOI: 10.1177/0093650215570653

LongLiveJanetFrasier. Comment on "Topic: 7.18 - Heroes (Part 2)." Stargate SG-1 & Atlantis Solutions Forum. November 7, 2006, 12:39:25 PM., http://www.stargate-sg1-solutions.com/forum/index.php?topic=164.0.

Lost-at-Sea. "Episode Rewrite: 2X14." *archiveofourown.org*. Web. https://archiveofourown.org/works/1855903.

Lothian, Alexis. "Archival Anarchies: Online Fandom, Subcultural Conservation, and the Transformative Work of Digital Ephemera." *International Journal of Cultural Studies* 16 (2013): 541–556. Print.

Lyell, Carrie. "Amanda Barrie: I was Terrified of Coming Out as Bisexual." *Diva Magazine*. August 8, 2016. Web.

_____. "The Dead Lesbian Trope That Won't Go Away." *Diva Magazine*. February 12, 2015. Web.

_____. "Did Call the Midwife just do a Last Tango in Halifax?" *Diva Magazine*. March 9, 2015. Web.

_____. "Last Tango Writer: Why I Killed Off Lesbian Character." *Diva Magazine*. January 16, 2015. Web.

Lunacy. "The History of Xena Fan Fiction on the Internet." *Whoosh!* Issue 25 (October 1998). Web.

_____. "A Very 'Good' Thing for Fan Fiction." *Whoosh!* Issue 46 (July 2000). Web.

Lynniethebeegirl. "Commanders of Peace." *archiveofourown.org*. Web. http://archiveofourown.org/works/6420295/chapters/14697865.

Mackey, Jill A. "Subtext and Countertext in *Muriel's Wedding*." *NWSA* 13.1 (2001): 86–104. Print.

Maggielassie. "Another Way." *academyofbards.org*. Web. http://www.academyofbards.org/fanfic/m/maggielassie_anotherway.html.

"Main/Bury Your Gays." TV Tropes.com. TV Tropes Foundation, n.d. Web. July 23, 2014.

Mangels, Andy. "Lesbian Sex = Death?" *The Advocate* August 20, 2001: 70–71. Print.

Mann, William J. *Kate: The Woman Who was Hepburn.* New York: Henry Holt, 2006. Print.

Maris, Elena. "Hacking Xena: Technological Innovation and Queer Influence in the Production of Mainstream Television." *Critical Studies in Media Communication* 33.1 (2016): 123–137. Print.

Marks, Elaine. "Lesbian Intertexuality." *Homosexualities and French Literature: Cultural Contexts/Critical Texts.* Eds. George Stambolian and Elaine Marks. Ithaca: Cornell University Press, 1979. 353–377. Print.

Martinez-Reyes, Consuelo. "Prodigal Daughters: Portraying Lesbians in Hispanic Caribbean Cinema." *Journal of Lesbian Studies* 16 (2012): 291–306. Print.

Mason, Gail. *The Spectacle of Violence: Homophobia, Gender and Knowledge.* London and New York: Routledge, 2003. Print.

Mayne, Judith. *Directed by Dorothy Arzner.* Bloomington: Indiana University Press, 1994.

_____. *Framed: Lesbians, Feminists, and Media Culture.* Minneapolis: University of Minnesota Press, 2000. Print.

McRobbie, Angela. "Postfeminism and Popular Culture: Bridget Jones and the New Gender Regime." *Interrogating Postfeminism: Gender and the Politics of Popular Culture.* Eds. Yvonne Tasker and Diane Negra. Durham: Duke University Press, 2007. 27–39. Print.

Medigovich, Lori. "Lucy Lawless." *Lesbian News.* 28.6 (June 2006). Web.

Mercer, Catherine H., et al. "Changes in Sexual Attitudes and Lifestyles in Britain through the Life Course and over Time: Findings from the National Surveys of Sexual Attitudes and Lifestyles (Natsal)." *The Lancet.* 382 (2013): 1781–1794. Print.

Millward, Liz. "New Xenaland: Lesbian Place Making, the Xenaverse, and Aotearoa New Zealand" *Gender, Place and Culture,* 14.4 (2007): 427–443. Print.

_____. "Xena and the Warrior Poets: Audre Lorde, Monique Wittig, and the Myths of Lesbian Origins." *Feminist Media Studies.* 14.1 (2014): 135–146. Print.

_____, and Janice G. Dodd. "Mid-Course Correction: 'Don't Ask, Don't Tell' and *Stargate SG-1* Femslash." *Queer Studies in Media & Popular Culture* 1.1 (2016): 41–59.

Minero, Emelina. "Chatting Up: "Kiss Me" Producer Josefine Tengblad." *Curve Magazine.* November 8, 2012. Web.

Minkowitz, Donna. "Xena: She's Big, Tall, Strong—and Popular." *Ms. Magazine* (July/August 1996): 74–77. Print.

Moore, Marlon Rachquel. "Close-up: Sexuality, Eroticism, and Gender in Black Films and New Media." *Black Camera: An International Film Journal* 6.2 (2015): 201–216. Print.

Morreale, Joanne. "*Xena: Warrior Princess* as Feminist Camp." *Journal of Popular Culture* 32.2 (1998): 79–86.

Moss, Kevin, and Mima Simić. "Post-Communist Lavender Menace: Lesbians in Mainstream East European Film." *Journal of Lesbian Studies* 15 (2011): 271–283. Print.

Msweener19. "Three Simple Words." *archiveofourown.org.* Web. http://archiveofourown.org/works/1354984/chapters/3092944.

Murphy, Amy. "Inside the Head of Pink Rabbit." *Whoosh.* Issue 70, July 2002. Web.

My Osage. "The Lie." *xenafiction.net.* Web. http://xenafiction.net/scrolls/myosage_tl.html.

Nazzaro, Joe. "Adventures in the Fantasy Trade." *Xena Magazine.* Issue 10, September 2000. 14–19.

Noland, Marcus, Tyler Moran, and Barbara Kotschwar. "*Is Gender Diversity Profitable?*

Evidence from a Global Survey." Working Paper 16–3, Peterson Institute for International Economics. February 2016.

O'Brien, Anne. "Producing Television and Reproducing Gender." *Television & New Media* 16.4 (2014): 259–274. Web. January 28, 2015.

O'Donnell, Shannon, Ilan Meyer, and Sharon Schwartz. "Increased Risk of Suicide Attempts Among Black and Latino Lesbians, Gay Men, and Bisexuals." *American Journal of Public Health* 101.6 (2011): 1055–1059. Web.

"'Orange' Creator Jenji Kohan: 'Piper Was My Trojan Horse.'" *Fresh Air.* NPR. August 13, 2013. Web.

Pendragon, Diane K. "Coping Behaviors among Sexual Minority Female Youth." *Journal of Lesbian Studies* 14 (2010): 5–15. Print.

Perriam, Chris. *Spanish Queer Cinema.* Edinburgh: Edinburgh University Press, 2013. Print.

Piccoli, Dana. "Why *Xena* Still Matters to Queer Women 20 Years Later." *AfterEllen.com* September 4, 2015. Web.

Prudom, Laura. "*The 100* Creator on Lexa Controversy: 'I Would've Done Some Things Differently.'" *Variety* March 27, 2016. Web.

Q with Shadrach Kabango. "Lesbian Deaths on TV: 'They're Dropping like Flies.'" *CBC Radio.* May 12, 2016.

Ralst. *Passion & Perfection.* Web. http://www.ralst.com/

Rich, Adrienne. "Compulsory Heterosexuality and Lesbian Existence." *Signs: Journal of Women in Culture and Society* 5.4 (1980): 631–660. Print.

Robinson, Joanna. "The Walking Dead's Latest Gruesome Death is Part of a Troubling TV Trend." *Vanity Fair.* March 20, 2016. Print.

Rockler, Naomi R. "A Wall on the Lesbian Continuum: Polysemy and *Fried Green Tomatoes,*" *Women's Studies in Communication.* 24.1 (2001): 90–106. Print.

Rogue_Mariah_Dare. "The Assassins Cry." *archiveofourown.org.* Web. http://archiveofourown.org/works/2577290/chapters/5735186.

Rollet, Brigitte. "In the Margins and Off-Centre: Lesbian Characters on French Television 1995–2005." *Lesbian Inscriptions in Francophone Society and Culture.* Eds. Renate Günther and Wendy Michallat. Manchester: Manchester University Press, 2011. 81–102. Print.

Romansilence. "Back From The Abyss." thealphagatewww. Web. http://www.thealphagate.com/viewstory.php?sid=3188.

_____. "When You Feel Longing, Sing of Women In Love." *thealphagate.com.* Web.

Romi364. "How Deep Is Your Love." *archiveofourown.org.* Web. http://archiveofourown.org/works/6198586/chapters/14200693.

Rooks. "The Other Side: Writing Alternative Xena Fan Fiction from a Male Point of View." *Whoosh!* Issue 46, July 2000. Web.

Ross, Sharon. "'Tough Enough': Female Friendship and Heroism in Xena and Buffy." *Action Chicks: New Images of Tough Women in Popular Culture.* Ed. Sherrie A. Inness. New York: Palgrave, 2004. 231–255. Print.

Roussanov, Bella. "The Disposable Lesbian: It's Time for Television to Let Us Live." *Harvard Political Review.* April 18, 2016. Web.

Russo, Julie Levin. "NEW VOY "cyborg sex" J/7 [NC-17] 1/1 new methodologies, new fantasies." *j-l-r.org,* n.d. Web.

Russo, Vito. *The Celluloid Closet: Homosexuality in the Movies* Rev. Ed. New York: Harper & Row, 1987. Print.

Ryan, Maureen. "'Anyone Can Die?' TV's Recent Death Toll Says Otherwise." *Variety* April 13, 2016. Web.

Saewyc, Elizabeth, Colleen Poon, Naren Wang, Yuko Homma, and Annie Smith. *Not Yet Equal: The Health of Lesbian, Gay, & Bisexual Youth in BC.* Vancouver: McCreary Centre Society, 2007. Web.

Saul, Jennifer Mather. *Feminism: Issues & Arguments.* Oxford: Oxford University Press, 2003.

Sgafirenity. "I Will See You Again." *archiveofourown.org.* Web. http://archiveofourown. org/works/6827470/chapters/15584233.

Sheffield, Vivian. "A Friend in Need: Xena Redeemed?" *Whoosh!* Issue 95, November 2004. Web.

Signorelli, Nancy, Douglas McLeod, and Elaine Healy. "Gender Stereotypes in MTV Commercials: The Beat Goes On." *Journal of Broadcasting & Electronic Media* 38.21(1994): 91–101. Web.

Silverman, Robin. "What Xena Giveth, Xena Taketh Away." *Gay and Lesbian Review* 8.5 (2001): 32–34. Print.

Smith, Stacy, et al. *Exploring the Barriers and Opportunities for Independent Women Film-makers.* Report by Sundance Institute and Women In Film Los Angeles. Women Filmmakers Initiative. University of Southern California Annenberg School for Communication and Journalism, 2013.

_____. *Gender Inequality in 500 Popular Films: Examining On-Screen Portrayals and Behind-the-Scenes Employment Patterns in Motion Pictures Released between 2007–2012.* Report by the Media, Diversity & Social Change Initiative. University of Southern California Annenberg School for Communication and Journalism, 2013.

_____. *Inclusion or Invisibility? Comprehensive Annenberg Report on Diversity in Enter-tainment.* Report by the Media, Diversity & Social Change Initiative. University of Southern California Annenberg School for Communication and Journalism, 2016.

Snarker, Dorothy. "Why Imaginary Deaths Matter to Real-World Queer Women." *IndieWire.com* March 28, 2016. Web.

Sommella, Laraine. "This is about People Dying: The Tactics of Early ACT UP and Lesbian Avengers in New York City: Interview with Maxine Wolfe." *Queers in Space: Communities, Public Spaces, Sites of Resistance.* Eds. Gordon Brent Ingram, Anne-Marie Bouthillette, and Yolanda Retter. Seattle: Bay Press, 1997. 407–437. Print.

Sontag, Susan. *Regarding the Pain of Others.* New York: Picador. 2003. Print.

Stacey, Jackie. "'If You Don't Play, You Can't Win': *Desert Hearts* and The Lesbian Romance Film." *Immortal Invisible: Lesbians and the Moving Image.* Ed. Tamsin Wilton. London: Routledge, 1995. 67–87. Print.

Stafford, Nikki, ed. *How Xena Changed our Lives: True Stories by Fans for Fans,* Toronto: ECW Press, 2002. Print.

Stanfill, Mel. "'They're Losers, but I Know Better': Intra-Fandom Stereotyping and the Normalization of the Fan Subject." *Critical Studies in Media Communication* 30.2 (2013): 117–134. Print.

Stanton, Gabrielle, and Harry Werksman. "The Universe Interview: Lucy Lawless." *Sci-Fi Universe* 3.9 (September 1997): 18–22. Print.

Stasi, Mafalda. "The Toy Soldiers from Leeds: The Slash Palimpest." *Fan Fiction and Fan Communities in the Age of the Internet: New Essays.* Eds. Karen Hellekson and Kristina Busse. Jefferson: McFarland, 2006. 115–33. Print.

Stolworthy, Jacob. "The Walking Dead Season 6 Sparks Backlash after Killing off Les-bian Character." *The Independent.* March 22, 2016. Web.

Streitmatter, Rodger. *From Perverts to "Fab Five": The Media's Changing Depiction of Gay Men and Lesbians.* New York: Routledge, 2009. Print.

Stockwell, Anne. "Flirting with Xena." *The Advocate*. August 20, 1996. 81–83.

Stuart, Jamie. *Performing Queer Female Identity on Screen: A Critical Analysis of Five Recent Films*. Jefferson: McFarland, 2008. Print.

"Sweeps Week Lesbian Kiss." Tvtropes.org/pmwiki.php/Main/SweepsWeekLesbianKiss. Retrieved January 2015.

Tabron, Judith L. "Girl on Girl Politics: Willow/Tara and New Approaches to Media Fandom." *Slayage* 4.1–4.2 (2004): 13–14. Print.

TaglarianMythicRites. "Holding Her." *archiveofourown.org*. Web. http://archiveofour own.org/works/1518266.

Taylor, Catherine and Tracey Peter, et.al. *Every Class in Every School: The First National Climate Survey on Homophobia, Biphobia, and Transphobia in Canadian Schools.* Toronto: Egale Canada Human Rights Trust, 2011. Print.

Thomas, Browen. "What is Fanfiction and Why Are People Saying Such Nice Things about It?" *Storyworlds* 3 (2012): 1–24. Print.

Torres, Sasha. "Television/Feminism: *HeartBeat* and Prime Time Lesbianism." *The Lesbian and Gay Studies Reader*. Eds. Henry Abelove, Michèle Aina Barale, and David M. Halperin,. London: Routledge, 1993. 176–185. Print.

"Tragic Lesbians and Clunky Love Stories: Does TV Have Trouble With Lesbian Love?" *The Gay UK.* April 15, 2015. Web.

Trancer. "Your Cheatin' Heart/Subterfuge." *area52hkh.net*. Web. http://www.area52hkh.net/author.php?name=Trancer.

Tuttle, Marion D. "Strange Alliances." *academyofbards.org*. Web. http://www.academy ofbards.org/amazontrails/xena/strangealliances.htm.

"Uncharted Terrain: *The L Word* Spawns a Network for Gay Women." *Newsweek* May 28, 2007. Web.

Unforciablecure. "Shine." *archiveofourown.org*. Web. https://archiveofourown.org/works/2626079.

Ventura, Michael. "Warrior Women." *Psychology Today* November/December 1998: 58 (4).

Verrath. "The Sad One." *academyofbards.org*. Web. http://www.academyofbards.org/fanfic/v/verrath_thesadone.html.

Vickers, Lu. "*Fried Green Tomatoes*: Excuse Me, Did We See the Same Movie?" *Jump Cut* 39 (1994): 25–30. Print.

Vincentelli, Elisabeth. "TV Shows Can't Stop Killing Off Their Lesbian Characters." *New York Post*. April 7, 2016. Print.

Wagmeister, Elizabeth. "'Empire' Showrunner Ilene Chaiken Responds to TV's Lesbian Death Trope." *Variety*. April 6, 2016. Web.

Walker, Alice. *The Same River Twice: Honoring the Difficult*. New York: Scribner, 1996. Print.

Wariangle. "Let This War Set You Free." archiveofourown.org. Web. http://archiveof ourown.org/works/2397920/chapters/5300885.

Watson, Julia. "BlogHer09: Ilene Chaiken and the Incredibly Disappearing Website." Velvetparkmediawww July 28, 2009.

Weisbrot, Robert. *Xena: Warrior Princess. The Official Guide to the Xenaverse*. New York: Doubleday, 1998.

Weiss, Andrea. *Vampires and Violets: Lesbians in the Cinema*. London: Jonathan Cape, 1992. Print.

_____. "'A Queer Feeling When I Look at You': Hollywood Stars and Lesbian Spectatorship in the 1930s." *Stardom: Industry of Desire*. Ed. Christine Gledhill. New York: Routledge, 1991. 287–304. Print.

Welsh, Kaite. "Last Tango in Halifax: The Latest Victim of The Dead Lesbian Cliché." *The Guardian.* January 20, 2015. Web.

Wereleopard58. "United." *fanfiction.net.* https://www.fanfiction.net/s/4063963/1/United.

"What is this ... Über?" *Whoosh!* 26 December 2001. Web.

White, Patricia. *UnInvited: Classical Hollywood Cinema and Lesbian Representation* Bloomington: Indiana University Press, 1999. Print.

White, Sherry. "Statement on Signing the Lexa Pledge." *LGBT Fans Deserve Better.* April 30, 2016. Web.

Whitt, Jan. "What Happened to Celie and Idgie?: 'Apparitional Lesbians' in American Film." *Studies in Popular Culture* 27.3 (2005): 43–57. Print.

Wilder, J.C. "Twenty-Seven Grilled Bards and One Reviewer: Rare, Medium and Supertoasty." *Whoosh!* Issue 25, October 1998. Web.

Willis, Ika. "Keeping Promises to Queer Children: Making Space (for Mary Sue) at Hogwarts." *Fan Fiction and Fan Communities in the Age of the Internet: New Essays.* Eds. Karen Hellekson and Kristina Busse. Jefferson: McFarland, 2006. 153–170. Print.

Wilton, Tamsin. "Introduction: On Invisibility and Mortality." *Immortal Invisible: Lesbians and the Moving Image.* Ed. Tamsin Wilton. London: Routledge, 1995. Print.

Winters, CN. "Bonding of Souls." *academyofbards.org.* Web. http://www.academyofbards. org/amazontrails/xena/friendindeed.htm.

_____. "Watching and Waiting." www.fanfiction.net. Web. https://www.fanfiction.net/s/8517984/1/Watching-and-Waiting.

Wittig, Monique. *The Straight Mind and Other Essays.* Boston: Beacon Press, 1992.

Woll, Allen. "*The Color Purple*: Translating the African American Novel for Hollywood." *Twentieth-Century American Fiction on Screen.* Ed. R. Barton Palmer. Cambridge: Cambridge University Press, 2007. 198–209.

Wong, Alvin Ka Hin. "From the Transnational to the Sinophone: Lesbian Representations in Chinese-Language Films." *Journal of Lesbian Studies* 16 (2012): 307–322. Print.

"Xena Draws Record Audiences." *Xena Magazine.* Issue 6, June 2000. Print.

Young, Cathy. "What We Owe Xena." Salonwww September 15, 2005. Web.

Websites

Australian Xena Information Page	ausxip.com
Christine Boese's Studies in Cyberculture	www.nutball.com
GLAAD	glaad.org
International Association of Xena Studies	whoosh.org
LGBT Fans Deserve Better	lgbtfansdeservebetter.com
Organization of Transformative Works	www.transformativeworks.org
The Trevor Project	www.thetrevorproject.org

Fan Fiction Archives

Archive of Our Own	archiveofourown.org
Dark Matters	www.freewebs.com
Fanfiction.net	www.fanfiction.net
Passion & Perfection	www.ralst.com
The Royal Academy of Bards	www.academyofbards.org
ShatterStorm Productions	www.shatterstorm.net
Tom's Xena Page	www.xenafan.com

INDEX